Labor's Millennium

Princeton Theological Monograph Series

K. C. Hanson, Charles M. Collier, and D. Christopher Spinks,
Series Editors

Recent volumes in the series:

Philip E. Harrold
*A Place Somewhat Apart:
The Private Worlds of a Late Nineteenth-Century Public University*

Poul F. Guttesen
Leaning into the Future

T. David Beck
The Holy Spirit and the Renewal of All Things

Ryan A. Neal
Theology as Hope

Abraham Kunnuthara
*Schleiermacher on Christian Consciousness
of God's Work in History*

Paul S. Chung
Martin Luther and Buddhism

Philip Ruge-Jones
Cross in Tensions

John A. Vissers
The Neo-Orthodox Theology of W. W. Bryden

Stephen Finlan and Vladimir Kharlamov, editors
Theosis: Deification in Christian Theology

Labor's Millennium

*Christianity, Industrial Education,
and the Founding of the University of Illinois*

BRETT H. SMITH

☙PICKWICK *Publications* · Eugene, Oregon

LABOR'S MILLENNIUM
Christianity, Industrial Education, and the Founding of the University of Illinois

Princeton Theological Monograph Series 124

Copyright © 2010 Brett H. Smith. All rights reserved. Except for brief quotations in critical publications or reviews, no part of this book may be reproduced in any manner without prior written permission from the publisher. Write: Permissions, Wipf and Stock Publishers, 199 W. 8th Ave., Suite 3, Eugene, OR 97401.

Pickwick Publications
An Imprint of Wipf and Stock Publishers
199 W. 8th Ave., Suite 3
Eugene, OR 97401

ISBN 13: 978-1-60608-067-2

Cataloging-in-Publication data:

Smith, Brett H.

Labor's millennium : Christianity, industrial education, and the founding of the University of Illinois / Brett H. Smith.

Princeton Theological Monograph Series 124

xii + 188 p. ; 23 cm. —Includes bibliographic citations.

ISBN 13: 978-1-60608-067-2

1. University of Illinois—History. 2. United States—Church history—19th century. 3. Church and state—United States—History. 4. Social gospel—History. 5. Turner, Jonathan Baldwin, 1805–1899. 6. Gregory, John Milton, 1822–1898. I. Title. II. Series.

BR515 .S56 2010

Manufactured in the U.S.A.

Earlier versions of chapters 2 and 3 were previously published: "Reversing the Curse: Agricultural Millennialism at the Illinois Industrial University," was first published in *Church History* 73 (2004) 759–91; and "'Men,' Not 'Monks': Teaching 'Christian Culture' at the Illinois Industrial University," was first published in *Fides et Historia* 38 (2006) 69–86. Both are used here with the permission of these journals.

All illustrations are courtesy of the University of Illinois Archives.

For Tammi

Contents

Acknowledgments / ix

List of Illustrations / xi

Introduction / 1

1. "A Good Time Coming" on "the Blessed Green Earth" / 11
2. Reversing the Curse / 32
3. "Men," not "Monks" / 63
4. Liturgies for "Learning and Labor" / 99
5. Preaching Labor's Millennium / 129

Conclusion / 162

Bibliography / 173

Acknowledgments

MANY PEOPLE HAVE CONTRIBUTED TO THE RESEARCH AND WRITING OF this book. Joe Barton, Larry Murphy, and Jack Seymour provided helpful feedback as my dissertation committee, suggesting ways a successful book revision could be undertaken. Bob Chapel, William Maher, Chris Prom, and the other staff members of the University of Illinois archives have been friendly and helpful fellow laborers during the various times I've visited their large and informative collection. Comments from persons at the "Fourth International Conference on Baptist Studies" at Acadia University, the "Eighth Annual Conference on Holidays, Ritual, Festival, Celebration, and Public Display" at Bowling Green State University, "The Schooled Heart: Moral Formation in American Higher Education" conference at Baylor University, and the "Illini Christian Faculty and Staff" and "Wednesday Forum" groups at the University of Illinois helped to hone the argument and find other sources to enrich it. Permission has been granted to use the material in this book which was published in a different form in two previous articles: "Reversing the Curse: Agricultural Millennialism at the Illinois Industrial University," *Church History* 73 (2004) 759–91; and "'Men,' Not 'Monks': Teaching 'Christian Culture' at the Illinois Industrial University," *Fides et Historia* 38 (2006) 69–86. In their editorial capacities for those journals, Will Katerberg, Amanda Porterfield, Ron Wells, and their staffs helped clarify and simplify my dissertation's rambling overabundance of primary sources, suggesting ways to locate the material in the leading secondary literature. Discussions with Greg Behle and Winton Solberg, who have capably plowed the early University of Illinois ground before, saved me from even more trial and error. Jerry Cain and Tammi Smith kindly read the chapters before publication, helping future readers to have a more readable book. Anita Bravo skillfully and cheerfully formatted the manuscript. K. C. Hanson, Diane Farley, Jeremy Funk, Patrick Harrison, and the staff at Wipf and Stock helped make doing my first book a pleasurable experience. The trustees of the Baptist Student Foundation at the University of Illinois graciously granted a leave of absence to write the final draft. They, the Foundation's staff members, the people of the University Baptist Church, and my family and friends have been amazingly patient and supportive during the ups and downs of this long process. For all of these kindnesses, I am deeply grateful.

Illustrations

1. Jonathan Baldwin Turner / 12
2. John M. Gregory surrounded by early faculty members / 38
3. The original I.I.U. building / 55
4. An early campus view looking northward (presumably from the new University Hall) toward the Drill Hall and the University Building / 58
5. I.I.U. students in military uniforms / 72
6. I.I.U. Women's Calisthenics Class / 74
7. The Art Gallery / 82
8. Alethenai literary society meeting room / 85
9. Seal adorning a certificate issued to James O. Pearman featuring the motto, "Learning and Labor" and the symbols of the plow, the anvil and the steam engine. (Image dated ca. 1881) / 100
10. The auditorium of University Hall, where chapel services were held / 118

Introduction

Prior to the University of Illinois' founding in 1867, higher education in the United States was predominately an affair of church groups. Inheriting the tradition of their European forbears, Americans saw learning as the cultivation of human faculties such as the mind and the will. Colonies and states would charter a school, usually in partnership with a particular Christian denomination. The understanding was that the church had a role, on behalf of the state, to train its future leaders. So most college faculty, and almost all presidents, were clergymen, to whom, as esteemed role models, the young were entrusted. A number of these schools did laudable work, especially in their missionary endeavors among underprivileged groups. Not many American young people attended colleges, though, because it was expensive, and the curriculum was narrow, designed mostly for training men to serve in law, medicine, or theology, or wealthy youths who might pursue other careers.[1] At its height during the mid-nineteenth century, American education featured what Carl F. Kaestle has called the Protestant-Republican ideology, which included "the sacredness and fragility" of republican government, including its key concepts like individualism, liberty, and virtue; "the importance of individual character in fostering social mobility"; the honor and necessity of personal initiative and labor; "the superiority of American Protestant culture; the grandeur of America's destiny"; and the need to unify America's diverse ethnic population into a national identity.[2] These values could generally be seen from schoolhouses to colleges throughout the United States.

During the period roughly between 1870 and 1920, though, American higher education experienced some major cultural transitions, including: the emergence of state-sponsored, land-grant universities; a democratic effort to include more and more students from all walks of life; the influence of European scholarship as imported by

---

1. Tewksbury, "Founding of American Colleges."
2. Kaestle, "Ideology," 127–28.

faculty and students studying abroad; the increasing priority of empirical scientific research; the establishment of distinct disciplines and departments; the priority of practicality and utility over classics; and the growth of technology and industry as factors driving education.³ With this curriculum change, college and now university life was increasingly understood less as a place for genteel cultural development and more as a means to utilitarian ends in the marketplace. Presidents and professors functioned less as moral guardians and more as dispensers of innovative techniques. Although religion did not disappear on college campuses, its location changed, moving increasingly from the administration and the classroom to the domain of voluntary student activities.⁴

The University of Illinois was founded during the transition period between these two eras, a time when many of the features of the antebellum college remained, including the missionary aspect of Christian education for the public good. The president of another state school, Wisconsin's John Bascom, would summarize the era's perspective by saying "that system of education is alone good which builds society together under spiritual law."⁵ He retained the perspective and language of the antebellum college president, but had broadened his scope to transforming the society as a whole. This was not unusual for public universities, including the land-grants, because the 1862 Morrill Act changed everything. Vermont congressman Justin S. Morrill sought to enlarge higher education beyond the professions by including a wider percentage of the population to train for commercial pursuits.⁶ He personally saw this expansion as an aid to the churches' educational ministry.⁷

When modern historians, though, have considered the land-grant movement, discussions about religion are minimal if not absent. Occasionally outward forms of religion are mentioned, like compulsory chapel attendance or participation in a voluntary student society. Agricultural historian Earle D. Ross, for example, says the clergyman

3. Roberts and Turner, *Sacred and the Secular*, 3; University of Illinois, *Memorial Convocation*, 14; Hoeveler, "University and the Social Gospel," 282.
4. Setran, *College "Y,"* 1–3.
5. Hoeveler, "University and the Social Gospel," 292.
6. Solberg, *University of Illinois*, 55–58.
7. Morrill, *Speech*, 14.

president and other leaders of the New York People's College in 1858 sought to teach "the revelations of the Bible" in a "perfect combination of Study with Labor" and "Justice to Woman," while Iowa State held Sunday chapel services and taught a course curiously called "Agricultural Theology."[8] But the normal theme of these histories is that land-grant colleges and universities were established with democratic and utilitarian motives, emphasizing the glories of westward expansion, technological sophistication, research, and professional specialization, available for any one regardless of class. Furthermore, says the American historian Allan Nevins, the land-grants "divorce[d] university work from religious trammels."[9] As land-grant college and university historian Edward Eddy put it, "One of the phases of the revolution ... was the break from the hold of orthodox religion on the minds of the people," with secularism's triumph over Christianity's tyrannical superstitions being a pervading theme throughout his book.[10]

Ross, though, disagrees with the secularization theme, claiming instead that, in the American Midwest, campus culture adopted and perpetuated the values instilled by the religious communities in a particular region.[11] Although not focusing specifically on land-grants, a later group of revisionists showed that North American universities, while beginning to show signs of religious decline, continued to demonstrate a Christian presence during the transitional period just after the Civil War.[12] Historians George Marsden and Julie Reuben developed this theme further, while Conrad Cherry postulated that an emerging "pan-Protestant" form of non-sectarian Christianity began to dominate the educational landscape during the period.[13] Since these authors' works were first published, a growing body of literature exists examining the place of religion in American higher education.

This book is one more contribution in that tradition, providing a new twist, since it is a case study of a land-grant, agricultural and

8. Ross, *Democracy's College*, 25, 109.
9. Nevins, *State Universities and Democracy*, 110.
10. Eddy, *Colleges for Our Land*, 1.
11. Ross, "Religious Influences"; Davis, "Frontier and Religious Influences on Higher Education, 1796–1860," agrees.
12. Marsden and Longfield, *Secularization of the Academy*.
13. Marsden, *Soul of the American University*; Reuben, *Making of the Modern University*; Cherry, *Hurrying toward Zion*.

mechanical public university. What follows, then, is a theological history of the founding University of Illinois community, from the mid 1840s through about 1880. This book demonstrates that the evangelical Christian founders of what was then called the Illinois Industrial University, or I.I.U., believed that agricultural and mechanical education would result in a millenarian blessing for the larger society by providing abundant food, economic prosperity, vocational dignity, and a charitable spirit of sacred unity and public service. It argues that Christian belief motivated their public educational theory and practice toward a social gospel of "labor's millennium"—their shorthand for God's Kingdom being advanced by the advent of scientific agricultural and mechanical education.

Innovations

The book is innovative in at least four areas. First, it locates an emerging agricultural social gospel one or two decades before current scholarly consensus. Early twentieth century British Protestants identified a mid-to-late-nineteenth-century "Christian socialism," but tended to think of it as a phenomenon of the urban industrial revolution.[14] American scholars also speak of the Social Gospel in urban terms, placing its origin in the latter part of the nineteenth century. Gary Dorrien, for example, traces the Social Gospel's emergence from Washington Gladden's Bushnellian pastoral reflections, ideas Gladden popularized while religion editor of *The Independent* in the 1870s. Dorrien claims the Social Gospel does not become a recognizable movement until coupled with labor and poverty in the 1880s and beyond.[15] This book adds to the discussion by telling the story of some rapidly industrializing rural and agricultural workers to whom the concept of a Social Gospel may be applied as well. Historian J. David Hoeveler, Jr., saw Wisconsin and its Baptist leader Bascom and others demonstrating "elements of continuity between the reform impulse of evangelical Protestantism in the antebellum period and the later Social Gospel movement."[16] For him, evangelicalism's twin towers—revivalism and voluntary organizations—are present in the notion of Christian higher education, includ-

---

14. Martin, *Christian Social Reformers*; Raven, *Christian Socialism*.
15. Dorrien, *Making of American Liberal Theology*, xix, 270–75, 304–14.
16. Hoeveler, "University and the Social Gospel," 283.

ing in public schools, as a means of social reform.[17] Bascom, who began his presidency in 1874 and was therefore a contemporary of Illinois' first President John M. Gregory, grew up, like Gregory, in western New York, an area well-known for revivalism.[18] This revivalistic, evangelical form of Christianity, says theologian Donald Dayton, birthed a number of social reform movements such as abolition, temperance, and suffrage.[19] Although some contemporary conservative evangelicals might question the wisdom of calling revivalists like those in the I.I.U. community adherents of the Social Gospel, one must remember that the sharp division between those advocating primarily personal salvation versus those emphasizing social change did not develop until the early twentieth century.[20] The Baptist minister Walter Rauschenbusch, sometimes called the "father" of the Social Gospel, maintained, throughout his lifetime, the need for a person's individual salvation from sin and hell through faith in Christ.[21] Historian Carl J. Guarneri reminds us that "In an era when religious ferment led thousands of Americans into reform movements, even supposedly secular radicals derived sustenance from Christian ideas and symbols and sought to infuse the new socialism with their power."[22] True, the University of Illinois' two founding clergy visionaries, J. B. Turner and J. M. Gregory, were not Socialists, but instead Republicans—as were the majority of students—and Gregory did his best to refrain from political and religious partisanship while leading University and other public affairs.[23] But the ideas of these key leaders and their educational peers nationwide featured a social progressiveness which opened the door for liberal theology. This book makes the case that the I.I.U. leaders and wider community lived during this period of theological transition, and that agricultural and mechanical education could be added to the evangelical social reform list as compiled by Dayton and others.

17. Ibid., 284.
18. Ibid., 284–85.
19. Dayton, *Evangelical Heritage*.
20. Marsden, *Fundamentalism and American Culture*.
21. Pitts, "Personal," 138–60.
22. Guarnari, "Associationists," 49.
23. Carriel, *Life of Jonathan Baldwin Turner*; Kersey, "John Milton Gregory as a Midwestern Educator," 20 passim.; Behle, "Scholars from the Sod," 204.

So a second innovation is that the book reveals a religious rationale for land-grant agricultural and mechanical education which is missing from prior histories. As discussed earlier, historians have tended to analyze the phenomenon from the contemporary scholarly lenses of politics, class, economics, or educational theory. While those have been helpful methods of analysis, this book adds a different dimension because it speaks from the perspective of historical theology, of how religious beliefs were embodied in the lives of a community and its individuals, in a dialogue with their larger culture.

In so doing, it adds a third innovation, because it provides insights into the era's public collegiate religious expression which are forgotten today. It does so by paying close attention to the religious rhetoric of key leaders and a sampling of students. It takes the I.I.U. community's ideas seriously, paying attention to how they are communicated through a common religious vernacular, where shifting cultural dynamics are interpreted as an interplay between leaders and their constituencies, formulating a public theology in order to motivate and explain. That is why their speeches and articles are often block-quoted at length, because if we endeavor to begin to understand the theological ideas and passion of the era and its people, we need to hear what they themselves say they believe, and how they said it in a way that was meaningful to them.

A fourth innovation, then, in demonstrating the religious vitality of the I.I.U. community, is that the book explains the era's transition not as secularization per se, but rather as a transformed understanding of Christian public service. As mentioned earlier, some land-grant historians have tended to link assumptions about educational secularization and apply it to the agricultural and mechanical milieu. The secularization thesis in American higher education has been widely debated in recent years. In the I.I.U.'s case, Winton U. Solberg first proposed it in 1966, tracing the move from non-sectarian Christian identity beginning in 1867 through waning Christian identity and the disestablishment of chapel by 1894.[24] Robert Bellah suggested a secularization thesis in 1984,[25] and by 1992, a flourish of publications on the topic emerged.[26]

---

24. Solberg, "Conflict between Religion and Secularism," 183–99.

25. Bellah, "Triumph of Secularism," 13–26.

26. Johnson, "'Down from the Mountain,'" 551–88; Hart, "Troubled Soul, of the Academy," 49–77; Cartwright, "Looking Both Ways," in Hauerwas and Westerhoff,

Major voices advocating the secularization thesis in the 1990s included the authors in George Marsden's and Bradley J. Longfield's book *The Secularization of the Academy*, and Marsden and Reuben in their excellent and influential monographs.[27] By the end of the decade, Jon H. Roberts and James Turner concluded that religion in American higher education declined in the latter nineteenth century due to a specializing professorate and an increasing empirical certainty that rendered religion irrelevant and therefore obsolete.[28] But some had been questioning the secularization thesis all along. In 1971, for example, David B. Potts argued that schools' denominational ties actually strengthened over the nineteenth century, with less of a conscious responsibility to the larger society outside of sectarian boundaries.[29] And strong arguments are found in a number of debates on the topic published within the last two decades.[30] More recently, scholars like Philip Harrold, David P. Setran, and John G. Turner have proposed a middle way by suggesting that universities did not actually secularize, but instead adjusted and reinvented the way religion was communicated and lived on campus.[31] This book proposes the same, mapping one institution's transition from the antebellum college ethos toward that of the new research model.

Content and Method

To explain this particular case study the book focuses upon two of the movement's key leaders, as well as I.I.U. trustees, faculty, guest lecturers, and students. The period of inquiry covers three and a half decades, from about 1845 until about 1880.

The first chapter, "A Good Time Coming" on "the Blessed Green Earth," traces the origin of the Labor's Millennium idea in the thought of Rev. Jonathan Baldwin Turner, a missionary educator and Yale University graduate. It will explain how the theological ideas there and elsewhere in Turner's writings, speeches, and endeavors provided an

---

Schooling Christians, 184–213; and Hauerwas, "On Witnessing Our Story," in Hauerwas and Westerhoff, *Schooling Christians*, 214–34.

27. See note 13 above.

28. Roberts and Turner, *Sacred and the Secular*.

29. Potts, "American Colleges," 363–80.

30. Bruce, *Religion and Modernization*; Hollinger, "'Secularization,' Question," 132–43; Sommerville, "Secular Society/Religious Population," 249–53.

31. Harrold, *Place Somewhat Apart*; Setran, *College "Y"*; Turner, *Bill Bright*.

ideology for the Illinois farmers' movement, which was instrumental in the eventual establishment of the I.I.U.

Chapter 2, "Reversing the Curse," demonstrates one example of the founders' vision of education as a means of public blessing, elevating humankind by eliminating the need for degrading and inefficient toil. Picking up where Turner left off, the Baptist minister and educator Dr. John Milton Gregory and other characters—including students—are introduced here, showing how the vision was cast, adopted, and put into practice.

Chapter 3, "'Men,' not 'Monks,'"—a concept of J. B. Turner's—moves from a collective promise toward a more individualistic focus, outlining what the I.I.U. community thought an educated person should become. Their leaders sought to form "Christian" people of high "character," graduates who would be dedicated to public service according to traditional and emerging conceptions of gender. Ethical topics like militarism, physical fitness, and temperance are covered here, as are pedagogical ones like curriculum, literary societies, the campus Y.M.C.A., and the student newspaper.

Chapter 4, "Liturgies for 'Learning and Labor,'" examines how the University's ceremonies and symbols communicated its shared values and mission as encapsulated in their motto "Learning and Labor." Attention is paid to the transition from inherited ceremonies from evangelical Christianity and church-based education into a more public realm, including the integration of civil religion into a low-church, pan-Protestant non-sectarianism.

Chapter 5, "Preaching Labor's Millennium," hones in on one aspect of the University's liturgical life, Regent Gregory's pulpit ministry, examining how he communicated the "Reversing the Curse" and "'Men,' not 'Monks'" visions. It charts the content and method of Gregory's influential preaching as a motivation for a new form of student piety and post-graduation public service, bridging antebellum evangelical education with an emerging Protestant liberalism and the rise of a public university.

The conclusion chapter summarizes the book's major themes, discussing the fruit of the I.I.U. experiment and lingering vestiges of the agricultural vision in American higher education and public life. It explains how the book adds to our understanding of the era's theological transitions in the realm of higher education and campus ministry.

A bibliography follows, listing primary and secondary sources consulted in order to compose the book.

A final word is worth mentioning regarding assumptions and philosophical leanings. James William McClendon's work regarding the relationship between faith, doctrine, and ethics has been highly influential in the research and writing of this book, as has his emphasis on the potential of narrative theology. Theology, he says, may be done through "the discovery of implicit religion lurking in society's crevices," keeping in mind that the Biblical narrative and the events of Christ's saving work impact a culture's story in such a way that a new creation is formed.[32] Similarly, the contemporary historian David W. Blight distinguishes between "History" and "Memory" as "two attitudes toward the past, two streams of historical consciousness that must at some point flow together." In his scheme, history, the domain of "trained historians," is "a reasoned reconstruction of the past rooted in research," while memory, the work of "poets and priests," is "often treated as a sacred set of potentially absolute meanings and stories." A history of memory, he says, can therefore be written studying "the power of myths that define societies and cultures."[33]

This book has been researched and written with the conviction that a community's dearest values reflect its understanding of the divine, and are embodied in its culture. As Robert A. Orsi has said, "Men, women, and children *together* make religious worlds in relationship with special beings and with each other."[34] Universities, acting as societal microcosms and centers for informational and ideational exchange, educate citizens according to the values of the university and the wider culture, which sometimes are congruent and sometimes are in tension with one another. The author confesses, despite the expanse of time separating our lives, a philosophical resonance with the Honorable Newton Bateman, Illinois' State Superintendent of Public Instruction, who told the crowd gathered at the I.I.U.'s March 11, 1868 inaugural ceremonies, "*Thought* rules the world, doubt it or deny it who may, and it will con-

---

32. McClendon, *Witness*, 26–37, 57, 97. See also his *Biography as Theology*.

33. Blight, "Civil War," B7. For a helpful exchange regarding history's self-imposed boundaries, the difference between historical theology and "faithful history," etc., see Yerxa, "That Embarrassing Dream," 63–64; McClay, "Thoughts on 'That Embarrassing Dream,'" 71; and Wells, "Donald Yerxa's 'Dream': A Reply," 67–70.

34. Orsi, *Between Heaven and Earth*, 2.

tinue to do so to the end of time."[35] As the Rev. Dr. John Milton Gregory said during the University's December 10, 1873 "Dedicatory Exercises" for their new University Building, one could read the events chronicled in the trustees' minutes and writings, but these would not be the truest histories. Instead, Gregory said, "at the centre and base of all true institutions lie ideas, . . . [and] an institution is but the incarnation of ideas; it exists for them, and its history is but the record of their development, progress and products."[36]

With these and similar thoughts in mind, let us now turn to the matter of how these persons' understandings regarding God and ultimate value[37] affected their teaching, learning, and other practices during the foundational years of their university.

---

35. Board of Trustees, I.I.U., *First Annual Report*, 165.
36. Board of Trustees, *Seventh Annual Report*, 63.
37. Grant, *God the Center of Value*.

1

"A Good Time Coming" on "the Blessed Green Earth"

THE LAND WHICH WOULD BECOME THE STATE OF ILLINOIS HAD ENJOYED centuries of human habitation, including a few French settlers who, in the seventeenth century, had come from the north and east in search of furs for the European market. Their Jesuit missionaries considered the indigenous Illinois people their most successfully evangelized mission in the entire region of what we now call the Midwest.[1] The earth itself allowed for relatively easy assimilation, being mostly flat, with a rich soil for planting, once one cleared and plowed the wide open areas of waving prairie grasses and other plants. And yet it was to the southern part of the state, in the thick woods along the many winding rivers and creeks, that the initial early national English-speaking settlers first came. At the time of Illinois' statehood in 1818, its U.S. citizens mostly hailed from Kentucky, Tennessee, and Virginia, bringing with them the customs of those places. Compared with its peer states in the Old Northwest—and certainly with states in the East—early Illinoisans were biased against the importance of public education, relying upon the religious schools to supplement the lack of a state-sponsored collegiate institutions.[2]

It was into this situation that seven young missionaries from Yale University arrived, establishing Jacksonville's Illinois College in 1830 as a means by which they could bring learning to the state.[3] One of these was a man named Jonathan Baldwin Turner, whose career exemplifies the Protestant theological evolution of the era, and the historical journey of Illinois. Born and raised a Connecticut Congregationalist, Turner

1. Leavelle, "'Bad Things' and 'Good Hearts,'" 393.
2. Howard, *Illinois: A History*, 173–74.
3. Solberg, *University of Illinois*, 16–17.

FIGURE 1: Jonathan Baldwin Turner

earned a BA from Yale's Classics department and pastored two churches before heeding the call of his fellow Yankees to become a missionary to the West. When he arrived at Illinois College, the campus consisted of a forty-foot square lecture building, a four-story dormitory, the head farmer's house, a cabinet shop, and the college barn, at that time reportedly the largest in the state. The college was a manual labor and classical school, and Turner served as the "Professor of Belles Lettres, Latin, and Greek," and a popular Sunday school teacher at the Congregational church for a decade and a half. Upon his arrival, Turner wrote to his fiancée, Rhodophia Kibbe, in Connecticut that Illinois was "indeed a land 'flowing with milk and honey.'" But, over time, the initial promise turned sour. Turner's outspokenness, abolitionism, and skepticism regarding divine election and predestination eventually got him into trouble with ex-Southerners generally, and specifically the Presbyterian Synod of Illinois, who, in 1844, launched an inquisition, questioning the doctrine of the faculty. By 1848, at the age of forty-five, Turner would resign his post at the college, "more feeble and broken in health," he would later write, than he was "at ninety-one years of age."[4]

As Turner's teaching career began to plummet, he spent an increasing amount of time gardening around his house in Jacksonville. Working in his extensive beds and groves—including some "cedars of Lebanon" which he had imported from Palestine—Turner eventually started engaging in horticultural experiments, most notably developing the Osage Orange hedgerow which became so popular in the Midwest. It wasn't long before he began advocating for agricultural education, and the word spread quickly. Jonathan Blanchard, President of Knox College in Galesburg, wrote "Brother" Turner in October of 1848, expressing his desire that a Mr. Kingsbury would endow Knox with "a Professorship of Agriculture, Horticulture, and Pomology" for Turner, "or at least pay [him] for a course of lectures." Turner liked the idea, saying "I pine for a professorship of the blessed green earth."[5] As early as 1840 the U.S. House of Representatives had proposed the establishment of a national agricultural school.[6] But for Turner and others of like mind

---

4. Carriel, *Life of Jonathan Baldwin Turner*, 9–61. President Beecher had already resigned in 1844 after going east on a fundraising trip and receiving a letter in Boston asking him not to return.

5. Ibid., 64, 73.

6. Cremin, *American Education: The National Experience*, 284.

the dream—which some mockingly called "Turner's folly"—would have to wait, as neither Illinois' churches nor their legislators were ready to pay for something which, they believed, could still be learned down on the farm.[7]

And yet, a movement was afoot which would enable Turner's vision to be fulfilled, because Illinois was a commonwealth of farmers who identified with romanticized notions of agriculturalism which were at least as old as the nation itself. In Illinois' earliest years of statehood, its politicians were predominately Jeffersonian Republicans, favoring a vision of self-employed, self-ruling agricultural entrepreneurs.[8] Historians often point to Thomas Jefferson as a leading theorist for American agrarian romanticism. Richard Bernstein, for example, says Jefferson had a "vision of the good society as an agrarian republic of independent yeoman farmers supporting themselves by their own labors. Self-sufficient to the greatest possible degree, they would maintain their virtue, the necessary ingredient for preserving a republic, refusing the seductive lures of manufactured luxury goods and the economic activities (trade and commerce) that created and distributed them."[9] On a 1786 trip to France, Jefferson said that, eschewing cities and dignitaries, he preferred to tour farms and visit with farmers, noting that the post-feudal village system of France was inferior to the family farm of the United States, and that Americans in France should concentrate on studying French agriculture, mechanics, and architecture.[10] Historian Merrill Peterson says "'[i]t was Jefferson more than any other man of his time who foresaw the fruitfulness of the application of science to agriculture.'"[11] Although at the time of the University of Illinois' founding an educational theorist from the U.S. Department of Agriculture would blame Jefferson's states' rights theory for the Confederacy's secession,[12] the University's first head farmer called Jefferson, along

7. Carriel, *Life of Jonathan Baldwin Turner*, 144–45.

8. Howard, *Illinois: A History*, 138.

9. Bernstein, *Thomas Jefferson*, x. Bernstein's contemporary, Joyce Appleby, disagrees: "Agrarian self-sufficiency never appealed to Jefferson; he plumped instead for a rural prosperity built on the export of America's bumper crops" (Appleby, *Thomas Jefferson*, 116).

10. Peterson, *Thomas Jefferson and the New Nation*, 350–52. These three fields would be emphasized in the early curriculum of the University of Illinois.

11. Peterson, *Jefferson Image*, 403.

12. Bollman, *Industrial Colleges*, 11. Bollman said, "Mr. Jefferson made [words] . . . poison; the Apostles, by [words], offered eternal life."

with George Washington one of only two American "fathers of modern Agriculture."[13]

Andrew Jackson's political revolution and 1828 election to the U.S. presidency encouraged poor westerners to improve their status.[14] Some two generations before, in 1785, in his *Observations on the Importance of the American Revolution*, the British Unitarian minister Richard Price—who was a friend of Benjamin Franklin and Thomas Jefferson—lauded the "independent and hardy yeomanry ... clothed in homespun—of simple manners—strangers to luxury—drawing plenty from the ground," blessed with health, long life, happy marriages, and numerous children: "O distinguished people!" he said. " ... [M]ay the happiness you enjoy spread over the face of the whole earth."[15] And Price was not alone in his enthusiasm. In that same year Celadon published a pamphlet foreseeing an American agricultural paradise. Two years earlier, Crevecoeur's popular *Letters from an American Farmer* did the same. And the Scottish cleric Hugh Blair's 1783 lectures lauding the "middle state" between prior civilizations' crude laborers and effete aristocrats became a popular textbook in American colleges through the mid-nineteenth century. It was a fruitful time for speculation about the promises of a new democratic agricultural age.[16]

Jefferson, in his *Notes on the State of Virginia*, had famously said: "Those who labour in the earth are the chosen people of God, if ever he had a chosen people, whose breasts he has made his peculiar deposit for substantial and genuine virtue." A few years later Philip Nicholas told the 1829–1830 Virginia Constitutional Convention, "I believe if there are any chosen people of God, they are the cultivators of the soil. If there be virtue to be found anywhere, it would be amongst the middling farmers, who constitute the yeomanry, the bone and sinew of our country."[17] Midwesterners generally believed in the morality and material progress

---

13. Periam, *Groundswell*, 33.

14. Solberg, *University of Illinois*, 22–40. Along with Jacksonian democracy, Solberg cites five other influences contributing to the agricultural education movement: an emerging practical curriculum as proposed by the leading Baptist educator Francis Wayland; romanticism of nature; economic changes requiring more precise methods; the rise of science; and agriculturalists' agitation.

15. Marx, *Machine in the Garden*, 105.

16. Ibid., 103–16.

17. Ibid. 43–44, 122.

of virtuous farmers, that human beings had the potential, through the dignity of hard work, to achieve a just, equal, and prosperous society.[18]

But there was still no organized means of collectively training people for the achievement of this goal. And into this dilemma stepped J. B. Turner as a leading prophet and catalyst of the movement. Jefferson, of course, was perhaps the preeminent American scholar of agriculture of his generation, experimenting at length on his Monticello farm. Turner's backyard research in Jacksonville mirrored Jefferson's example. But what about those hardworking Illinoisans who did not have the wealth, education, and leisure to study their vocation on their own?

In the early 1850s, Turner began to actively work toward establishing a public agricultural and industrial university.[19] Concurrently, he was involved in the advent of state farmers' conventions that would meet throughout the decade, resulting in the founding of the Illinois State Agricultural Society. The first of these met on November 18, 1851, in Granville, Putnam County, with a "quite large" attendance "from various parts of the State."[20] Oaks Turner of Hennepin—who was not a relative of J. B.—was elected chairman, and J. B. Turner, though not an officer, was appointed to a committee determining items of business. At the evening session, he proposed that, since the "professional, scientific, and literary" classes enjoyed the blessing of educational institutions, so should "the industrial classes" have "the same privileges and advantages . . . in each of our several pursuits and callings." And so, Turner moved, "we take immediate measures for the establishment of a University, in the State of Illinois, expressly to meet those felt wants of each and all the industrial classes of our State." His proposal included the founding of high schools and the like in each county which would serve these populations as well.[21]

Turner then read at length from his "Plan for an Industrial University, for the State of Illinois." Beginning with the premise that the "professional" and "industrial" classes are "not antagonistic" toward one another, he mused that "we do not really need over one professional man for every hundred, leaving ninety-nine in the industrial class." The vast majority, then, still had no advanced education "to elevate them,

18. Cayton and Gray, *American Midwest*, 10–12.
19. Turner, *Plan for an Industrial University*, 1851, n.p.
20. Ibid., 14–15.
21. Ibid., 14–15.

their pursuits, and their posterity to that relative position in human society for which God designed them." Professionals, he said, are "laborious thinkers," while industrials should be trained to be "thinking laborers"—one for helping the mind, the other the body: "But neither mind nor body can feed on the offals of preceding generations," he said. An entirely new mode of education must be established. History had taught, he said, that "higher institutions" impacted the quality of the lower schools, rather than the other way around. So, he proposed, a "National Institute of Science" was of primary importance—already available in the Smithsonian Institute—which could be networked with an industrial university in every state.[22]

Such a university, he said, may or may not teach classics, as was the norm among his contemporaries. But research should definitely, he said, be a cornerstone, "to facilitate the increase and practical application and diffusion of knowledge." Apparatuses would therefore be necessary, as would public lectures and means of communicating with the farmers in practice around the state. To those who might think the subject matter beneath the dignity of higher learning he said, "the field embraces all that God has made, and all that human art has done; and if the created universe of God and the highest art of man are too gross for our refined uses, it is a pity the 'morning stars and the sons of God' did not find it out as soon as the blunder was made." Agriculture, he said, was every bit as noble as medicine, theology, law, astronomy, or Greek. Appealing to Illinois' naturally fertile prairie soil, he asked the audience, "is not such an object worthy of at least an effort, and worthy of a state which God himself, in the very act of creation, designed to be the first agricultural and commercial State on the face of the globe?"[23]

The next morning, after considering Turner's elaborate plan for a public agricultural university, the convention moved to adopt his proposal and publicize it throughout the state via newspapers, *The Prairie Farmer*, and a thousand of their own pamphlets. They also agreed to solicit the governor, senators, representatives, and state officers regarding the cause, insisting that an entirely new university be established, rather than organizing multiple agricultural programs in the existing colleges.[24] Perhaps ironic that a clergymen would argue against clerical oversight,

22. Ibid., 18–21, 28–29.
23. Ibid., 22, 25, 29.
24. Ibid., 16–17.

Turner had said the University must be "at once and forever beyond all legislative and ecclesiastical control," since partisanship would inevitably corrupt the mission and limit its access to all.[25] This was, of course, a hot-button issue, prompting "a controversy" and much discussion at the second convention, held in Springfield on June 8 of 1852. Advocates for the established denominational colleges were admitted to the meeting, stumping for state funding to be directed their way to enable industrial education, but they failed to persuade the agriculturists to their cause.[26] Ohio's denominational colleges would do the same thing, failing as well.[27] In Kentucky and Oregon, though, as strange as it might sound to readers today, the state legislatures initially attached their tax-funded agricultural education to existing denominational colleges.[28]

As early as 1874, the University of Wisconsin's Baptist President John Bascom would begin telling audiences that Kingdom work transcended the narrow pettiness of sectarian religion, and that a Christian state could be a great means of public good.[29] It is possible that such thinking informed Turner's liberal opinion that a non-sectarian and non-partisan university should be established for the toiling majority of it's population. This controversial idea prompted a barrage of mudslinging in the Illinois press, with the churches crying foul to Caesar's meddling with impressionable young minds and souls, and the agriculturists—including Turner—countering that anticlericalism should prevail. Public opinion increasingly sided with Turner. This parallels historian James Dombrowski's claim that organized labor impacted mainstream Protestant theology and vice versa, and that "many labor leaders, while disavowing ecclesiastical religion, were professed followers of Jesus."[30] Yet he says that the U.S. Christian labor movement began in the 1870s, while Turner and the Illinois farmer's alliance predates him by two decades.

At least one other Midwestern state experienced a similar pattern. Minnesota had a man named Oliver H. Kelley who, according to historian James Gray, by "the middle of the 1850s . . . had already become

25. Ibid., 30–31.
26. Ibid., 34–36.
27. Cope, *History of the Ohio State University*, xii.
28. Edmond, *Magnificent Charter*, 33–35.
29. Hoeveler, "Universities and the Social Gospel," 289, 292.
30. Dombrowski, *Early Days of Christian Socialism in America*, 5–7.

a sort of agricultural John the Baptist."[31] Kelley's and others' promptings would lead Minnesota to, like Illinois, eventually establish an agricultural university. Perhaps there are unknown others like Turner and Kelley in this prophetic band. But still, historians generally locate Christian Socialism and the Social Gospel in the U.S. as beginning no earlier than the 1870s or 1880s.[32] Along with agricultural movements like the Grangers, the 1870s marked the beginning of organized labor movements among Illinois' factory and railroad workers.[33] Quite possibly, then, the 1850s farmers' movement led the way regarding organized labor in Illinois, and perhaps elsewhere.

By the third state farmer's convention, held in Chicago on November 24, 1852, momentum was building, and a host of activities had been initiated. "The Industrial League of the State of Illinois" was created, and chartered by the legislature in February of 1853, with J. B. Turner serving as a paid Director. His "Plan for an Industrial University" was further commended, and he, along with L. S. Bullock and Ira L. Peck, were commissioned "to prepare an address to the citizens of this State, on the subject of Industrial Education, and the establishment of an Industrial Institution."[34] By the time of the fourth convention, in January of 1853, Turner was well on his way in preparing a speech that would become the movement's manifesto: "The Millenium of Labor."[35]

"The Millenium of Labor"

The concept of "the millennium" was familiar in a nation of persons steeped in Christian doctrine. Rooted in the teachings of the biblical book of Revelation, it literally meant the thousand year rule of God on earth, often expanded and interpreted symbolically as God's eternal presence and reign as seen in the prophecy's final chapters. The "city on a hill" (Matthew 5:14) vision of Puritan colonists was prompted by

---

31. Gray, *University of Minnesota*, 33.

32. Dorrien, *Making of American Liberal Theology*, 270–75, 304–14; Buckingham, *Expectations for the Millennium*, 1–18, 35–54; Phillips, *Kingdom on Earth*.

33. Howard, *Illinois: A History*, 375–79; Scott, "Grangerism in Champaign County," 139–63.

34. Turner, *Industrial Universities*, 37, 56–59.

35. Throughout this book, original spelling, capitalization, and punctuation will be maintained in quotations from and bibliographic entries for nineteenth-century works.

postmillennial theology, a divine mission to work with God to establish, in the Christian era, a heavenly society on earth. As historian Carl Guarneri has said, by the mid-1800s the vision had expanded into the public consciousness in myriad ways, as "millennial longings could be found among a wide spectrum of Americans that included Mormons, abolitionists, presidents, business leaders, revivalists, and Fourth of July orators."[36]

Although not an Independence Day celebration, speeches were a top attraction at the first Illinois State Fair, which was held in the capital city of Springfield in October of 1853, after the Illinois Agricultural Society donated funding for the event.[37] The Society had invited Jonathan Baldwin Turner to speak specifically on the topic of "the Millenium [sic] of Labor," which he did, at the fairgrounds, on October 14th.[38] The following will summarize the speech's major themes and flow, quoting some phrases at length to get a feel for the explicitly religious rhetoric.

Throughout the speech, in order to promote hope, clarity and build momentum, Turner frequently repeated the line "there is a good time coming." He begins:

> There is a good time coming. Poets have sung of their golden era. The devout of all ages have clung to this hope, and their sages and prophets in the hour of their darkest gloom have ever fixed their eye upon the future risings of this millenium [sic] dawn. God seems to have impressed the conviction of its approach upon the mind and heart of the race.
>
> But when poetry and art, and philosophy and faith, shall greet the first rising of this long desired day, labor shall be there—labor—first in the primeval paradise before the fall—first companion of the Son of God; first at the cross and first at the tomb; first and almost sole to bear the triumphs of that cross abroad. *labor*—the source and producer of all else shall be there, too, acknowledged triumphant, and crowned as the true glory and giver of all.
>
> This millenium [sic] of labor is fast coming. I see it in its errand-boys, born from the thunder cloud, outracing the sun; in its horses and chariots of fire and of steel, that dart with light-

---

36. Guarnari, "Associationists," 43; Gaustad, *Rise of Adventism*.

37. Howard, *Illinois: A History*, 264. The fair would rotate annually from city to city during its early years.

38. Turner, "Millenium of Labor," 51.

ning speed across every continent and over every mountain height.

The enraptured and almost incredible visions of prophets and seers of old already begin to grow tame and common-place, when read along side of the existing realities of its progress and its triumphs.[39]

Turner suggests that the industrial age is a fulfilment of God's progressive intention for humankind. Those who had lived before them in all places and ages had longed for this day, and, good news!, it was being fulfilled before their very eyes. As extreme as it might sound, this idea would successfully resonate with Turner's audience as a link between mechanization and millennial deliverance. For example, a Harvard-trained lawyer named Timothy Walker argued in his 1831 "Defence of Mechanical Philosophy" that a society "will make the greatest intellectual progress, [sic] in which the greatest number of labor-saving machines has been devised," prophesying a millennial utopia where "machines are to perform all the drudgery of man, while he is to look on in self-complacent ease."[40] And similarly, the I. I. U.'s contemporaries who authored an 1860 article called "Improved Hay-Maker," asked, "Are not our inventors absolutely ushering in the very dawn of the millennium?"[41]

Turner continues:

There is a good time coming . . .

I see it in the congregated masses of free and independent artisans and yeomen around me, assembled here under nature's great crystal palace, which a few years since over-arched only the wigwam and the war dance, to take each other by the hand, exhibit the products of their toil and their skill, toward their mutual faith, and fire their hearts anew by a reiteration, even from this new land, of the peals of that anthem that already swells and resounds over earth and sea. Dandyism, sham and humbug crucified—labor, merit, worth exalted, crowned—peace on earth, good will to man, and glory to God in the highest.[42]

Here, familiar millennial themes are invoked regarding America as a New Eden, and City on a Hill, achieving its manifest destiny through

39. Ibid., 51–52.
40. Marx, *Machine in the Garden*, 185.
41. Ibid., 198.
42. Turner, "Millenium of Labor," 52.

the virtue of the noble laborer, who has been modeled, Turner said, by great men of the past: Socrates, "the sculptor"; Cincinnatus; Washington, "the farmer, and model chief"; "the tent-makers and fishermen of Judea"; and "their Divine Master, the Son of God himself, whose hands here on earth were hardened with the saw and axe of the carpenter, as well as pierced by the nails of the Pharisees." Christ, Turner said, "has evidently crowned these varied efforts of labor with his divine blessing, and granted them a success and a power on earth which all their adversaries can neither gain nor resist, and against which neither the insolences of cockneyism nor the jeers of idleness and vice, nor the gates of Hell shall ever prevail."[43]

The final line prompts the listener to deduce that perhaps one should interpret this movement of God as a sign of the true church invisible and universal. Yes, Turner implied, the fulfilment of God's divine intent for human history was occurring in his audience's own lifetime.

"There is a good time coming," he said again, "and that time shall be the millenium of labor. But," he said, evoking an image from Revelation 6:9-10, "the souls of the toiling millions, like those crying from out of the altar, still ask, how long—how long before these things shall be?"[44] When would this long awaited judgment and deliverance come, and by what means?

The answer, Turner then said, was beginning to unfold: technological progress, especially in the industrial realm. Citing example after example of recent material advancement, he appealed to his audience to romantically remember the rapid march of mechanization during their lifetime, reminding them of how much better off their children now are.[45] "The millennium of labor is coming" with a Promethean flourish, he said,

> and when it comes it will prance with its ten thousand chariots of fire over all these prairies and these plains. The west is the great green ocean of that iron commerce that is to mark its triumph, and of which or own state is to be the central port of entry and of exit. Fellow citizens, there is a good time coming for industrial labor and skill, and we have assigned us a noble part to play in the face of the world for its advance.

43. Ibid., 52–53.
44. Ibid., 53–54.
45. Ibid.

> Shall we play it well?
> SHALL WE PLAY IT WELL? That is the only question?[sic]⁴⁶

Turning the responsibility of completing labor's millennium, then, upon his listeners, Turner's answer somewhat curiously begins with an appeal:

> It has been said that the aboriginal inhabitants who preceded us on this soil were the first men then upon the continent. They were called the "Illini"—which means pre-eminently "the men"—and their country "Illinois" or "the land of the men." We have taken their name and their heritage; shall we show ourselves worthy of the name and that inheritance, and to bear down through all coming time the memorials of that once proud and noble though now unfortunate and extinct race?
>
> We thus call ourselves "the men" and our state "the land of the men." Shall we be such in fact? Then great will be the labor, and great the good, and great the renown, that shall result from the part we play in ushering into the world the good time coming—the millenium [sic] of labor.⁴⁷

Earlier in the speech, Turner implied that Illinois' native peoples were an inferior civilization. Yet here he says that the settlers have a responsibility to carry on their predecessors' dignity by becoming "men," a theme which will be discussed at length in chapter three. He does tell his audience that Illinois' native inhabitants had "perished" because "a higher civilization came," but then Turner warns his listeners that the same thing could happen to them.⁴⁸ But thankfully, he said, there was a key difference between the two civilizations. Unlike the native peoples, the new settlers had

> *mind*, which [the natives] had not ... the great motive power of the universe ... the steam power of the eternities. It is the high prerogative of this mind to overmaster and enslave all matter and reduce it to a perfect subjection to its wants and its uses. Mind is the only freeman and matter the only slave God ever made. That man, therefore, or that class of men who have most mind will most nearly approximate the condition of freedom,

---

46. Ibid., 54.
47. Ibid.
48. Ibid., 54–55.

and those who have least will inevitably sink to the nearest level with the slave.[49]

So education, Turner said, is what makes the difference. And how one stewards it affects the outcomes. After all, he reminded his listeners:

> It was the triumph of mind over matter that produced your products and bore them to this fair with railroad speed and I may add railroad gratuity, too.
> Thus much, then, this power of mind has already done for you. But all this, vast as it may seem to you, is but a drop in the bucket compared with what that same power of mind is ready to do for you, if you will but invoke its continued presence and aid; for its powers and its resources are infinite and eternal.[50]

Here Turner sets the groundwork for the pinnacle of his speech. If his listeners are to "play well" the advent of labor's millennium, then they need to improve their minds, which can cause even more advancements than already accomplished:

> The same power that has brought us up from the barbarism in which our ancestors lived can bear us with equal ease still higher aloft, and that is the power of mind—mind not applied to barbarian mythologies and still more barbarian abstractions, mystics, and metaphysics, but mind applied to our daily avocations and pursuits.[51]

So the next question before them, Turner continued, is how they might put mind power to work to enhance their own industries as it has already been put to work in others. For example, in an earlier era, "labor wield[ed] the power of faith and of God, for the *eternal* salvation of man" in "the person and mission of our Saviour," in whom "labor became incarnate in the highest specimen of humanity and seized upon the highest attributes of the human soul . . ." Depicting the incarnation of Christ as a sign of labor's millennium would doubtless leave a powerful impression on the minds of those present. And then next in history, Turner said, came another messianic figure, George Washington,

---

49. Ibid., 55.
50. Ibid.
51. Ibid., 57

through whom "in this second great drama of labor was enacted the *political* salvation of man."⁵²

But now, Turner said, it was the Illinoisans' turn. Because

> it was reserved for the laborers in this great valley of the far west to take under their charge the last great social and moral interest and necessity of man—*the cause of liberal industrial education*—and thus prepare the way fully for the great triumph and millenium of labor; and as in other lands and other times this labor has already begun to wield the powers of piety and polity for man's eternal and civil salvation, shall it not here also begin to wield the powers of education and intellect for his *industrial* and *social* salvation?

> This question you are now called upon to answer ... You must also take in charge the education of [the world's] coming teeming millions or you fail at once of your duty and your destiny too. You must teach earth's millions as the great apostle of the Gentiles directed, "How to study, to be quiet, to work with their own hands, that they may walk honestly and have need of nothing."⁵³ For in this world of ours God has foreordained that ignorant and idle men must either be dishonest or lack many things. This is the only predestination of earth to which we are all alike fated.⁵⁴

So theirs was a divine mission, Turner said. But this new education would depart from the past curriculum of ancient languages and metaphysics. Instead, Illinoisans would "look abroad upon the green earth, as God made it, and view at one and the same glance, with the true poet's and philosopher's eye." Empirical observation—science—would be the way toward industrial agricultural improvement, producing "the finest products and greatest amount of human weal with the least amount of human toil." This work would please God, he said, and help them attain "the entire perfection of [their] manhood." And if they do it, he told them, twenty years from now people would admire their vision and progress. But better still, in fifty years their offspring "will look back upon us this day as we do now upon our swarthy predecessors—as being only in the barbarism of agriculture and art." Why? Because their current agricultural practices, he explained, were inefficient, wasteful, and

---

52. Ibid., 55.
53. This is the Apostle Paul's advice as found in 1 Thessalonians 4: 11.
54. Turner, "Millenium of Labor," 56.

often ecologically disastrous, "deteriorating" soil quality and potentially yielding "starvation or emigration." Such future foundational agricultural practices, which would meet everyday needs, were "as unknown to the wisest among us as they were to the savages who preceded us."[55]

So if such progress was to happen, it was up to them to do something about it:

> Our brethren of the professional classes ... have not studied science and Providence so long and so vainly as not to know that in this world's affairs, at least, God helps only those who help themselves. He has given them their place of labor and duty to take care of, and in that respect they have done it. They have founded schools and universities--libraries and apparatus—for the application of knowledge to their several arts; and now, with all the advantages which they have derived from this foresight and wisdom fully before our eyes, they call upon us to do the same for ourselves ...
>
> Fellow-citizens, the moment you do this, and do it effectually, you have struck the next most important and most needed blow for the proper dignity of your profession—the millenium [sic] of labor—and the amelioration and civilization of man; and until you do this you have done nothing, as a class, effectual for your profession, your posterity or your race.
>
> Until our fellow laborers the world over arm themselves with this panoply of light and of power they cannot be otherwise than the virtual servitors of those who do; for God has ordained that knowledge is power; and those who will not take the needful steps to secure the knowledge must live and die without the power.[56]

Just in case appealing to inter-class competition and the world-wide movement of labor's upward mobility were not enough to motivate his audience, Turner reminded them of Jeffersonian romanticism regarding the nobility of their profession:

> I would covet for myself and for my children no higher earthly distinction than the capacity, the knowledge and science requisite to cultivate in the best possible manner 160 acres of our prairie land, and discharge thereon all the necessary duties of an American free laborer. And if I had it I should know more at

55. Ibid., 57.
56. Ibid., 58.

this moment than all the professors and teachers and scholars, statesmen, lawyers and divines, that have ever trod this continent since Columbus first bowed his knee upon its eastern sands.[57]

Having made his case, then, that an industrial education would be the highest and most practical form of human knowledge, he gave one final appeal to his listeners. After politely thanking the citizens of Springfield and of Sangamon County for their hospitality,[58] he encouraged the farmers to take the matter into their own hands and agitate for the establishment of the University. He ended the speech by asking:

> have you done enough? Are your energies ... for Good ... to man—and to God—all exhausted?
> Shall not the millions of free laborers that are in all coming time to throng and till the vast plains of our great western green ocean home, rise up hereafter, and over your prairie graves pronounce your names blessed, and your very dust sacred and hallowed, for one more act of imperishable beneficence done to them and theirs?
> In your hearts let this, this day, be decided, and at your homes, and at the polls let it be enacted—and posterity shall declare you worthy of the name you have assumed for yourselves and your state,
> "ILLINOIS"—"THE MEN"—"THE MEN."[59]

Turner's "The Millenium of Labor" speech was not only heard by those in attendance that day at the fairgrounds, but was sent, via the society's journal *Transactions*, to individuals and libraries throughout the state. The farmer's movement continued to grow, and Turner remained its primary spokesman.[60] In 1858 he further solidified his status as an educational leader and scholar by being elected the first president of the Illinois State Natural History Society. As the farmer's movement gained speed, the passage of the 1862 Morrill Act, which provided land for the establishment of new colleges and universities, aided its cause. Although the church-related colleges repeatedly appealed to the state to grant Morrill funding to them, Turner's vision of non-sectarian public

57. Ibid., 59.
58. Ibid., 61.
59. Ibid., 61.
60. Periam, *Groundswell*.

education eventually prevailed, contributing to the Illinois Industrial University's founding in 1867.[61]

Turner's Footprint

When J. B. Turner began calling for the establishment of an industrial university in Illinois, agricultural research was a new field. In retrospect, it is staggering to consider how quickly the movement expanded, and what an influential role Turner played in its inception and implementation.

In a "Memorial" of the fourth farmer's convention written for the Illinois Senate and House of Representatives, for example, agricultural society president Bronson Murray imitated, almost verbatim, Turner's ideology and rhetorical style.[62] It was apparently effective, because on February 8, 1853, just a few months prior to the "Millenium of Labor" speech, the Illinois General Assembly unanimously adopted an appeal to the U.S. Congress for "the Establishment of Industrial Universities, and for the Encouragement of Practical and General Education among the People." It contained a summary of Turner's plan, including cooperation with the Smithsonian. Illinois asked for this almost a decade before the passage of the Morrill Land Grant Act. The move captivated attention in the press, with the *New York Tribune* and *Illinois Journal* commenting on the appeal.[63]

At about the same time, on January 26, 1853, a national convention commenced in Albany, New York, featuring prominent leaders in church, state, and education. They met to consider the potential establishment of a "practical" national system of higher education. A committee of twenty-one was appointed, including clergymen like famed Baptist educator Francis Wayland, Bishop Potter, Rev. Dr. Kennedy, Rev. Ray Palmer, and Rev. Dr. Wykoff, all of whom agreed that the industrial classes needed a university education, too. Furthermore, the group lauded J. B. Turner, noting that he had been commended by esteemed publications such as the *Horticulturalist*, the *New York Tribune*, and the *Southern Cultivator*.[64] *The North American*, for example, said: "The

---

61. Smith, "Envisioning and Embodying a Public, Protestant Paideia," 29–41.
62. Turner, *Industrial Universities*, 38–42.
63. Ibid., 43–44.
64. Ibid., 47–53.

proposition of Professor Turner seems to be entitled to peculiar and favorable consideration, and it is urged with a force of argument and eloquence that cannot fail to secure it."[65]

Along with his persuasive eloquence, it did not hurt that Turner was from a thriving state. As he and his fellow agriculturalists were agitating for the new university, a population and railroad boom was happening throughout Illinois.[66] Less than a decade later, in 1862, a federal Department of Agriculture was created, fueling the Northern push for scientific farming.[67] Illinois' own Abraham Lincoln, the President under whom the Department was founded, would also sign bills to establish two other key movements in U.S. agriculture: the aforementioned Morrill Act, and the Homestead Act, which provided farms to landless persons seeking to improve their lives.[68] Turner actually knew Lincoln personally, having conversed with him on multiple occasions in Lincoln's rural summer home during the Civil War.[69] After the war Illinois enjoyed national celebrity and notoriety through new heroes like Ulysses S. Grant. This growth period resulted in the commissioning of both a new constitution and a new capitol building. A good time had definitely come to the people of the prairie state.[70]

According to J. B. Turner, Illinois' legislature led the nation by asking the federal government for $500,000 worth of land granted for an industrial university, while giving Illinois' state "Industrial League" $20,000 to do so. He urged Illinoisans to do what New Yorkers did-- take Illinois' reports (which Turner claimed New York had plagiarized) and ask their industrial population to endow a university.[71] They did, along with help from *The Prairie Farmer*, which organized a series of meetings to accomplish what twentieth-century historian Robert P. Howard calls Turner's "dream of a single state institution supported by land grants."[72] Although others have disputed Turner's leadership in this area, the earliest Illinois Industrial University trustees minutes

---

65. Ibid., 49.
66. Howard, *Illinois: A History*, 255–57.
67. Phillips, "Antebellum Agriculture Reform," 799–822.
68. Dil, *Norman Borlaug*, 228.
69. Carriel, *Life of Jonathan Baldwin Turner*, 277–85.
70. Howard, *Illinois: A History*, 331–38.
71. Turner, "Millenium of Labor," 60.
72. Howard, *Illinois: A History*, 277, 339.

occasionally quote Turner in their frontispieces, and their rhetoric is reminiscent of Turner's speeches and reports. In 1898, long-time I. I. U. Professor Thomas J. Burrill recalled that the 1851 Granville Convention began not only advocacy in Illinois, but also nationally, resulting in a February 1853 request from Illinois' General Assembly to the U.S. Congress "praying for the endowment and establishment in each state of industrial universities for the promotion of the more 'liberal and varied education adapted to the manifold wants of a practical and enterprising people.'"[73] Three years after Burrill's speech, University of Illinois Professor Eugene Davenport paid homage to Turner's millennial vision when the University dedicated a building for the study of agriculture.[74] And three years after that, historian Paul Selby would assert that Illinois played a leading role in the movement.[75]

A half century after Burrill, Davenport and Selby made these claims, Cornell University historian Carl Becker called Turner *the* seminal theorist for land-grants, and leading land-grant historian Edward Eddy wrote that J. B. Turner's was the earliest voice calling for mechanical and industrial education, and personally had a key influence upon Justin Morrill's decision to establish the movement.[76] Eddy and others of his era identified political and economic reasons why this was the case. What has not been previously discussed, though, is the impact of the theological ideas and rhetoric upon labor's millennium. J. B. Turner was a deeply religious man who was Yale-educated and ordained in a mainstream American denomination. A former pastor and educational missionary, he continued to remain active in church affairs. And Illinoisans themselves were a religious people, belonging mostly to evangelical churches. In the 1870 census, Illinois' largest denominations reported the following number of churches and/or ministries: 1,426 Methodist, 722 Baptist, 595 Presbyterian, 290 Roman Catholic, and 212 Congregational, which was Turner's denomination. Other less prominent Christian groups were present, while Jewish and other non-Christian religious communities were numerically small by comparison.[77] So when J. B. Turner would speak or write of a good time coming

---

73. University of Illinois, *Memorial Convocation*, 12.
74. Davenport, "Dedication Speech for Davenport Hall."
75. Selby, "National Education Movement," 214–29.
76. Eddy, *Colleges for Our Land*, 23–27; Kammen, *Cornell: Glorious to View*, 4.
77. Behle, "Educating 'The Lord's Redeemed and Anointed,'" 61.

on the blessed green earth, most Illinoisans surely knew what he meant: that God, in Christ, was making things better, and God's purposes were being fulfilled in their own era and place through agricultural and industrial education. Now it was time to put the dream into practice, as the University opened its doors and commenced its teaching and research function.

2

Reversing the Curse

AFTER SOLICITATIONS FROM A NUMBER OF ILLINOIS COMMUNITIES, Champaign-Urbana was selected as the site for the new university.[1] In the Spring of 1868, sixty-eight students gathered there to become the first matriculants. They had responded to a summons by the state legislature and undoubtedly hoped that the University would bring prosperity to their fellow citizens and themselves. As land-grant historians have shown, utilitarian and nationalistic rationales motivated the founders of such colleges, and the I.I.U. leadership was no different in that regard.[2] Quoting their commission by the Morrill Act, they said the University's "chief aim" was to educate "the industrial classes" by teaching "such branches of learning as are related to Agriculture and the Mechanic Arts, and Military Tactics, without excluding other scientific and classical studies."[3] They intended that farmer's children would come and help fulfill their radical and compelling vision, one which was intrinsically theological: "The hope of the Trustees and Faculty," they said, "is that the Institution will produce ... men of Christian culture ... able and willing to lend a helping hand in all the great practical enterprises of this most practical age."[4]

Although perhaps surprising in today's academic climate, making claims to promote Christian civilization was not unusual for some of the early land grants. An official document of the Massachusetts Agricultural College, for example, said "the Bible is adapted as an invaluable textbook, and its teachings regarded as constituting the best

1. Solberg, *University of Illinois*, 59–85.
2. Eddy, *Colleges for Our Land*; Edmond, *Magnificent Charter*; Nevins, *State Universities and Democracy*; Ross, *Democracy's College*.
3. Illinois Industrial University, *Circular and Catalogue*, 4.
4. Ibid.

rules for the conduct of life."[5] New York's agricultural school, in its 1867 "Features of the University," said "The Cornell University, as its highest aim, seeks to promote Christian civilization."[6] Neither Cornell faculty nor students, however, would be judged based upon doctrinal opinions. Illinois, too, did not require student assent to a creed, but still had a reputation for being quite religious.[7] The "majority" of I.I.U. students, says Greg Behle, grew up in "frontier denominations known for their evangelistic fervor."[8] Other public schools in the Midwest consciously cultivated a Christian identity, ethos, and self-understanding,[9] although, ironically, land-grants around the nation were sometimes attacked as godless and immoral institutions.[10]

The motivating vision at the I.I.U., though, was articulated in the language of Christian belief. One specific feature of the founding vision involved the reversal of Adam's curse as described in Genesis 3:17–19. Humankind, the I.I.U. visionaries believed, had toiled miserably for their sustenance since time immemorial. But now, by God's grace, the divinely ordained dignity of farming as covenantal co-laboring with God would be restored. After completing an agricultural education, said I.I.U. head farmer Jonathan Periam, students, "instead of despising the labors of the farm, will glory in the fulfillment of the great command—far less a curse than blessing—which says, 'In the sweat of thy brow shalt thou eat they bread.'"[11] Furthermore, they believed, emerging technologies were going to lessen the quantity of sweat, because God's gift of empirical science would enable them to feed themselves and their neighbors more efficiently, while granting them intellectual stimulation, physical exercise, and spiritual benefit at the same time. By putting their hands to the plow of agricultural education, they claimed, the Lord would usher in nothing less than what J. B. Turner prophesied as a "Millennium of Labor," liberating, the I.I.U. trustees said, "the toiling millions of man-

---

5. Ross, *Democracy's College*, 132, 217.
6. Eddy, *Colleges for Our Land*, 56.
7. Solberg, "Conflict between Religion and Secularism," 185–86.
8. Behle, "Scholars from the Sod," 204.
9. Longfield, "From Evangelicalism to Liberalism."
10. Nevins, *State Universities and Democracy*, 53.
11. Periam, *Groundswell*, 541.

kind" who "must still, by the stern but beneficent ordination of Heaven, 'eat their bread in the sweat of their brows.'"[12]

Citing the Biblical "sweat-of-their-brows" idea of Genesis 3:19 was an ongoing literary tradition, having appeared in some earlier American writings. The colonial author Robert Beverly, for example, thought of North America as a pre-lapsarian Eden, with the native peoples retaining their purity by missing Europe's corrupting artificial vanities, having "'seem'd to have escaped, or rather not to have been concern'd in the first Curse, *Of getting their Bread by the Sweat of their Brows* . . .'"[13] In 1846, Charles Fraser published a magazine article on "The Moral Influence of Steam" in which he said "for so wonderfully does [steam power] relieve the necessity of physical exertion, that it seems destined . . . to disturb the moral economy of the world, by opposing that great law of the universe, which makes labor the portion of man, and condemns him to earn his bread by the sweat of his brow . . . "[14] Illinois' own Abraham Lincoln often spoke of the "the sweat of thy brow" when referring to labor.[15] His disdain for slavery was expressed as the intrinsic injustice of one person's work to feed someone else while not feeding himself or herself, a basic concept among the era's labor proponents which achieved theological weight when considering Adam's—and his farmer offspring's—lot in life.[16]

As discussed in the previous chapter, Illinois' farmers and laborers, who were familiar with daily exertion for their physical sustenance, resonated with the curse-reversing good news proclaimed by Jonathan Baldwin Turner. As part of labor's millennium, he said, the worker's status would be elevated. As early as 1853 he expressed an interesting hermeneutic regarding labor's simultaneously condemning and salvific affect on the human condition. He said

> God, himself, made the first Adam a gardener or farmer, and kept him so till he fell from his high state. The second Adam, sent to repair the ruin of his fall, he made a poor mechanic called "the son of a carpenter," who chose all his personal followers from the same humble class. Deity has pronounced his

12. Illinois Industrial University Board of Trustees, *First Annual Report*, 64.
13. Beverly, *History and Present State of Virginia*, 17.
14. Marx, *Machine in the Garden*, 199.
15. Smith, "Uncommon Man," B7.
16. Ibid., B8.

opinion on the dignity and value of these pursuits, by the repeated acts of his wisdom and grace, as well as by the inflexible laws of his providence compelling industrial labor as the only means of preserving health of body, vigor, purity of mind and even life itself.[17]

In Turner's Christology here, the second Adam—Jesus—functions not as a crucified atoner, but instead as a hard-working example of labor's redemptive qualities. Historian James Dombrowski says that, in the emerging Social Gospel theology, "In the passion of Jesus was seen the crowning achievement of a life spent freely in the service of man, the symbol for all time of the social passion that should characterize all human relationships."[18] Evil social forces, therefore, could be overcome through collective service to society, as Jesus had done in his day. Taking on these forces for the uplift and restoration of the worker were in the forefront of Turner's mind. Unequal educational opportunity, he said, "generates clans and castes, and breaks in upon that natural order, equality, and harmony which God has ordained . . . produc[ing] a bedlam rather than a kingdom on earth . . . as sure as God lives and reigns . . ."[19] During his famous "Millenium [sic] of Labor" speech he said: "We must respect ourselves and our professions, as God and nature designed that we should, and then we shall have no need to challenge the respect of mankind. We are not oppressed by our brethren of the professional classes; we are simply depressed by neglecting to do for ourselves what they have already wisely and properly done for themselves; and they now exhort us to do the same; and we must do it."[20]

Turner believed that by reaffirming the divinely-ordained dignity of the farmer's vocation, and its resulting self esteem, public opinion could be swayed by this new army of confident, educated planters. But unfortunately, too many thought too lowly of the vocation the I.I.U. visionaries claimed was closest to God. Turner asked his audience:

> What then, my friends, is your idea of a farmer or a mechanic? Is it merely a mass of meat and bones, six feet by two, that can hold a plow, fat a steer, feed a pig, or drive a jack-plane, or swing a trowel? I have met men who had about them that high con-

17. Turner, "Industrial Universities," 374.
18. Dombrowski, *Christian Socialism in America*, 17.
19. Turner, *Industrial Universities*, 5.
20. Turner, "Millenium of Labor," 57.

ception of the proper dignity of their calling and I dare say you have.

Shall I then attempt to give the outline of the true farmer and the true mechanic—such as they ought to be and shall be when the millenium [sic] of labor shall fully come?

It is the conception of a man who has such an intimate knowledge of all the hidden processes of nature—such a practical skill in combining all the laws and resources of the universe—meteorological, geological, chemical and physiological and the great art of production—such fullness, breadth, amplitude and power of mind on all practical subjects of industry, morals, policy and faith as would cause all the school-men and professors of our day to hang their heads and blush for shame in his presence—a hard-handed, able-bodied, strong-minded, whole-souled, all-knowing, all-conquering man, worthy of himself and of the God who made him such—not a mere machine to hold plows and feed pigs. This and this only is the true farmer when the millenium [sic] of labor shall come—as much above all other professions in the natural and necessary development and vigor of his intellect, as he now is in the natural health and vigor of this body or as farmer Adam was before the fall above that same fallen farmer now.[21]

Becoming such a "man" was no small undertaking, and the I.I.U.'s curriculum toward achieving that end will be discussed in the following chapter. But once such an educated farmer was produced, and he, through research, began to invent and manufacture labor-saving devices, Turner told his audience this good news:

Fellow citizens, God made us all intellectual beings, and to do the work of intelligence and freedom, not the drudgery of ignorance and servitude. And when the millenium [sic] of labor comes, brute beasts will perform less really hard service than we and our children do now, and brute matter, enslaved by free mind—iron and steel and steam, without weariness or disease, will become the bone and sinew of our industry, as God designed they should, instead of living flesh and living souls."[22]

About two decades later, when the cornerstone of the I.I.U.'s new University Hall was laid in September of 1872, Turner triumphantly told the crowd that the Lord's purposes had been accomplished, since

21. Ibid., 58–59.
22. Ibid., 60.

the "sons of our farmers and our friends" would now become "true sons of the Republic and true sons of God . . ." They would be educated "in institutions which are in no sense conventional, partisan, or sectarian, but in all their methods, ends and aims truly, grandly, and broadly industrial, natural, scientific, and American, and therefore christian [sic] . . ."[23] But Turner, the budding movement's leading theologian, spoke that day only as an invited guest. He had turned down a bid to lead the University as its first "Regent," which was the term they selected rather than "President."[24] The trustees had chosen a man perhaps, in hindsight, even more fit for the job than Turner: the Rev. John Milton Gregory, L.L.D., who faithfully and tirelessly served the I.I.U. from its founding in 1867 until his departure in 1880.

A Pastoral Regent

During a Monday morning chapel talk in 1874 Regent Gregory expressed beliefs similar to J. B. Turner's: "Labor gives health," he said. As "both the Bible and Nature" say: "'work if you will live.'"[25] Gregory explained to the I.I.U. faculty and students that God designed the earth for people to cooperate by laboring. God, he said, did not curse humanity by establishing work, because "Labor is Honorable . . . Has God made the daily doom of so many of His intelligent creatures low in its nature and necessarily degrading? . . . How mean and how unchristian the thought!" Labor itself was not the problem, Gregory said; *sin* was the problem. The world's prior history of toiling serfs and leisured nobles was a diabolical corruption of God's intended laboring order for humankind, because labor, he said, "transforms the world itself from the savage wild to the fruitful Eden."[26]

It was exactly this type of leader the I.I.U. founders needed: some one with the gentility of a scholar, the golden tongue of a preacher, and the chameleon-like adaptability of a diplomat. How did Regent Gregory arrive at this point, where he could so skillfully comingle evangelical

---

23. Illinois Industrial University Board of Trustees, *Fourth Annual Report*, 354.

24. Kersey, *John Milton Gregory and the University of Illinois*, 66; Carriel, *Life of Jonathan Baldwin Turner*, 55.

25. Illinois Industrial University, *The Illini* 4/2 (November 1874) 34.

26. Ibid., 35.

FIGURE 2: John M. Gregory surrounded by early faculty members.

theology with public practice, and communicate it in such a way that all parties—secularist and sectarian alike—could be satisfied?

John M. Gregory was born and raised in Sand Lake, New York, in a Baptist family originally from Connecticut.[27] His mother, Rachel Bullock Gregory, was a religious woman who loved books. A capable teacher in the home, two of her children would become pastors, and two others university presidents. Yet she died in childbirth when John was only four. His father, Joseph Gregory, soon married Almira Foster, and she brought her eleven children to join Joseph's eleven, resulting in a large and busy household which, along with its twenty-two children, held the village library. Baptized at thirteen, John showed an early interest in both faith and learning, favoring reading in solitude over working in his father's busy tannery and fields. After teaching at his brother Lewis' school in Gilboa, John attended Union College in Schenectady, where President Eliphalet Nott's influence would shape Gregory's own eventual university leadership. John graduated Phi Beta Kappa in 1846, began to study law, but soon abruptly abandoned it—following a significant religious awakening—to become the Baptist pastor in Hoosick Falls. A self-taught Bible scholar, long-time I.I.U. professor Thomas J. Burrill once said of Gregory: "Among those who pass judgment in such matters he was considered to have attained eminence in theology, though never having taken a regular course of instruction of this nature."[28]

John married his second cousin Julia Gregory in 1848. They turned down a call from the Sand Lake church, leaving New York for the First Baptist Church of Akron, Ohio. By 1852, though, the couple left full-time pastoral ministry altogether, primarily because it was difficult for Julia, who suffered from poor health. John launched his career as a full-time educator, teaching at his brother Uriah's Detroit Commercial College, and founding the *Michigan Journal of Education* in 1854, which he edited until 1859. After being nominated by the fledgling Republican party, he served three terms as Michigan's superintendent of public instruction, and, from 1859 to 1865, was a member of the Michigan Board of Education, giving him first-hand experience in the establishment and

---

27. Kersey, *John Milton Gregory and the University of Illinois*; Kersey, "John Milton Gregory as a Midwestern Educator"; Allene Gregory, *John Milton Gregory*; Smith, "Envisioning and Embodying a Protestant Paideia," 15–22.

28. Roberts and Turner, *Sacred and the Secular*, 16.

governance of the State Agricultural College of Michigan, which would later become Michigan State University.[29]

By 1864, Gregory brought all of these prior experiences together, resulting in a theoretical framework which would aid the I.I.U. Becoming president of the Michigan Baptists' Kalamazoo College that year, his published inaugural speech, *The Right and Duty of Christianity to Educate*, provided a public apologetic for understanding state-sponsored education as a form of Christian ministry. This idea was not only expressed by Gregory, as Wisconsin's President, John Bascom, said in an 1876 baccalaureate address that "the state like the individual has the duty to be righteous. It has the right and the duty to push to completion ... its own highest attainments in itself and its citizens."[30] Gregory and J. B. Turner had similar thoughts to Bascom regarding religion's place in public university life. Turner believed that an industrial university should maintain the wider American culture's integration of family, school, church, and state, as each facet depended upon one another.[31] And Christianity, Gregory said, had the "right" to be foundational in American higher education because it "holds in its keeping some of the most potential agencies of instruction—the grandest and most fruitful ideas that ever enter the human mind, and the most impressive motives that ever influence human action."[32] This classically Protestant understanding of education builds upon a theological assumption regarding God's self-disclosure through scripture and the church. And because, Gregory said, the church stewarded the Word of God,

> Christianity cannot be shut out of the world's great school rooms. To banish it is to banish the only adequate agent for a full and rounded development of human souls ... Mutually co-working with all parties—with the parent, the child and society—welcoming, and co-operating with, the State in all that the State can be permitted to do, prompting the parent to a higher solicitude, and the child to nobler aspirations and to more diligence, and stimulating society, to a juster regard for public virtue and public intelligence, Christianity yet claims for itself a further and higher field of educational work, a field where it labors peerless and alone.

29. Powell, *Semi-Centennial History*, 275.
30. Hoeveler, "University and the Social Gospel," 292.
31. Turner, "Industrial Universities," 368.
32. Gregory, *Right and Duty*, 7.

Only Christianity, he argued, could meet the needs of "the religious nature in man"; the State could not help in that particular area. After all, Jesus was primarily a "Teacher"; that is why the church had established schools in the first place. "Education," Gregory said, "assuredly, cannot be neutral. It must either be Christian, Jewish, or Infidel . . . Hence in making such an exclusive selection, the State must enter into alliance with one or the other of those forms . . ." Since most Americans were Christians, he said, it would not be unethical for a public school classroom to teach a Christian world view. In fact, according to Gregory, it would be unethical *not* to, because

> The grand elements of modern civilization are found not in the ideas of Plato and Aristotle but in the ideas of Jesus of Nazareth. Human brotherhood—the inalienable and equal rights of mankind—the sole sovereignty of God, and the sole accountability of man to God for his religious opinions—the duty of doing to others as we would be done by,—all these are christian [sic] ideas, and they lie at the very center of our Christian civilization.—Strike these out from the popular mind and heart, and how speedily should we return to the old barbarisms, from which all its science could not save ancient Greece. And how shall these ideas continue current in the nation's life, when they are no longer plainly recognized in the nation's schools, or appear there stripped of the divine sanctions that give them authority and power?

Capping his argument, Gregory said that teaching is the "divinely appointed mission of Christian men," and quoted the "great commission" of Matthew 28:18-20 to "go and teach all nations" as his proof text. But here the mission's scope was expanded from specifically religious teaching to the larger acquisition of knowledge. "All sciences," he said, "even the merest physical science, have a divine side; and the true scholars, in every department of learning, as they approach the grand ultimate truths in their studies, find themselves in the presence of the Creator." All learning, he believed, was religious work—a seeking of God's mind.[33]

Guided by this doctrinally evangelical and yet inclusively public theology, it is easy to see how Gregory and others of like mind could jus-

---

33. Gregory, *Right and Duty*, 7-8, 11, 14, 15. Bascom echoed similar ideas in an 1887 baccalaureate address called "The Christian State." See Curti and Carstensen, *University of Wisconsin*, 287-88.

tify establishing a new type of research university on religious grounds. Indeed, Gregory was a perfect fit for the I.I.U. presidency. His lifetime of educational and pastoral experience prepared him to quite competently teach, lead, and relate to the public. He was so revered by his peers that he was elected the first president of the national organization called the "Friends of Agricultural Education" during their inaugural convention in Chicago in 1871, selected from among the top educators of the at least eleven different colleges and universities from across the U.S. which were represented at the conference.[34] Gregory's abilities nicely fit the I.I.U.'s needs.

But, as will be discussed at length in chapter 5, perhaps Gregory's greatest contribution to the I.I.U. cause came from his pulpit presence. Consider the power unleashed by the vision-setting address called "The University," which Gregory gave at the I.I.U.'s "Dedicatory Exercises" for the new University Hall, held on December 10, 1873. "At the centre and base of all true institutions lie ideas," Gregory said, "and "an institution is but the incarnation of ideas; it exists for them, and its history is but the record of their development, progress, and products." He then proceeded to explain for them the core ideas which had been so foundational for the I.I.U. Rebuking Princeton University's president James McCosh, who had recently criticized the absence of academic rigor in agricultural education, Gregory said, in tones reminiscent of Jonathan B. Turner, that the I.I.U. faithful were "in the midst of a great conflict— the battle of the ages." He told them he was fully devoted to "the great cause" of industrial education, "whose principles," he said, "are to me as God's truths." That's why, he said, he had willingly endured persecutions like incessant public criticism, his family's exile due to "their inability to endure the [Illinois] climate," and his own poor health resulting from his unceasing toil for the University's cause. Gregory then invoked the memory of a colleague, Professor William M. Baker, whose "labors on earth [had] ceased . . . While the spring flowers were yet blooming," Gregory said, "we laid his mortal remains away in the grave which he believed to be but the portal to a better world. A genuine worker, and a noble, christian [sic] man, history will embalm his memory among those who toiled faithfully for the good of the University and of mankind."[35]

34. Board of Trustees, *Fourth Annual Report*, 221.
35. Board of Trustees, *Seventh Annual Report*, 63, 67–69, 73.

After this emotional appeal came the crux of Gregory's speech: the salvific necessity of omnipresent, luminous, "Learning and Labor"—the I.I.U.'s official motto—with its radiant "coronal [sic] of light." Gregory said "the *spirit* of scientific industry and education rules in our midst, fills our halls, haunts every lecture room, breathes in every recitation, and does its rich and beneficent work."[36] So

> There is no mockery—there is no lurking sarcasm—there is no humbug in [the University's] yonder motto [, "Learning and Labor," literally] written in this great auditorium where we meet daily to worship God, and ask His blessing on our efforts. There is a prophecy in it grand as science and its future, grand as the God of science, who was the first Worker—the great Author of both learning an labor—a prophecy of the coming time when you and I shall lay our heads under the sod, and leave to younger hands to clasp and bear onward down the march of time the banner upon which we have written that motto, till they plant it in the culmination of history over the crowned humanity of free, enlightened and regenerated man.
>
> The work which we have roughly outlined will be accomplished, and in the end God will not leave on this earth one single one of the necessary employments of mankind, or of womankind, unredeemed from that old, clinging curse which reduced labor to ignorant, sweating toil—will not leave a single avocation necessary to the maintenance or civilization of mankind, which shall not demand and receive its own share of all that guiding and glorifying light that He has written in the starry skies above, in the petals of flowers beneath, and on this whole framework of things—not a machine, but a book. And labor thus linked to learning become the mightiest education of the soul, working out the problems of truth in the laboratory of God, shall reinterpret this might [sic] divine volume of worlds, out of which shall come grander conceptions of the author than ever yet swept through the heart of the wildest dreamer, or penetrated the brain of the profoundest theologian.

Gregory prophesied to the youngest there assembled that, when they became "gray-haired and sage," they would remember the day's "predictions," that "there lie in these two words, Learning and Labor, the clasped hands of the marriage tie," the "sworn oaths of love and mutual service, between the Brain of man—God's Senate Chamber on

---

36. Italics added.

the earth—and the Hand of man, God's vicegerent [sic] on the earth of noblest work and worship."³⁷

After ending the speech abruptly with that line, the University's choir responded by singing a "dedication ode" entitled "Learning and Labor" which was "written for the occasion." Its lyrics, in their entirety, are as follows:

> DOWN the line of struggling ages,
> Swells the cry for truth and light,
> Wrung from bosoms of the peoples,
> Dimly yearning for the right.
> Toiling millions, bravely bearing
> All the burdens of the day,
> Supplicate the ear all-hearing,
> For to labor is to pray.
>
> Down the line of ages flaming,
> Glow the kindling fires of thought;
> Flashing 'neath the stroke of hammers,
> Light, as well as iron, is wrought.
> And the mighty schools of labor,
> With their problems deep and stern,
> Educate the toiling peoples,
> For to labor is to learn.
>
> Thus the Father's wisdom giveth
> Answer, from the prayer outwrought:
> From the furrowed fields of labor
> Come the harvest sheaves of thought;
> And from out the lines of ages,
> Gleams the truth of Christly birth—
> Learning, incarnate in labor,
> Shall regenerate the earth.
>
> Then to labor and to learning
> Let us consecrate these halls:
> Lo! they come as God's strong angels
> Bringing light and breaking thralls;
> Kindling in us hopes supernal
> Of a glorious coming time,
> When the love and might eternal
> Shall work out God's will sublime.³⁸

---

37. Board of Trustees, *Seventh Annual Report*, 74–76.
38. Ibid., 62.

By comparison, Cornell University's "Alma Mater," composed during the same period, contains no explicitly Christian references as does the I.I.U.'s.[39] In Regent Gregory's mind, though, Learning and Labor were nothing less than means of grace, beckoning the faithful to respond with reverent worship. When Illinois' governor, J. L. Beveridge, stood up to speak after the audience had finished singing "Learning and Labor," he said "Now I do not feel like Moses, standing upon holy ground, but I feel that I tread upon very delicate ground."[40] True, they may not have been at church, it apparently felt mighty close. The "ode" was so revered that it was adopted as the "University Hymn."[41] As the audience left the new building, they could see the phrase "Learning and Labor" literally carved, as trustee J. O. Cunningham had suggested, in the stone frieze above the pillars surrounding the front doorway, an icon to help the I.I.U. faithful remember how they had pledged their troth to the God who would bring labor's millennium to their prairie land.[42]

There was something contagious about Gregory's vision as expressed through his person and leadership. Alumni would recall the power of his sermons and lectures, and their long term effect upon them. Gregory's love for learning itself enlightened the prairie community. Lorado Taft remembered observing, at the age of thirteen or fourteen, Gregory lecturing, with stereoptical illustrations, on the topic of sculpture. "The enthusiasm of the speaker made my blood tingle!" Taft said. "A new heaven and a new earth were opened up to my imagination. Unconsciously that night settled my fate ..."[43] Taft's vocational conversion in response to the I.I.U.'s premier educational evangelist was not unique. The curse-reversing, millennial vision of "Learning and Labor" so eloquently expressed by Gregory permeated the I.I.U. community, influencing some remarkable ideas, speeches, policies, and behaviors.

The Community Concurs

"The good providence that has thus far prospered us," Regent Gregory told the I.I.U. trustees at their 1871 annual meeting, "will still be over

39. Kammen, *Cornell: Glorious to View*, vi.
40. Board of Trustees, *Seventh Annual Report*, 77.
41. Unknown, "Decennial Anniversary."
42. Students of the Senior Class, *The Student (Illinois Industrial University)* 2/1 (January 1873) 7; Board of Trustees, *Seventh Annual Report*, 105.
43. Powell, *Semi-Centennial History*, 314–15.

us . . ."[44] Like many of their time and place, people at the I.I.U. believed in a benevolent, providential God who had called them into a covenant of stewardship. Six of the twenty-nine founding trustees—all appointed by Governor Oglesby—were active members, like Gregory, in Baptist churches, and two of them had even led Baptist colleges.[45] Almost all of the rest were active in other Christian denominations. It is not surprising, then, that they would support views like those of guest lecturer Samuel Edwards, who said "Our Allwise Father made no mistake when He gave man the fruits of Eden for his food, nor has man, by his wisdom, found a diet more wholesome or acceptable."[46] Farming, they believed, was therefore foundational for human existence, and was upheld as the ultimate vocation for any man created in God's image.[47] Ralph Waldo Emerson said all people believed that farming had "its ancient charm, as standing nearest to God, the first cause."[48] During an 1870 public lecture sponsored by the I.I.U., Trustee Willard Flagg agreed, asking his audience, given that "on a well regulated farm . . . where the beautiful birds will want to linger and discourse their cheerful songs of praise; out in the pure breeze and sunshine of heaven; away from the throng and vices of the city; where all nature is spread out before us, suggesting the wisdom, power and goodness of the Great Ruler of the Universe . . . who would not be a FARMER?"[49]

Flagg's audience may well have nodded in agreement. Illinoisans had romanticized about nature's Edenic properties for some time. Ever since God had placed Adam in a garden and made Eve from his rib, humanity's ideal place was understood to be on the farm.[50] The U.S. Department of Agriculture echoed this view, saying that "The Creator" has "given dominion" over the animals to the farmer."[51] These examples are consistent with the larger American experience. As historian Henry Nash Smith explains, Americans moved west to cultivate their "Garden

44. Board of Trustees, *Seventh Annual Report*, 71.
45. Powell, *Semi-Centennial History*, 340–41.
46. Board of Trustees, *Second Annual Report*, 273. For an excellent study of humankind's search for Eden, see Delumeau, *History of Paradise*.
47. Marx, *Machine in the Garden*, 122; Peterson, *Jefferson Image*, 43–44.
48. Board of Trustees, *Third Annual Report*, ii.
49. Ibid., 247.
50. Ibid., 351–52.
51. Bollman, *Industrial Colleges*, 8.

of the World" which "became one of the dominant symbols of nineteenth-century American society—a collective representation, a poetic idea (as Tocqueville noted in the early 1830's) that defined the promise of American life. The master symbol of the garden," Smith said, "embraced a cluster of metaphors expressing fecundity, growth, increase, and blissful labor in the earth, all centering about the heroic figure of the idealized frontier farmer armed with that supreme agrarian weapon, the sacred plow."[52] In the Midwest, "the idealized Western yeoman" was thought to be the cultivator of the Garden, sometimes expressed in millenarian ways.[53] As discussed in the prior chapter, Jefferson is attributed with starting the dream of cultivating the West's garden. But Smith concludes that the failure of the Republicans' 1862 Homestead Act and the aridity of the high plains and far west dashed any hope of agricultural utopia.[54]

Despite the flurry of optimistic rhetoric, during the I.I.U.'s founding period farmers were actually struggling financially. The "Panic of 1873" was a depression which historian Robert P. Howard says "lasted a decade" and was "the severest the nation experienced."[55] Agricultural overproduction coupled with mortgage financing left farmers vulnerable, as did concern over railroad tariffs and grain elevator monopolies.[56] As a result, agriculturalists banded into various societies, most notably the Grangers, although they did not last as long as in neighboring states, primarily because Illinois' Republicans were able to effectively solve the railroad regulation problem and appease the farmers.[57] Trustee Flagg, who became renowned for taking on the powerful railroads, led the Independent Farmers Organization, which highly affected the 1873 state judicial election.[58] The following year these antimonopolists, along with Democrats, elected the state superintendent of public instruction

---

52. Smith, *Virgin Land*, 12, 123. Gail Finney argues for a similar romanticism in Europe in *Counterfeit Idyll*.

53. Smith, *Virgin Land*, 133–44.

54. Ibid., 15–18, 165–83, 189–94.

55. Howard, *Illinois: A History*, 359.

56. Ibid., 358–64.

57. Ibid., 357.

58. Ibid., 363. Grangers in Wisconsin were able to elect their candidate for governor during this same year.

and made gains in the General Assembly.[59] Those within the I.I.U. orbit were familiar with and active in the affairs of the day.

Following conventional wisdom, previous rural manual labor schools like Turner's Illinois College had required students to farm, not only to help feed their community, but to build piety and character as well, a notion which will be explored in more detail in the next chapter. Agricultural historian J. B. Edmond says that manual labor was normative for land-grants during the early period, as specified by the Morrill Act, but makes no mention of any one providing a theological rationale for labor as Turner and Gregory had done.[60] The I.I.U. trustees, however, agreed with Emerson that "labor is God's education."[61] No other calling, said I.I.U. Head Farmer E. L. Lawrence, "requires . . . so many of the qualities . . . that go to make up the perfect man as designed by an all-wise Creator," the farmer needing "the skill of the mechanic and engineer; the tact of a lawyer; the sagacity of a judge; the capacity of a governor; the perseverance of a saint, and the faith of a christian [sic]; all these combined with the powers of a Hercules."[62] Reputable I.I.U. dignitaries like trustee Matthias Dunlap of Savoy captained vast, bountiful farms throughout the state. And both Flagg and fellow I.I.U. guest lecturer Elmer Baldwin told their audiences that indeed, people may have made towns, but to remember that *God* had made the country.[63]

This popular agrarian theology solidified in Illinois among those joining Turner in the movement, achieving millennial proportions as time went on. Owen Lovejoy, writing to Turner, hoped that someday "every one of the human family" would "have a part of the great farm of the Heavenly Father."[64] Baldwin prophesied a realized eschatology and millennium of labor for an audience gathered for an 1870 I.I.U. extension lecture in Rockford. Describing the advent of the "hardy son of toil," Baldwin said:

> Deriving his support and rewards of his labor direct from the hand of Providence, and living in close contact with the grandeur and beauty of nature's handiwork, seeing the imprint of di-

59. Howard, *Illinois: A History*, 364.
60. Edmond, *Magnificent Charter*, 162–65.
61. Board of Trustees, *First Annual Report*, frontispiece.
62. Board of Trustees, *Fifth Annual Report*, 227.
63. Ibid., 233; Board of Trustees, *Third Annual Report*, 397.
64. Carriel, *Life of Jonathan Baldwin Turner*, 151.

vine intelligence on every leaf and breathing from every flower, he can [sic] but be devout.

Old age to such a man comes not with disease and pain, and with dwarfed and dying sensibilities, but his faculties become brighter and more highly appreciative as he approaches the immortal.

Were such the character and such the life lived by the rural population, our political economists would have no reason to speculate on the decline and extinction of the race. A higher and more glorious destiny would await them[,] class legislation and class privilege would disappear before their intelligence, and a more perfect intellectual, physical and moral man would convert our country into a modern Eden.[65]

Baldwin's rhetoric encapsulates the I.I.U.'s mission of forming "hardy sons of toil" who would carry the torch of Learning and Labor into the hamlets of rural Illinois, restoring its Edenic righteousness. This, too, was a familiar notion in American lore. Celadon's 1785 pamphlet *The Golden Age* foresaw America as a millennial paradise, and in Crevecoeur's popular *Letters from an American Farmer* [1783] his farmer-hero says "Sometimes I delight in inventing and executing machines, which simplify my wife's labor," as, in America, "human industry has acquired a boundless field to exert itself in—a field which will not be fully cultivated in many ages!"[66] The future was bright for both the prairie state and the nation.

Jacksonville's Newton Bateman became corresponding secretary and traveling agent for the newly formed Illinois State Teachers Association in 1853, two years after the Granville farmers' convention and the founding of the state's first free public high school in his and J. B. Turner's community.[67] A graduate of Illinois College, former high school superintendent, and future president of Knox College, Bateman served as an ex-officio I.I.U. trustee via his post as Illinois' State Superintendent of Public Instruction.[68] He succinctly and passionately expressed the missionary necessity for a millennium of Learning and Labor when he told the crowd assembled for the new University Hall's cornerstone laying ceremony on September 13, 1872: "The cry of the disappointed and

---

65. Board of Trustees, *Third Annual Report*, 398–99.
66. Marx, *Machine in the Garden*, 105–7, 116.
67. Howard, *Illinois: A History*, 275–76.
68. Powell, *Semi-Centennial History*, 339.

tired world is 'Give us the true bread and water of life—we are starving upon husks and fleshless bones. If there is balm in the Gilead of science, bring it down to us, for we are sick unto death. If there is blessing and power in philosophy and learning, dispense them to the toiling millions. We would not know less of the world to come, but more of these visible heavens and this solid earth.'"[69]

Responding "to this long and bitter cry of the ages," Bateman said, "we have at last a *new departure* in education," with the motto, "The invisible things of God from the creation of the world are clearly seen, being understood by the *things that are made*."[70] This gospel was no mere hope in the comfort of spiritual salvation, but rather a tangible, visible, and realized eschatology of cornucopia. "Bowing to the truth that by the sweat of his face shall man eat bread," Bateman continued, labor's millennium "seeks to lessen the sweat and increase the quantity of bread" by "invit[ing] desponding farmers to the cheering revelations of vegetable physiology." Let industry, democracy, commerce, agriculture, and education serve the multitudes, he said, bringing economy, efficiency, and beauty, "for it is the will of God that *earth*, as well as heaven, shall be filled with brightness and glory."[71]

Bateman had publicly expressed a similar hope and mission a few years prior when he addressed the audience gathered for the I.I.U. inauguration ceremony on March 11, 1868. Regent Gregory had proposed the motto "Learning and Labor" for the school, and the phrase, spelled in green letters, adorned the chapel wall, along with a lithograph of George Washington, "the great Farmer of the Revolutionary period."[72] After various choral and instrumental musical selections were performed, a number of political and educational dignitaries made short speeches. Then, the crowd rose to its feet, and sang, along with the choir, the University Anthem, with lyrics composed by Regent Gregory and music by Chicago's famous George Root:

I

We hail thee! Great Fountain of learning and light;
There's life in thy radiance, there's hope in thy might;

69. Board of Trustees, *Eighth Annual Report*, 358.
70. Bateman is referring to Colossians 1:16 here.
71. Board of Trustees, *Eighth Annual Report*, 358–59.
72. Board of Trustees, *First Annual Report*, 149.

We greet now thy dawning, but what singer's rhyme,
Shall follow thy course down the ages of time?

II

O'er homes of the millions, o'er fields of rich toil,
Thy science shall shine as the Sun shines on soil,
And Learning and Labor—fit head for fit hand—
Shall crown with twin glories our broad prairie land.

III

And as generations, in the grand march of time,
Shall toil the long ages with numbers sublime,
Thy portals shall throng with the lowly and the great,
Thy science-crowned children shall bless all the State.

IV

Then hail thee! Blest fountain of learning and light,
Shine in thy glory, raise ever in might;
We greet now thy dawning; but ages to come
Must tell of thy grandeur, and shout Harvest Home.[73]

After this reverent and motivational song, Bateman gave a sermonic speech outlining the history of the Illinois agricultural movement, urging the people to usher in labor's millennium. He finished with this striking benediction:

> May the God of light and knowledge and love smile upon the transactions of this day—may He accept and bless the offering we here lay upon the altar of truth and liberty. We have waited long for this Institution and for this hour—both have come at last. With beaming garments and glorious prophecies of good to all the people of this Commonwealth, the Illinois Industrial University, escorted and upborne, I trust, by the heartiest benedictions of all, to-day moves grandly to the front, and assumes her position at the head of the imperial line of forces by which the State would draw the whole people up to light and knowledge. Well may every mind be impressed as we stand at the head-springs of this new fountain, and pray that its streams may be *pure, copious,* and *perennial* . . . Henceforth the inscription upon the temples of highest learning, as well as of the common

---

73. Ibid., 154–55. This University Anthem remained in use until at least 1877: see Unknown, "Decennial Anniversary."

school, is to be: "*Whosoever will*, let him come . . ."[74] Glory be to God in the highest, and on earth, peace, good will to men.[75]

In order for learning's fountain to flow, or course, some labor in the form of research would be required. Though decidedly Turneresque "Men," the Christian faculty of the I.I.U. would embrace their work with monk-like devotion. Consider perhaps the most exemplary faculty example, the Methodist Thomas Burrill, who was the I.I.U.'s Professor of Botany. In a January, 1869 public lecture, Burrill quoted Genesis 1:28–30, saying that humankind was given "dominion" over all things. But the dominion, he argued, did not make humanity "an absolute monarch" over the creation.[76] Instead, Burrill said, human rule required responsibility: "Like every other gift of the Creator," he said, plants "are ours to improve. [God] always gives us elements from which we must develop their possibilities . . . He furnishes the materials; we, by patient study and consummate skill, must learn how to use them."[77] Guest lecturer Elmer Baldwin agreed with Burrill's humane attitude toward Christian stewardship, telling his audience that farmers should allow ample warmth and protection for pigs in the winter, "where their owner will not have the nightmare from listening to their unearthly screams from suffering from the biting cold . . . I do not believe that any good christian [sic] can say his prayers and sleep easily and quietly while the whole neighborhood is made vocal by the cries of his freezing pigs."[78]

Numerous other I.I.U. lecturers said things similar to Burrill and Baldwin, citing a covenant between God and humanity to righteously cultivate the Garden, cooperating with the divinely established agricultural, geological, and meteorological laws of nature, and even the guidance of scripture.[79] With this theology in place, a commission was there for research and practice which would inevitably lead, or so they thought, to labor's millennium.

The I.I.U. students, arriving on campus with, for the most part, their evangelical theology intact, welcomed what educational historian

74. Bateman quotes Revelation 22:17 here, a millennial vision of invitation to eternal life with the victorious Christ in the new creation.

75. Board of Trustees, *First Annual Report*, 172.

76. Board of Trustees, *Second Annual Report*, 321–22.

77. Ibid., 320.

78. Ibid., 295.

79. Smith, "Envisioning and Embodying a Protestant Paideia," 163–67.

Lawrence Cremin calls the "paideia"—the educational ethos—of their university.[80] The religious essays cited by students in the University journal called first the *Student* and then the *Illini* reflect a common popular genre of the period.[81] A student author named Del. (the name included the period), for example, noted how, once the new Eden arrived, proper gender relations would be restored. Del. said: "God gave woman her rights, and in Eden she stood, *not* man's superior as some would now contend, but his equal, and competent to fill her position as his companion and helpmeet. But society, in the ages since then, has taken from her those rights, and for centuries she has been man's toy or slave, and circumstances have decided which."[82]

But Del. hoped that the curse of womankind's fall would be reversed. Citing his or her advocacy of evangelical feminism, Del. said "Our Regent" had recently told the I.I.U. community that "'Eden will be restored to the earth when woman is restored to the position she held there.'" As John Gregory's personal papers show, he was clearly a feminist according the progressive evangelical views of his day.[83] The Christian feminism embraced by the I.I.U. community and others of like mind prompted them to work hard to make it happen.

Another benefit of restoring Eden, the I.I.U. community believed, would be the grace bestowed by beauty itself. Agriculture and horticulture not only brought a material blessing to God's people, but an aesthetic one as well. An I.I.U. student wrote that nature's beauty provided spiritual uplift, wonder, and conviction of one's need for God. The author quoted this uncited poem:

> "God might have made the Earth bring forth
> Enough for great and small,
> The oak tree and the cedar tree
> Without one flower at all."
>
> "Our outward life requires them not,
> Then whyfore had they birth?

80. Lawrence Cremin employs the term *paideia* throughout his two volumes *American Education: The Colonial Experience, 1607–1783*; and *American Education: The National Experience, 1783–1876*.

81. Brown, *Word in the World*.

82. Illinois Industrial University, *The Illini* III, no. 6 (June 1874) 147.

83. Gregory, "Women Manuscripts c. 1875."

> To minister delight to man
> To beautify the earth."
>
> "To comfort man, to whisper hope
> When e'er his faith is dim,
> For who so careth for the flowers
> Will care much more for Him."[84]

Similarly, Regent Gregory, addressing the State Horticultural Society at Jacksonville in December of 1871, called flowers "reminiscences of Eden and prophecies of Heaven," being "God's incarnated smiles ... teaching us a theology better than creeds" through "unending illustrations" of "infinite trust in that divine Fatherhood which gives their splendor to the lilies and tells us that 'Solomon in all his glory was not arrayed like one of these.'"[85]

Valuing horticultural beauty translated into an emphasis upon improving the University's grounds. Alumna F. Adelia (Potter) Reynolds, class of 1874, remembers her initial impression of the first University building: "A large, plain, red brick five story building set down flat, in the black Illinois mud, with not a tree nor a shrub, a spear of grass nor a fence. It was as desolate a place as possible to imagine, and to us, just from a pretty little village home (in Wisconsin), surrounded by trees and flowers, it was enough to make us homesick."[86]

The Grand Prairie section upon which the campus lay was part of a flat, grassy plain stretching southward from the shore of Lake Michigan. Although fertile, it lacked variety, so in 1868, the trustees' Horticulture Committee suggested planting a one hundred sixty acre strip on campus in orchards and forest plantations, with the north part designated as an arboretum "for the use of the University, and the citizens of Urbana and Champaign." They asked the state legislature for $22,000 to do this project, which was their first official request.[87] The following year, Regent Gregory reported upon a detailed study of the campus, suggesting, among other things, "a colored plan for the ornamental grounds about the University building."[88] Gregory was so intent

---

84. Illinois Industrial University, *The Illini* III, no. 2 (February 1874) 41–42.

85. Students of the Senior Class, *The Student (Illinois Industrial University)* 1, no. 3 (January 1872) 9. Gregory quotes Jesus in Matthew 6:29 here.

86. Powell, *Semi-Centennial History*, 316.

87. Tilton and O'Donnell, *History of the Growth and Development*, 6.

88. Ibid., 7–8.

FIGURE 3: The original I.I.U. building.

on improving the University's landscaping that he sought out Frederick Law Olmsted, the famed architect of New York's Central Park, who advised the Regent to plant around the current grounds, and then wait until further building plans were made.[89] They did so, with the campus being comprised of "over one thousand acres of land," surrounded by "ornamental and parade grounds, experimental and model farms, gardens, etc."[90] Reynolds recalls that students built fences, planted trees, shrubs, and grass, so "the refreshing green took the place of the mud. Gravel walks were laid out," making it "possible to step without sinking shoe deep in the mud. Altogether, at the end of the second spring the surroundings were entirely changed."[91] By 1870, there was a twenty acre forest plantation, an experimental apple orchard with over three thousand trees of more than a thousand varieties, and an orchard boasting

---

89. Solberg, *University of Illinois*, 93.
90. Board of Trustees, *First Annual Report* 185.
91. Powell, *Semi-Centennial History*, 317.

over four hundred different kinds of pears.⁹² Improvements continued to be made, with Professor Burrill planting elms along one avenue, and various trees throughout the campus. By 1875, about twenty acres of ornamental grounds surrounded the new University building, and the landscape of the entire school had been altered.⁹³

The original University Building had been inherited from a failed seminary called the "Urbana and Champaign Institute." Built of bricks and lit by oil lamps, the five story building could allow about four hundred students and house one hundred and thirty.⁹⁴ It featured, the trustees said, "about sixty-five private rooms" which were each "designed for the accommodation of two students."⁹⁵ Each room was "fourteen feet long and ten feet wide." Having a flue but no furniture, students were required to provide their own. The trustees "earnestly recommended for health's sake that each student have a separate bed," including "a narrow bedstead and mattress, with suitable clothing," which students were to supply themselves. Jointly, roommates were to make sure that, between the two of them, "a study table, chairs, and a small coal stove" were provided, and coal was purchased by students from the University. Though students could cook for themselves in their rooms for a dollar or so per week, board "not exceeding $3.50 per week" could be had in the building itself, provided by F. Adelia (Potter) Reynolds' parents. Alumnus and long-time I.I.U. professor Nathan Ricker recalls that some students chose to live on fifty or sixty cents worth of milk and mush per week, plus the cost of coal—or time spent gathering wood kindling for their stove.⁹⁶

Reynolds says the basement had "the long kitchen, and a large dumb waiter carried the food to the dining room."⁹⁷ Her mother, she said, sought to "carry out Dr. Gregory's wishes with regard to having a home-like table for a reasonable price." Describing the dining room, she remembered

> six, and sometimes eight long tables each seating ten persons. These were always nicely set with white linen and pretty china.

92. Illinois Industrial University, *Catalogue and Circular*, 12.
93. Tilton and O'Donnell, *History of the Growth and Development*, 113.
94. Board of Trustees, *First Annual Report*, 126, 185.
95. Ibid., 200.
96. Kersey, *John Milton Gregory and the University of Illinois*, 183.
97. Powell, *Semi-Centennial History*, 316–17.

There were generally sixty or over at table for the first term. Professor Atherton boarded at the Hall, most of the time he was there . . . the boarders . . . I presume . . . all remember bright red-cheeked Lucy and her quiet assistant who waited on table. We had a good cook, and there was an effort to make the table attractive to the boys from the farms who had always had good living. The result was that in a little over a year's time we found it could not be done, and the boarding-hall was given up. The boys boarded in clubs, or took care of themselves in their rooms, or roomed and boarded with near-bye [sic] residents."

Indeed, as the Trustees noted, board could be found in "good private boarding houses" which were "already springing up around the University."[98] Students could room at such houses if they wished, granting them, of course, "the advantages of the family circle."

Daily necessities were obtained by students through the labor that coupled their learning. Student James Matthews described how, during a drought in the autumn of 1871, "both of the University wells are exhausted and we have to carry water from new wells at the Mechanic Hall."[99] Students apparently carried water from wells as a normal procedure. Water closets were not used, but public "glory holes" provided toilet facilities for students. Even just getting around campus was a struggle. In his diary, student Arthur Talbot said, "The weather! What an unfathomable subject! That is, the mud has been unfathomable. From Oct. 1 until Jan. 1, the roads have been very bad—during the latter part almost impassable."[100]

Still, though, the trustees worked hard to improve facilities. In April of 1871 they voted to build a new University Hall at an estimated cost of $143,700.[101] Its designer was John Mills Van Osdel, an I.I.U. trustee and Chicago architect who also conceived the Governor's Mansion in Springfield and was instrumental in rebuilding Chicago after its great fire.[102] A University Drill Hall was commissioned in 1871, complete with a mechanical shop and workshop, and was in use by the fall term of 1872.[103] A number of functional buildings, like the model farm

98. Board of Trustees, *First Annual Report*, 200.
99. Matthews, Papers, letter, 10/7/1871.
100. Talbot, *Diary*, 3.
101. Board of Trustees, *Eleventh Annual Report*, 113.
102. Howard, *Illinois: A History*, 353.
103. Nevins, *Illinois*, 360.

FIGURE 4: An early campus view looking northward
(presumably from the new University Hall)
toward the Drill Hall and the University Building

house, stock farm barn, and storage sheds were erected.[104] Gregory proposed a lavish ornamental grounds plan which sadly never came into fruition.[105] But University Hall itself was larger than the old University Building, and well constructed, described as "one of the most spacious and convenient to be found on this continent," being "214 feet in length, with a depth on the wings of 122 feet," including a "fire-proof" library wing and a "chapel wing."[106] It was crowned by a mansard roof and featured two "companile towers for clock and bells" on each side.[107] By the University's tenth anniversary, a variety of upgrades were introduced

---

104. Illinois Industrial University, *Catalogue and Circular*, 16–18.
105. Tilton and O'Donnell, *History of Growth and Development*, 12.
106. Illinois Industrial University, *Catalogue and Circular*, 16.
107. Ibid., 13.

to improve existing facilities.[108] New, large scale projects like a chemical laboratory and greenhouse were begun. Heating improvements and water closet upgrades commenced the following year, and Gregory called for the construction of a new women's building.[109] The campus had come a long way from its early days.

In 1879, Edward Orton, President and Professor of Geology at the Ohio Agricultural and Mechanical University, led a delegation to the I.I.U. to observe the progress of their peer institution. Here's Orton's description of what he saw:

> [We] stood near the center of one of the great prairies of Illinois. Its undulations stretched away on every side like ocean wastes. Upon its slopes stately halls and ambitious towers arose, consecrated to learning and labor. [We] entered the doors and passed from room to room, finding a score of departments replete with the best facilities that the world knows, for teaching the various branches of modern culture. A library of 13,000 volumes, selected from all the great centers of literature and science, offered knowledge to all comers—nor offered in vain, for throngs of eager-minded youths were watching at the posts of the doors. [We] passed with awakened curiousity [sic] to the art gallery ... Ranged [sic] around the ample room were one hundred or more thoroughly faithful copies of the masterpieces of sculpture, that all the ages have preserved. Photographs and engravings of famous architectural and historic scenes were added. Leaving the main building [we] found on one side a chemical laboratory. On another side a spacious greenhouse, . . . filled with rare and beautiful exotics, drawn from every clime and station. Beyond was a machine shop, well appointed and ringing with busy and successful labor. Herds of stately Shorthorns and deerlike Alderneys grazed in the fertile fields. A veterinary stable stood ready to receive the ailing animal, and to make the sickness or suffering of one, save, by the examples of treatment given, scores on every side, while orchards and gardens, and broad fields of grain, covered the square mile which was the site of the institution.[110]

In short, by seeing the fruits of a decade of Learning and Labor while Regent Gregory's hand was upon the plow, the Ohio General

---

108. Board of Trustees, *Ninth Report*, 47–55.
109. Board of Trustees, *Tenth Report*, 138.
110. Cope, *History of the Ohio State University*, 109.

60   LABOR'S MILLENNIUM

Assemblymen and University Trustees were inspired to return to their struggling school and work hard to make what would soon be called the Ohio State University as Edenic as the utopia they'd seen at Illinois.[111]

The Curse Reversed

The historian Paul Boyer once said, "From the days of the Puritans to the latest California commune, the impulse to form highly cohesive communities knit together by a common ideology and a shared vision of social harmony has been a constant in American history."[112] More precisely, says Paul Buhle, "Guilty Calvinism and innocent utopianism mixed strangely together in virtually every American radical reform movement from the seventeenth century."[113] The utopian agricultural millennialism of Calvin's evangelical heirs like Turner, Gregory, and other I.I.U. visionaries anticipated the appearance of a visible American Christian theory of social salvation—the soil from which the Social Gospel would grow—by almost two decades. While J. B. Turner was formulating his ideas in the late 1840s and articulating them by the early 1850s, with J. M. Gregory preaching labor's millennium by the late 1860s, historians like Paul Phillips usually start the Social Gospel in the 1870s or 80s instead.[114] James Dombrowski begins the movement with wealthy manufacturer and Princeton Seminary trustee Stephen Colwell's publication of *New Themes for the Protestant Clergy* and his endowing a chair in Christian ethics at Princeton in 1871.[115] Jacob Dorn cites examples of socialism rising within mainstream Christianity, but reluctantly, and no

---

111. Ibid., 110.

112. Pitzer, *America's Communal Utopias*, xi.

113. Buhle, *Marxism*, 59. For the impact of Calvinism on Illinois colleges, see Johnson, "Puritan Power."

114. Phillips, *Kingdom on Earth*.

115. Dombrowski, *Christian Socialism in America*, 31–34, 60. Dombroski also cites the impact of the "Christian Labor Union," organized in Boston in 1872 and disbanded in 1878 (77–83); emerging national conventions of socialist groups from the 1870s forward (74–76); Henry George's troubled reflections on poverty in the 1870s, leading to his influential writings and speeches in the 1880s and 90s (35–49); the advent of sociology in the seminaries (60–73); and Richard Ely's pioneering work in economics (50–59). Interestingly, by the end of his own career, John M. Gregory was moving increasingly away from history and toward economics instead, as was Wisconsin's John Bascom, who was, by the late 1880s, a fan of Ely's as well (Curti and Carstensen, 287–88).

earlier than the 1880s.[116] But as Gary Dorrien reminds us, Christianity provided a framework for commonwealth communities in the United States as early as the colonial period.[117] In 1870, when the I.I.U. was just three years old, utopian leader John Humphrey Noyes said that revivalism and socialism are interdependent and necessary in America, as they were in ancient Christianity.[118] Five years later Charles Nordhoff claimed that utopian religious societies work while labor unions fail.[119] Although nineteenth century millennialistic evangelical revivals had frequently influenced the piety of American college communities, it was a new thing for an emerging public university like the I.I.U. to advocate the industrial transformation of society based upon religious grounds. Usually utopian religious enclaves focused their energies on achieving the ideal society within their own community, rather than transforming the larger state or nation.[120] But the I.I.U. visionaries perceived of themselves as being engaged in a broader mission, one that would positively benefit the commonweal for generations to come.

Reflecting in 1898 upon the University's pioneering work during the Gregory years, long-time I.I.U. professor Thomas J. Burrill said:

> Never before in the history of the world has there been in an equal length of time such accomplishments, such a stupendous forward movement in the assertion of the dominion of man over nature, in controlling and managing the forces and forms of nature for the good of man and the uplifting of his race ... During this half century how the elements and forces of nature have sprung into use at the command of man! ... the waste places have been recovered and beautified as a garden for the king ... Heavy loads, then borne by human machines, have been transferred to those framed of oak and of steel, transforming a race of slaves into masters and conquerors, subjugating not nations, but nature ... even the cannon of these later times are noisy with proclamations of peace.[121]

116. Buckingham, *Expectations for the Millennium*, 1–18, 35–54.
117. Dorrien, *Reconstructing the Common Good*.
118. Noyes, *History of American Socialisms*, 25–29.
119. Nordhoff, *Communistic Societies*.

120. Guarnari, "Associationists," 36–49. See also Mandelker, *Religion, Society, and Utopia in Nineteenth-Century America*; Sutton, *Communal Utopias and the American Experience*; Shor, *Utopianism and Radicalism*; and the classic by Alice Felt Tyler, *Freedom's Ferment: Phases of American Social History to 1860*.

121. University of Illinois, *Memorial Convocation*, 13.

From Burrill's perspective, many of J. B. Turner's and J. M. Gregory's prophesies had been fulfilled. Now, at last, farmers would be free to do the kind of thoughtful, noble work which God intended for Adam and everyone since. Yet part of reversing the curse meant developing the personal qualities of a people who would be fit for labor's millennium. To this matter we now turn.

3

"Men," not "Monks"

Though expressly designed to break with the normative church-related educational tradition of its day—including the absence of theological studies or the training of clergy—the I.I.U. trustees and faculty were quite intentional about offering a Christian education, as informed by their progressive evangelical heritage. As we have seen, in their first advertising pamphlet sent to Illinois high schools the I.I.U. trustees said that, even though theirs was a *public* university, "the hope of the Trustees and Faculty is that the Institution will produce ... men of Christian culture ... "[1] This chapter examines the theory and practice of establishing the I.I.U. leaders' notion of "Christian culture" as the education of young adults within a public land-grant university. It will first consider how the I.I.U. founders understood ideal personhood—as being a "man" rather than a "monk"—and then discuss how the implementation of this vision was attempted, through educational innovations, adaptations, and continuities in the curriculum and student life.

The idea of Christian "manhood" was a popular social construction of the time. The Civil War and other trends of the era prompted theologians to emphasize rugged discipleship over timidity.[2] On campuses, says historian Kim Townsend, a "scholarly manliness" developed, featuring what historian Philip Harrold calls "mental toughness, courage, and noble purpose" and "the distinctive personality of the individual."[3] Michigan's President, James Angell, for example, gave a Sunday afternoon lecture called "The Manliness of the Christian Life,"

---

1. Illinois Industrial University, *Circular and Catalogue*, 4.

2. Carnes, *Secret Ritual and Manhood in Victorian America*; Kimmel, *Manhood in America*.

3. Harrold, *A Place Somewhat Apart*, 56; Townsend, *Manhood at Harvard*.

speaking of young male "pulses," "passions," and "virile strength."[4] A "muscular Christianity" movement was blossoming among English speaking Protestants which would continue well into the twentieth century.[5] Early in this development, Jonathan Baldwin Turner invented an attention-grabbing contrast between "men" and "monks." As discussed in chapter one, Turner, noting that, in the native peoples' language the word "Illinois" translated into "the land of the men," thought "men" meant the kind of noble laborers who would honorably represent the supplanted indigenous peoples who had previously populated the land.[6] Though he himself had spent his childhood immersed in New England's version of Old England's monkish learning, Turner possessed a strong physical constitution, being perhaps the most gregarious in a family of over-achievers. Active in athletics while at Yale, he had an adventurous side, making frequent horseback and walking trips across Illinois' prairie frontier with Native American guides. He was one of the few who remained physically able to aid others during a series of cholera epidemics that hit Jacksonville. In general, he enjoyed his missionary life.[7] But as discussed in prior chapters, he was adamant that the churches had done a poor job of educating the public. The old, clerical-style classical and literary education produced, he said, poor specimens of humanity. Turner's own experience at Illinois College too closely resembled, in his opinion, the European and early American clerical model with its cloistered, fraternal community, keeping rigidly structured hours for work, study, and daily prayers beginning at six in the morning.[8] Modern, nonsectarian America required a new way, he argued, saying "the end of all education should be the development of a TRUE MANHOOD, or the natural, proportionate and healthful culture and growth of all the powers and faculties of the human being—physical, mental, moral, and social: and any system which attempts the exclusive or even inordinate

---

4. Harrold, *Place Somewhat Apart*, 30–31.

5. Ladd and Mathisen, *Muscular Christianity*; Putney, *Manhood and Sports*. David Setran explains that fears of collegiate male effeminacy, and accusations of the church's cultivating milquetoast Christians, were foremost in the minds of educators in the early twentieth century, too: see Setran, *College "Y,"* 107–11.

6. Turner, "Millenium of Labor," 54–55.

7. Carriel, *Life of Jonathan Baldwin Turner*, 1–46, 61.

8. Ibid., 45.

culture of any one class of these faculties, will fail of its end—it will make mushrooms and monks, rather than manhood and men."[9]

Curiously, Turner uses a largely non-Protestant concept—"monks"—to describe pre-land-grant education in the U.S., which was historically inaccurate because the curriculum's designers were the Reformation-era Protestants and American colonials from whom Turner himself descended theologically.[10] By using such a loaded word Turner bluntly and pejoratively made his point: pan-Protestant piety in the U.S. must become industrialized and active rather than clerical and contemplative.

The problem with the old schooling, he said, was its impracticality. "A real grammar boy of such schools," he said in 1854, "can have no other idea than that God made the world out of the nine parts of speech, and in English, at least, spelled it all wrong."[11] How much wiser it would be, he said, to study "God's laws and ordinances" which "govern the world," rather than "men's opinions and usages." The educational tradition inherited from Europe and New England "engenders an undue deference to mere learned authority, a spirit of effeminate timidity and pedantic servility, rather than one of true wisdom, true freedom, and true manhood, such as has shone in the prophets, apostles, and martyrs of every age." Its graduates have "learning," but not "mind"; "scholarship," but not "intellect." They can "prove either side of any proposition, but [are] not real men, who can discharge the hard side of any duty." How much better it would be, Turner said, to look less toward "books and the laws of verbiage" and more toward "facts and the laws of God," from "nature, as it comes all radiant and instinct with life, beauty, and glory, from the Hand Divine . . . What a monstrosity was that which some years since took little boys and girls, not yet seven years old, out of God's clear sunshine, away from the birds and the breezes, the flowers and the trees, and set them, for six hours in the day, bolt upright on a wooden bench, to look at big letters and triangles made of cotton rags and lampblack!!—and all this, only to educate them!!!"[12] Wherever such an education exists, he said, "the necessary result must be a monstrosity, not a manhood; a monk, rather than a man," replete with "the

9. Board of Trustees, *First Annual Report*, ii.
10. Tewksbury, "Founding of American Colleges," 56–57.
11. Turner, *Industrial Universities*, 6.
12. Ibid, 6–7.

supercilious pride of a conceited monk or an India Brahman, instead of that brave, generous, and steadfast heroism that should characterize the true man."[13] Such educational deception, he said, is the work of "Satan," but thankfully, "God has, in his mercy, hitherto sheltered his defenceless poor."[14]

Sixteen years later, after the new University had begun, Turner continued to discuss this theme. On March 2, 1870, at Bloomington, Turner told the Northern Illinois Horticultural Society "the feudal theory of curriculum" advocated by monks should be abolished, since "scholarship was not the chief end of life"; rather, "elevated upright manhood was the great end of life." America's "greatest curse," he said, was "the fatal mistake of confounding schooling with education." Why was this a problem? Because, he said,

> Our theory of education does not develop the muscle, does not strengthen the nerves, does not give breadth to the imagination or depth to thought. It is words, words. It teaches to avoid labor, to avoid solitude, and to evade the responsibility of actual life.
>
> We have too much intellectual education, creating the crowd who throng our cities, who hang out their shingles on every street, who want to be supervisors, governors, congressmen, or presidents. We are growing into a nation of intellect to the default of will, energy, muscle, and power. We are growing fast toward becoming a nation of supervisors and officials. We are growing out of the age of physical and intellectual development properly allied and combined into an age of brain-work. Never was a more fatal error ...
>
> If a man has peculiar faculties for blacksmithing, in God's name, let him be a blacksmith. Metaphysics, what is it? Ten pages will contain the substance of the labors of all the metaphysical fools from Aristotle down. All the new theories are simply changes of words.[15]

During the 1860s a transition was beginning to happen in American higher education broadly, eschewing traditional recitations and the classics while favoring research and modern topics.[16] A former classicist himself, Turner disdained the idea of teaching ancient languages and

---

13. Ibid., 7–8.
14. Ibid., 13.
15. Carriel, *Life of Jonathan Baldwin Turner*, 230–31.
16. Nevins, *State Universities and Democracy*, 1–2, 53–54.

theology at the I.I.U., since, though perhaps useful for clergy, these studies provided no practical industrial benefit. And regarding already existing tax-supported military education, Turner scathingly asked, "Has God so made the world, that peculiar schools, peculiar applications of science, and a peculiar resultant literature are found indispensable to the highest success in the art of killing men, in all states, while nothing of the kind can be based on the infinitely multifarious arts and processes of feeding, clothing and housing them?"[17]

So, as his writings show, Turner, a prophetic, progressive evangelical, advocated a benevolent, active and utilitarian spirituality, allowing little room for speculation alone. His ideas about "manhood" and education set the stage in Illinois for a growing movement toward establishing a new type of public university with in implicit Christian piety. But his voice was not the lone inspiration for the I.I.U. As Regent, John M. Gregory would build upon the foundation established by Turner and other early theorists of agricultural education. Eventually eulogized by Thomas J. Burrill as a "manly Christian man," Gregory had the respect of others in this important regard.[18] The Chicago alumni club called the Regent "a man of pure life, of high ideals, a leader of men, a friend of humanity, devoted to the progress and advancement of those whose education was intrusted to his care, faithful and watchful as a parent, he stands as a model for imitation in all those virtues which crown a Christian manhood."[19] Charles G. Neely of the class of 1880 concurred, calling Gregory "a leader of men" who "was naturally first in a distinguished company. Sincerity of purpose was his chief characteristic."[20] In the eyes of his University, only a Christian "man" like Gregory could successfully lead in such a time as this.

"Learning and Labor"

In John Gregory's anthropology, mind and body were integrated parts of the whole. During his first year at the I.I.U., he said "that education is most practical which develops brain power ... to perceive, judge, and act ... The skilled hand and the thinking brain will be found compat-

---

17. Turner, "Industrial Universities, 375.
18. University of Illinois, *Memorial Convocation*, 11.
19. Ibid., 31.
20. Roberts and Turner, *Sacred and the Secular*, 24.

ible members of the same body . . . thus, these two, Thought and Work, which God designed to go together will no longer remain asunder."[21]

Early in his tenure Gregory established, as discussed earlier, the phrase "Learning and Labor" as the school's motto. The concept was so important it was pinned in green letters to the chapel walls as an iconic reminder of the community's common purpose.[22] Years of experience as an educator led Gregory to conclude that college life was usually too heavy on the Learning but too light on the Labor. So, to complement his and other I.I.U. leaders' devotion to cerebral growth through empirical study, they, like other land-grant innovators, adopted the practice of the era's existing manual labor colleges.[23] Gregory and his colleagues, though, added a re-worked theological emphasis, trusting that hard farm work would ensure their vision of Christian manhood. Indeed, as Gregory wrote in his hymn "Learning and Labor," "To labor is to pray." And God, he said, answers the laborer's prayer.[24] The *New York Tribune* reported that "The students at Champaign, Illinois, 'are not only not ashamed of labor,' says Prof. Gregory—'they love it.'"[25] After all, the article said, labor led directly to "the high moral character of the graduates." Yet the editors of the student paper mocked the I.I.U. *Catalogue*'s "Is it possible to work my way through the Illinois Industrial University?" article's cheery "yes" by satirizing the expectation as unrealistic and excessively ascetic, more fitting, perhaps, for pious monks than fallible men.[26]

Following Turner's and Gregory's theoretical lead, the I.I.U. trustees said they sought to educate a person with "a highly cultured mind . . . linked to a brawny hand," a "classical scholar feel[ing] at home in a workshop . . . find[ing] use for all his scholarship and taste in the successful practice of this art."[27] Departing slightly from Turner's non-elitist vision, they wanted to form people "fit for society and citizenship," since an I .I. U. graduate, on track to become a future agricultural or

21. Board of Trustees, *First Annual Report*, 179.

22. Ibid., 149.

23. Ross, "Manual Labor Experiment," 513–28.

24. Board of Trustees, *Seventh Annual Report*, 62.

25. Board of Trustees, *Fourth Annual Report*, 350. The quotation is from the September 6, 1871, issue.

26. Ebert, *Illini Century*, 30.

27. Board of Trustees, *Report of Committee*, 21; Board of Trustees, *First Annual Report*, 63.

industrial baron, would "not infrequently be called to serve in Senate Chambers and gubernatorial chairs," requiring "an education broader and better than the simple knowledge of his art." Other early land grants held varying points of view on this issue. Where agricultural education bubbled up from farmer's movements, there was usually more suspicion of a perceived elitism in higher education. Penn State, for example, was initially called the "Farmer's High School."[28] Michigan State's founders likewise faced suspicion from agricultural interests.[29] Cornell, on the other hand, because of the initial impetus of the state legislature, Ezra Cornell, and Andrew Dickson White, thought their "People's College" should help the students to become more genteel. A. D. White and J. M. Gregory apparently had a collegial relationship, with Gregory sending at least sixteen surviving letters to White, and White visiting the I.I.U. in 1871 and speaking at the University's commencement in 1873.[30] Cornell's view won out at the I.I.U., and Regent Gregory's personal preferences may have impacted this outcome.[31] As his trustees said when the University began, even though farming was considered the noblest profession, still, "man is something more than an artisan," and "manhood has duties and interests higher and grander than those of the workshop and the farm."[32] So these future leaders must therefore become adept enough at "literary culture" to communicate well in both public oration and the local press. In the end, they hoped that "the light of high and classic learning will be found as beautiful and becoming when it shines in an educated farmer's home, as when it gilds the residence of the graduated lawyer or physician."[33] In truth, though, it was more likely that an I.I.U. grad would not come from a farm family or leave school and farm, since the proposed democratization of higher education championed by the era's politicians did not in fact happen at Illinois.[34] Despite the rhetoric of utility and egalitarianism, the I.I.U and its peer university at Minnesota soon became elitist by Midwestern

---

28. Bezilla, *Penn State*, 3–14.
29. Widder, *Michigan Agricultural College*, 15–29.
30. Solberg, *University of Illinois*, 121, note 2.
31. Ibid., 111–13.
32. Board of Trustees, *First Annual Report*, 49.
33. Ibid., 64.
34. Behle, "Scholars from the Sod."

middle-class Protestant standards, maintaining a lingering devotion to the liberal arts after all.[35]

Still, though, in the early days, the ideology, at least, was alive and well. One can hear Turner and Gregory being echoed by the I.I.U. trustees in their earliest University catalogue, where, extolling the benefits of the labor system, they boasted that the "union and alternation of mental and muscular effort" would "not only give the 'sound mind in a sound body,'" but would "help to produce educated men who will be strong, practical, and self-reliant, full of resource, and the mental peers of the wisest . . ."[36] This would result in "redeeming higher education from the odium of puny forms and pallid faces, and restoring the long lost and much needed sympathy between educated men and the great industrial and business classes." Despite their firm belief in equality as noted above, the manly virtue of competition, they said, would bring out the best in a student, a "healthful stimulation" resulting from "competitive examination."[37]

"Man"hood and Womanhood

Of course, all this testosterone-laden rhetoric posed a problem for the I.I.U.'s trustees, since they voted to become a coeducational university in early 1870.[38] This was not unusual, as the era was generally one of rapid growth for women's higher education.[39] The 1854 initial "Plan of Action" to establish an agricultural university which was presented by J. B. Turner and the Industrial League argued for both male and female students.[40] Regent Gregory, the father of daughters enrolled at the I.I.U., held a similar view to Rev. Samuel May, an advisor to Cornell's President White, who explained that he "would have both sexes educated equally well—educated together" because "God made man dual and he cannot be singular in anything, without detriment to some part

---

35. Fitzgerald, "Two Land-Grant Colleges."

36. Board of Trustees, *First Annual Report*, 198. J. B. Edmond claims that manual labor and military drill were normative for the early land grants but mentions no theological rationale for their inclusion: see his *Magnificent Charter*, 162–65.

37. Board of Trustees, *Report of Committee*, 16.

38. Board of Trustees, *First Annual Report*, 198; Board of Trustees, *Third Annual Report*, 84–85.

39. Geiger, *American College*, 181–95.

40. Turner, *Industrial Universities*, 55.

of his character."[41] So now that the I.I.U. had women on campus, if they wanted to form "men" rather than "monks," did that mean they also wanted to form "women" rather than "nuns"? No such explicit talk exists in their writings, so one *might* conclude that their concept of "men" was an inclusive one, meaning that they assumed, regardless of gender, that their students should attain the same slate of admirable character traits. In practice, though, their culturally-conditioned notions of gentility shaped their expectations regarding appropriate behavior for men and women.[42] Though egalitarianism toward the sexes was voiced by the trustees as early as 1867—with Regent Gregory saying women would equal or even outscore men in the classroom—they debated for months whether women should be excluded from military drill, and, more importantly, whether men and women should reside in the same college building. Their eventual answer to both questions was "no." Victorian decorum would prohibit co-ed dormitories, and only men, they decided, would be soldiers, while women would not.[43]

Military drill was a vital part of the I.I.U. regimen, for a variety of reasons. Enacted during the American Civil War, the Morrill Act stipulated that land grants would establish militias. A number of the early I.I.U. students were recently-returned Civil War veterans.[44] As the new University commenced just two years after the war's end, the Illinois legislature mandated that the I.I.U. would comply, initially requiring the students to wear military uniforms.[45] These uniforms were quite expensive—far more than even tuition, and by March of 1869 the trustees decided to only require uniform wearing for those having completed at least one term of study.[46] All male students were required to wear cadet caps beginning with their first term.[47] Much like con-

41. Kammen, *Cornell: Glorious to View*, 42.

42. Bloch, *Gender and Morality in Anglo-American Culture*; Collins, *America's Women*, 85–238. In *Manliness*, Harvey C. Mansfield suggests that twentieth-century feminism hindered the necessary social concept of "manliness," which had been so helpful to Western society prior.

43. Board of Trustees, *First Annual Report*, 45, 86; *Second Annual Report*, 54–55, 75, 83; *Third Annual Report*, 84–85; *Fourth Annual Report*, 117, 135; Powell, *Semi-Centennial History*, 327, 331.

44. Kersey, "John Milton Gregory," 184.

45. Illinois General Assembly, "An Act to Provide," 590–98.

46. Board of Trustees, *Second Annual Report*, 82.

47. Kersey, *John Milton Gregory and the University of Illinois*, 163.

FIGURE 5: I.I.U. students in military uniforms

temporary advocates of school dress codes, the trustees said uniforms would "secure personal neatness, and place all students upon a footing of republican equality," conferring a distinction which "awakens an honorable ambition to excel, refines, [sic] the manners, gives a *manly* tone to the character and, in some sort, makes each individual student feel that the reputation of his class and the honor of the institution are in his keeping."[48] They considered the "neat and striking" I.I.U. uniform "a badge of honor.... bring[ing] respect and caus[ing] the wearer to respect himself."[49] Uniform wearing itself was believed to be "a pledge of good behavior, of genteel deportment and a security against vicious habits and associations." Indeed, any student "recommended to the Governor for a commission" must "be conspicuous for high character both as a student and a gentleman..."[50]

Along with the attitudinal benefit of wearing a uniform, the trustees said "daily martial exercises" provided the physical culture of collegiate gymnastics while keeping young men from "a class of amuse-

48. Board of Trustees, *First Annual Report*, 84 (italics added).
49. Illinois Board of Trustees, *Sixth Annual Report*, 110.
50. Solberg, *University of Illinois*, 207–8.

ments scarcely beneficial, sometimes injurious . . ."[51] It was normative for land-grants to extol military drill for the cultivation of masculine posture.[52] Cornell, Michigan State, and Penn State, for examples, all had it.[53] Likewise, the I.I.U. trustees believed that

> military drill . . . will rescue [a student] from the rust of inaction, and secure the "erect carriage, the firm graceful, manly bearing, the expansion of chest, the harmonious action of every limb and muscle; in fine, that perfect physical development" . . . The race of wretched dyspeptics, consumptives and hypochondriacs, which crowd the learned professions and go trembling to their graves before the work of their lives is half done, are eloquent witnesses against that system in which the education of the mind is sought in violation of the laws of health . . .

So, contrasting Turner's earlier critique of military education, the early trustees believed that preparing for war was healthy, ensuring manly vitality rather than monkish pathology.[54] But they did allow for conscientious objectors citing religious grounds for their omission. And by early 1880, the trustees dropped the uniform-wearing requirement, with Regent Gregory requesting that Juniors and Seniors be entirely exempted from military drill.[55] It's possible that Gregory's personal stance on this issue contributed toward his resignation that same year.[56]

The evidence indicates that the I.I.U. did not allow its women students to train for combat. Instead, they taught women to be scientific homemakers, a view which was normative for other land grants as well.[57] The "School of Domestic Science & Art" was established by

51. For a Methodist minister's list of the era's vices, see Crane, *Popular Amusements*.

52. Ross, *Democracy's College*, 123.

53. Bezilla, *Penn State*, 17, 46; Kammen, *Cornell*, 54; Widder, *Michigan Agricultural College*, 128–30.

54. Board of Trustees, *Eighth Report*, 152, 163.

55. Board of Trustees, *Tenth Report*, 192, 221.

56. Solberg, *University of Illinois*, 207–12.

57. Ross, *Democracy's College*, 129; Eddy, *Colleges for Our Land*, 61–62; Ross and Eddy may, though, be making generalized assumptions. Bezilla says, "about twenty institutions [nationwide] were then [1907] awarding degrees in home economics, but a lack of money delayed the start of a degree program at Penn State" (79). Michigan State was co-educational by 1870, but did not establish a women's program until 1896, despite the agitation for home economics by Granger Mary Bryant Mayo (Widder, *Michigan Agricultural College*, 101). Cornell's vision for co-education was broader from the start,

Figure 6: I.I.U. Women's Calisthenics Class

1871, offering courses in chemistry, anatomy, dietetics, physiology, hygiene, "Household Aesthetics," "Usages of Society" (etiquette), landscape gardening and domestic architecture.[58] Using Catherine Beecher's and Harriet Beecher Stowe's book *The American Woman's Home: Or, Principles of Domestic Science; Being a Guide to the Formation and Maintenance of Economical, Healthful, Beautiful, and Christian Homes* as their guide, the I.I.U.'s women's course, striving for the establishment of "a Zentmeyer grand microscope [to test for food impurities] along with a Chickering grand piano in every household," emphasized, in Professor Louisa C. Allen's words, "the strong moral influences exerted by good bread, wholesome food, and healthful, attractive homes."[59] The Rev. A. N. Page was hired by the school to "Steward" the women's boarding house, providing a pastoral presence to shepherd the young women entrusted to him by their parents.[60] Apparently, though, Rev. Page was unable to protect them from the admiring gaze of the I.I.U. trustees, who left a December, 1875 board meeting "to witness the exhibition of the class in Calisthenics" led by Professor Allen, and returned for repeat

---

with their women's college featuring a wider curriculum than just home economics (Kammen, *Cornell: Glorious to View*, 42–53).

58. Illinois Industrial University, *Catalogue and Circular* (1873), 42; Board of Trustees, *Third Annual Report*, 285.

59. Solberg, *University of Illinois*, 161–63.

60. Board of Trustees, *Seventh Annual Report*, 46.

performances during successive trustees' meetings. "*Resolved*," wrote Trustee Willard Flagg, "That the Board of Trustees have witnessed, with much gratification, the calisthenic exercises of the young ladies, under the instruction of Miss Allen, and that they strongly recommend that all the female pupils participate in these exercises." They quickly authorized $2.50 to rent a piano to use in the class.[61]

Although the I.I.U. leaders pushed the School of Domestic Science & Art, by 1881 only seven students had graduated from the program, prompting the faculty and new regent, Selim Peabody, to persuade the trustees to close the School. Women were favoring the College of Literature and Science instead, outnumbering men in liberal arts courses.[62] Still, though, gender stereotypes remained among at least some of the male students. "L. E. Williams, class of '77," for example, said an ideal bride "must be good looking, amiable, of kind disposition and a Christian ... well versed in domestic affairs, wealthy, charitable, and last but not least she should be a granger."[63] Echoing Williams' romanticized ideal of agrarian womanhood, a writer in the May, 1879 issue of the student paper asked, "Wouldn't it astonish our Eastern college friends to see our lady taxidermists out before sun-rise, with shot-guns, ammunition, young men and other accoutrements 'chasing the antelope over the plain,' and returning to breakfast with pockets full of birds. It's a very exhilarating sight—from a safe distance. Can you beat it, Vassar?"[64]

Whether or not they were entirely successful in their task, in theory, when the I.I.U. leaders said they wanted to form "men," they meant people exhibiting traits appropriate to their generalized perceptions of ideal men and women. Despite the founders' rhetoric regarding egalitarianism and co-education, though, Charles Wesley Rolfe, a member of the class of 1872 and an I.I.U. professor for thirty-seven years, said in retrospect that other than "modify[ing]" the "roughness" of the farm boys, the presence of "girls" did not have "any other appreciable effect for a considerable number of years. The University," he said, "was a boys' school to which girls were admitted."[65]

61. Board of Trustees, *Eighth Report*, 149, 179.
62. Solberg, *University of Illinois*, 243, 156.
63. Ebert, *Illini Century*, 9. "Grangers" were members of contemporary agricultural societies. See, for example, Scott, "Grangerism," 139–63.
64. Ebert, *Illini Century*, 32.
65. Quoted in Powell, *Semi-Centennial History*, 319–20.

A Public yet "Christian" University

Regent Gregory assumed that it was morally acceptable to implement his religious vision of Learning and Labor in a tax-supported university. As outlined in the prior chapter, his 1864 inaugural speech for the Kalamazoo College presidency called *The Right and Duty of Christianity to Educate* provided an apologetic for understanding state-sponsored education as a form of Christian ministry. He said it would be a mistake for Christian truth to not be taught and applied in public education, since—despite church-state separation—American civilization literally depended on it.[66] Although himself an advocate of an intentionally non-sectarian Christianity at the I.I.U., Gregory's theory here contrasts drastically with that of Cornell's A. D. White, who, in his *The Cornell University: What It Is and What It Is Not*, does not support a distinctively church-based mission extended through the land-grants.[67] Others in Ithaca felt otherwise. Before his untimely death, for example, benefactor Ezra Cornell said that their University should "make men more . . . manly," specifically by preparing them to serve family, country, and God.[68] However, he said, "It shall be our aim and our constant effort to make true Christian men without dwarfing or paring them down to fit the narrow gauge of any sect." The *Ithaca Journal*, too, prescribed a "true Christian culture . . . untrammelled by the fetters of narrow minded sectarianism and bigotry."[69] Cornell's trustees even turned down an offer to endow a seminary in Ithaca, citing the subjective, sectarian, divisive, and therefore "evil" nature of theology as a discipline.[70] Gregory and the majority of I.I.U. trustees did not share this view. Although they were clear that theology would not be part of a practical curriculum fit for industrial education, they still followed a distinctively evangelical and yet inclusively public theology, seeking to establish a new type of research university based upon religious grounds.[71] With the theory intact, the next step was to make the type of disciples Gregory longed for.

---

66. Gregory, *Right and Duty*, 7–8, 11, 14–15.
67. Kammen, *Cornell: Glorious to View*, 23–24.
68. Ibid., 29.
69. Ibid., 30.
70. Ibid., 23–24.
71. Ross, *Democracy's College*, 37.

To accomplish his vision, Gregory found allies in the other agricultural and industrial educators throughout the nation, even among those who did not share his religious beliefs. Although Cornell's White despised ecclesial authority and revealed religion, dreaming of a new type of university entirely free from imposed religious world views,[72] Gregory was still able to find common ground with him and those like him because, when one looked at the big picture, they and their peers were in the same boat—leading a new, untested enterprise. Due to the Morrill Act's stipulations and a perceived need for a new education appropriate for industrializing America, the development of a new curriculum was being debated by land-grant leaders throughout the country. They needed to establish what J. B. Turner had called "a literature of their own."[73] The newly-formed U.S. Department of Agriculture provided a written guideline to assist their deliberation.[74] They also looked back to monk-infested but industrially progressive Europe, where, in 1869, Regent Gregory wrote home praising the polytechnic schools of Germany and France, saying that, although originating to educate the poor in trades, they had evolved into respectable universities.[75] By and large, a practical and applied viewpoint prevailed at the land-grants, whether a Christian apologetic was included or not. While serving as Michigan's state superintendent of public instruction, for example, Gregory himself advocated, for budgetary reasons, shortening the course at Michigan State, eliminating literary courses in favor of the strictly practical.[76] Public pressures and fiscal realities sometimes forced leaders to reign in their ideology for the sake of institutional survival. But despite early utilitarian ideology and financial concern, schools eventually added literature and arts as funding and public sympathy allowed.[77]

72. Kammen, *Cornell: Glorious to View*, 10–11, 22–23, 30.

73. Turner, *Industrial Universities*, 8.

74. Bollman, *Industrial Colleges*.

75. Gregory, "Agricultural Education in Germany," 4–6; Gregory, "Agricultural Education in France," 6–8. Writing these articles for the Western Rural, Gregory makes no mention of a theological rationale in European polytechnic education. Similarly, he wrote two more articles for the Western Rural on "Agricultural Education" in which he did not mention any explicitly religious reasons; see Gregory, "Industrial Education," 48–49.

76. Widder, *Michigan Agricultural College*, 40.

77. Kammen, *Cornell: Glorious to View*, 16–17; Widder, *Michigan Agricultural*

As the new curriculum would show, the I.I.U. departed from what J. B. Turner perceived as the traditional monkish liberal training required for service in the learned professions, though not as drastically as some agriculturists would have liked. Perhaps most illustrative of this tension is the lengthy debate among the I.I.U.'s earliest leaders about whether or not classical and romance languages and literature should be studied.[78] Turner said he wasn't against classical languages per se, but unfortunately they had been used by the "aristocracy of pedantry" to keep the unlettered down.[79] English alone, he said, was enough to be successful, as Abe Lincoln himself had shown. This debate was not unique to the I.I.U. Michigan State's founders, for example, decided against all languages except English.[80] But the I.I.U. trustees, while unashamedly emphasizing the utilitarianism of their new university, still desired—according to Morrill Act mandate—to "teach such branches of learning as are related to agricultural and the mechanic arts, *without excluding* other scientific and classical studies, and including military tactics."[81] Though trying to form "men" rather than "monks," the general course they selected retained some traditional emphases, reflecting a value for well-roundedness and general preparedness for original thought. In the trustees' words, "while it affords a sound and liberal education, it provides for the students of the various industrial courses, the scientific knowledge they may need for a thorough mastery of those conrses [sic],"[82] imparted through the "high-toned, gentlemanly character and culture" of the faculty.[83]

Clearly, though, the emphasis on the utility of the agricultural and mechanical was at the top of the I.I.U. leaders' agenda. Following the Morrill Act's mandate for industrial and agricultural education "to the very letter,"[84] the I.I.U. trustees affirmed their belief in a "common sense" which would allow phenomena to be observed and quantified.[85]

College, 34.
- 78. Solberg, *University of Illinois*, 113.
- 79. Powell, *Semi-Centennial History*, 234–35.
- 80. Widder, *Michigan Agricultural College*, 34.
- 81. Board of Trustees, *First Annual Report*, 47 (italics added).
- 82. Ibid., 91.
- 83. Ibid., 61.
- 84. Ibid., 48.
- 85. Board of Trustees, *Report of Committee*, 13.

As J. B. Turner had said years earlier, "the laws of God are everywhere, and to all persons and classes, the same . . . based upon these uniform laws."[86] Head Farmer Jonathan Periam, reminiscing about the existing church-related schools' vain attempts to land Morrill Act money in the 1850s and 1860s, said the conservative denominationalists

> told wild stories that science, if not tempered with the old dogmas, would overturn society and bring the earth back again to the darkness of paganism, forgetting that true science conflicts with no law that is capable of demonstration, but only attacks and demolishes the weak dogmas of mere theorists. They have stated that scientists were infidels, when the fact is that the true scientist is nearly always a firm, unwavering believer in the One Great Cause, the Supreme Ruler of the Universe, fashioning its materials through the operation of uniform, undeviating law, directing its infinity of operations, and controlling all things 'in the heavens above and the earth beneath, and the water that is under the earth.'[87]

Not all traditional Protestants felt the need to jettison the old faith in order to embrace the new science. "[T]o science," John Gregory said, "Christianity owes a high duty."[88] Educators of the era saw much potential in the new empiricism, emphasizing the virtues of free inquiry not only in scientific research, but also as a means of moral formation along with explicit religious education.[89] The I.I.U. leaders, seeking to make "men" instead of "monks," taught their pupils to value physical, quantifiable research over what they deemed mere mystical speculation. But theirs would be a theistic science, theologically congruent with the challenges posed by Darwin and other thinkers of the day.[90] In fact, a number of the era's evangelicals were able to integrate Darwinism and Christian thought, such as Gregory's fellow Baptist John Bascom, whose "New Theology" equated evolution with progress toward the realization of God's Kingdom, an ongoing unfolding of God's natural revelation,

---

86. Turner, *Industrial Universities*, 9.

87. Periam, *Groundswell*, 542–43.

88. Gregory, *Right and Duty*, 13–14.

89. Reuben, *Making of the Modern University*, 75–76, 133.

90. Smith, "Envisioning and Embodying a Public, Protestant Paideia," 118–31; Roberts, *Darwinism and the Divine in America*. Michigan State's students likewise struggled with Darwinian evolution, eventually adopting it for the most part (Widder, *Michigan Agricultural College*, 294–95).

with science being nothing less than "the thought of God" and "the omnipresence of his wisdom."⁹¹ Through the gift of science, many of the faithful believed, God would provide blessing on both corporate and individual levels. Agricultural and industrial education would enable a more efficient use of resources and effort, reversing Adam's curse of earning his bread through the sweat of his brow.⁹²

Despite this new apologetic for Labor's millennium and the reverse of Adam's curse, though, there was little in the University library and curriculum which could be called particularly "Christian." According to the report of the trustees' Library Committee on March 11, 1868, for example, none of the books was categorized as "theological" or "religious,"⁹³ and the library additions for the following year in the fields of history, biography, and literature were entirely of political ideology, with the lone exception of Cotton Mather's *Magnalia Christi Americana*.⁹⁴ Democratic heroes of the Revolution were favored over colonial theologians. At Kansas State, the clergy president valued American republican ideas so much that he even frowned upon reading Charles Dickens, who, he said, created an "undercurrent of caricature" deemed "not Christlike."⁹⁵

The course catalogue does indicate that religion *was* formally studied—though only in two courses—for those seniors enrolled in the "General Course" of the "Department of Science, Literature, and the Arts." During their fourth and final year, students were required to take a course in "Moral Philosophy" with Regent Gregory, and one course in "Evidences of Christianity," both offered in the same quarter.⁹⁶ Moral Philosophy, of course, had a long and stellar history in American collegiate life, and to not include it at the I.I.U. would have seemed radical.⁹⁷

91. Hoeveler, "University and the Social Gospel," 286–87. Bascom's views were not without controversy, however. The Wisconsin campus YMCA thought him too liberal (Setran, *College "Y,"* 30–32).

92. Board of Trustees, *First Annual Report*, 63, 67–68, 73–74.

93. Ibid., 124.

94. Board of Trustees, *Second Annual Report*, 42.

95. Ross, *Democracy's College*, 217, note 63.

96. Illinois Industrial University, *Circular and Catalogue* (1873), 7. The textbooks used for those courses were Joseph Butler's *The Analogy of Religion, Natural and Revealed* (London, 1736) and William Paley's *A View of the Evidences of Christianity* (3 vols., London, 1794), which were popular during the era (Solberg, *University of Illinois*, 98, note 21).

97. Cremin, *American Education*, vol. 2, 27; Reuben, *Modern University*, 3, 19.

Plus, Regent Gregory believed in the primacy of scriptural revelation being available to all, but rejected his peers' belief in an innate moral sense, making it necessary to help students develop a conscience by applying reason to concrete, real life situations.[98] But overall, the I.I.U.'s lack of specifically religious coursework is especially noteworthy when compared to Harvard's "Classical Course of Instruction," curiously listed in the I.I.U. catalogue, in which students studied Moral Philosophy, the English Bible, metaphysics, and patristic Greek during their four year course toward a bachelor's degree.[99] At Wisconsin in the 1860s, courses in Natural Theology and Evidences of Christianity were required.[100] Even Cornell offered instruction in the Hebrew Bible, but "as a purely human production" rather than divine revelation.[101]

Along with the courses and texts offered in the I.I.U.'s formal curriculum and library, the I.I.U. leaders approved Regent Gregory's recommendation that "Miss Lottie E. Patchen be appointed teacher of instrumental music ... and that she receive the fees charged for instruction on the piano, as her salary."[102] And the I.I.U. also established both natural history and art museums.[103] The former, which began in 1869 with specimens from both John Wesley Powell's Rockies expedition and botany professor Thomas J. Burrill's jaunts through Illinois, became a public showcase of the University and brought renown throughout the country. The art gallery—which the *Chicago Tribune* called "the largest west of New York"[104]—provided a "healthful, refining and stimulating influence ... on the minds of the young,"[105] opening, recalled alumnus and famed sculptor Lorado Taft, "A new heaven and a new earth ... to my imagination."[106] Students were also required to keep a vacation jour-

98. Kersey, "John Milton Gregory," 170.

99. Illinois Industrial University, *Circular and Catalogue* (Champaign, IL: Church, Goodman, and Donnelley, Printers, 1868), 32–34.

100. Curti and Carstensen, *University of Wisconsin*, 407.

101. Kammen, *Cornell: Glorious to View*, 40.

102. Board of Trustees, *Fifth Annual Report*, 160.

103. Illinois Industrial University, *Catalogue and Circular* (1878), 17. Similarly, Cornell's president installed "plaster casts of classical statuary" and "acquired collections of fossils and shells for research" (Kammen, 37). Gregory purchased plaster statues for the I.I.U. (Solberg, *University of Illinois*, 172–73).

104. Solberg, *University of Illinois*, 172.

105. Board of Trustees, *Report of Committee*, 18.

106. Powell, *Semi-Centennial History*, 314–15.

FIGURE 7: The Art Gallery.

nal chronicling their extracurricular readings and knowledge of current events, and were expected to submit "a Thesis on some philological subject" upon their return to campus.[107] The I.I.U. students were not only required to work, however, but to also observe Sabbath rest, a time to remember, Regent Gregory said in a chapel sermon, "the mingled light of the paradise that was, and the paradise that is to be. *Fifty two times each year,*" he said, "it comes authoritatively bidding man to pause in his career of sensuality & sin, and listen to the voices of conscience & truth. The sabbath is a *mighty power in the earth* [.]"[108] That is why, he told them on a different occasion, Sundays "ought to be held sacred among you, as the day of Religious thought and study. The day that our maker has set apart as a day in which we may give attention to the interests of our souls."[109]

Yet another educational innovation present at the I.I.U. was the institutions known as the Y.M.C.A. and the Y.W.C.A.[110] During this era before denominational or parachurch campus ministries existed, the Ys constituted a new phenomenon in American collegiate life. They flour-

107. Illinois Industrial University, *Catalogue* (1871), 48.
108. Gregory, "Sermon on Luke 12:32."
109. Gregory, "Lecture, Sunday Sep. 22," 3–4.
110. Morgan, *Student Religion*; Setran, *College "Y."*

ished at Illinois, providing such ministries as Bible studies, evangelistic outreach, temperance efforts, helping students find housing, and even sponsoring the tuition of a Native American student.[111] And along with the Ys, some other student-led religious organizations met in the I.I.U. building, including a "Students' Daily Prayer meeting" at 6:30 every evening[112] and a student choir, which was, ironically, criticized in the school paper for "Sabbath desecration" due to their Sunday rehearsals and performances.[113]

Religion and Extracurricular Student Activities

Along with the innovative approaches used by the Y.M.C.A. and Y.W.C.A., the I.I.U. continued the American collegiate tradition of required daily and Sunday chapel services for students, with Regent Gregory frequently preaching. There was also a mandatory "weekly lecture" which was "delivered to all the students, on manners, formation of habits and character; on the conditions of health, happiness, and success in life; [and] on the general duties and affairs of life . . ."[114] In order to assist the cultivation of moral behavior, the I.I.U. published formal conduct rules, with high expectations for student ethics. An early recruitment catalogue states: "The University is designed for *men*, not *children*, and its government rests in an appeal to the manly feeling and sense of honor of its students. It has but one law, and that is, "Do RIGHT."[115]

To help promote proper behavior, the I.I.U. established the peer pressure of student government, "to establish and maintain," the trustees said, "that high toned, refined, and honorable public sentiment, which is at once the best safeguard against meanness and vice, and a constant inspiration to nobleness and virtue."[116]

The I.I.U. also continued the tradition of campus literary societies. Remnants of the older colleges, the Lits were heartily welcomed by

---

111. Solberg, *University of Illinois*, 179–80, 302; Peters, *Promise of Association*.

112. Students of the Senior Class, "'Student's Organizations,'" 4.

113. Students of the Senior Class, *The Student (Illinois Industrial University)* 2/1 (January 1873) 11.

114. Board of Trustees, *First Annual Report*, 196.

115. Ibid., 201 (emphasis original).

116. Ibid., 202; Solberg, *University of Illinois*, 183–84.

land-grant leaders throughout the nation.[117] Penn State, for example, had literary societies from its origin, as did Michigan State.[118] In both cases, geographical and social isolation made the Lits especially important. I.I.U. Alumnus Charles Albert Kiler recalled that

> the social life of the students up to 1891 was confined almost wholly to the literary societies ... The programs at the Friday night meetings attracted not only students and faculty but the townspeople as well. Generally the halls were filled every Friday night. Music of all kinds, orations, essays, recitations, book reviews, and debates constituted the programs. Musical talent from the two towns supplemented that in the University ... [and] the debates between the two men's societies always attracted a crowd ...[119]

Kiler said "many an alumnus ... got as much good from his membership in [the literary societies] as he got from class work in his particular field of study," including "learn[ing] how to get up on [their] feet and express [them]selves." He concluded that "the passing of these societies was a distinct loss in student life."

The I.I.U.'s Lits sponsored social events, including a year-end banquet, and brought famous religious speakers to campus such as Henry Ward Beecher, Wendell Phillips, Elizabeth Cady Stanton, and David Swing.[120] Despite their supposedly non-religious purpose, the Literary Societies displayed noteworthy Christian influence. At least one literary society, the Adelphic, had a student "Chaplain," who "invoked ... the blessings of God" at their 1873 banquet.[121] (The evening, incidentally, ended with a temperate "toast to the host [in lemonade].") And the societies sometimes debated explicitly theological topics. In January, 1878, for example, Frank Brown spoke before the Philomatheans regarding "The Origin and Destiny of Man," in which he said both Christian and Darwinian theories of origin are unknowable, advocating agnosticism

117. Ross, *Democracy's College*, 130; Horowitz, *Campus Life*, 24–31.
118. Bezilla, *Penn State*, 9; Widder, *Michigan Agricultural College*, 292–301.
119. Kiler, *On the Banks of the Boneyard*, 11.
120. Illinois Industrial University, *The Illini IV*, no. 1 (October 1874): 21; Talbot, Diary. Talbot said a large crowd turned out for Beecher, who lived "fully up to his reputation—that of being America's best living orator." Beecher spoke at the I.I.U. chapel on "The Wastes and Burdens of Society."
121. Students of the Senior Class, *The Student (Illinois Industrial University)* II, no. 7 (July 1873): 77.

FIGURE 8: Alethenai literary society meeting room.

on the subject.[122] At their next meeting, student Arthur Talbot said, "the question, Resolved [sic] that God teaches endless punishment was ably discussed but was not decided . . ."[123] According to programs of student William Curtiss, who was an Adelphic, their June 3, 1882, meeting opened with prayer, and the May 22, 1880, "Inter-Society Oratorical Contest" featured a speech by F. M. McKay entitled "There's a Divinity that Shapes our Ends."[124] Similarly, the April 22, 1881 "Alethenai Oratorical Contest" had orations called "Fly Forth, O, Gentle Dove" and "Labor: as wide as the earth, has its summit in Heaven." C. L. Smith asked, during the Adelphic's April 29, 1881, contest, "Are We Governed by Destiny?" And A. M. Bridge spoke on "Religion a Civilizer" at the May 14, 1881 inter-society contest.

The I.I.U. student newspaper provided yet another extracurricular way for the community to express and learn their understanding of

---

122. Talbot, *Diary*, 11.
123. Ibid., 21.
124. Curtiss, *Scrapbook*, 6, 21.

Christian belief.[125] One student, for example, published an article commending Jesus of Nazareth for modeling salvific "character," which the student defined as "the Golden Rule and more; it means that one shall, in every thought, word and deed, side with the right and the good."[126] Even though "mankind is subject to error," the student said, through imitating Jesus "it is possible to approximate to that one type of ideal character found in the Son of man ... " And furthermore, he said, "The Christian religion is clearly 'the survival of the fittest' ... All other systems are narrow and insufficient because wanting in characteristics essential to high *manhood*."[127]

Regarding the meaning of suffering, another student said:

> Surely "long suffering" is one of the royal steps ... and with bowed hearts we pray for this long suffering toward others which our Heavenly Father has shown so wonderfully toward us, and the love of Christ comes into our hearts, giving us that "peace which passeth all understanding," and makes us long for that joy which is the endowment of the Holy Spirit, and we can say with Thomas a Kempis: "We will seek no other way than this royal way, which is the way of the holy cross. And we will therefore, [sic] set ourselves, like a faithful servant of Christ, to bear *manfully* the cross of our Lord ... "[128]

It is ironic that this student—who belongs to a university community which supposedly prided itself for being masculine rather than monastic—would quote Thomas á Kempis, who was, of course, a monk, although, as his classic *Of the Imitation of Christ* demonstrates, he did busy himself with labor as well as learning. By fondly mentioning Thomas, though, the student author demonstrates an awareness of a broad, popular Christian tradition. As these and numerous other articles indicate, ongoing peer reflections in the student paper—like the theologically-themed orations of the literary societies—provided a key way for I.I.U. students to learn and teach their faith in a new type of

---

125. A similar journal to the I.I.U.'s *Student* and later *Illini* emerged at Michigan State, although Widder does not mention whether religion is freely discussed within the *Bubble*'s pages: see Widder, *Michigan Agricultural College*, 292–98.

126. Illinois Industrial University, *The Illini* 5/3 (December 1875) 63–64.

127. Ibid. (italics added).

128. Students of the Senior Class, *The Student (Illinois Industrial University)* 2/9 (September 1873) 108 (italics added).

university which, although public and utilitarian, still sought to impart the University's reworked version of Christian higher education.

Cultivating "Character"

The student author mentioned above was typical in his concern about cultivating "character." The topic was in the forefront of the minds of I.I.U. students and faculty alike. Character development was a primary concern for Victorian American educators, who borrowed from a long tradition of classical and Christian sources.[129] As historian Candy Gunther Brown puts it, "Nineteenth-century Americans were obsessed with character formation ... Evangelicals associated character with habits of the mind and heart that led to habitual actions calculated to promote growth in holiness."[130] According to Thomas Jefferson's thinking, an agricultural school like the I.I.U. would already have an advantage in this pursuit, since immorality, he said, is rare in any agrarian society, while "the mobs of great cities" inevitably succumb to "a degeneracy" which becomes a "canker" to a republic.[131] Theodore Parker called the farmer's farm "a gospel," every animal "a heaven-sent prophet to refine his mind and heart," and "the stars his guides to virtue and to God."[132] Ezra Cornell said his agricultural university "shall make men more truthful, more honest, more virtuous, more noble, more manly . . . to better comprehend their higher and holier relations to their families and their God."[133] Gregory's contemporary, University of Michigan president James Angell, wanted his school to cultivate "Christian character and Christian life," since Michigan was a "Christian State governed by Christian principles" and its University a place where "Christianity . . . is honored and cherished."[134]

In a talk called "The Cultivation of Character," Angell urged Michigan students to consciously imitate the "perfect model" exemplified in Jesus Christ.[135] In 1872 Regent Gregory preached a similar

---

129. Kiefer, *Mantle of Maturity*; Marx, *Machine in the Garden*, 124–25.
130. Brown, *Word in the World*, 88.
131. Peterson, *Jefferson Image*, 43–44.
132. Board of Trustees, *First Annual Report*, frontispiece.
133. Kammen, *Cornell: Glorious to View*, 29.
134. Harrold, *Place Somewhat Apart*, 21, 24.
135. Ibid., 51.

sermon on "The Christian Elements of Character" during I.I.U. chapel.[136] At least one student, his daughter Carrie, took this and other such messages to heart. She gave a speech at the 1874 union meeting of the I.I.U. literary societies which brought down the house. Printed afterward in the student paper, her composition epitomizes the Christian virtues sought for the holiness of a young person. One should obtain "Truth, Temperance, and Aspiration," which lead to "*Character*."[137] "Education," leading to "Knowledge," assisted the process. To go even higher, one needed to "combine the elements of unselfishness and charity and polish them with those of cheerfulness and politeness." And in the end? Achieving "the Golden City with its River of Life, where is needed no sun, for the great glory of its King is sufficient light." Carrie Gregory ended her address by saying,

> This beautiful land he must also gain; on, on, he would still press, shaping as he went a key formed of Purity and Christian Love. Presenting this at the pearly gate, wide open it swung, and he was ushered in to the presence of the Great King. Overpowered by this majesty, the young man fell at His feet to praise and adore. To Him he gave up his ring of keys and received for his labors a crown and palm, then joining his voice with the heavenly choir, he sang the victor's song: "Joy! Joy! forever! my task is done, The gates are passed, and Heaven is won."

The next year a different student commended Jesus for modeling salvific "character," saying Jesus, "a Jewish philosopher" is "he himself, with his life . . . that philosophy."[138] The ideal that Jesus embodied, "The Christian religion . . . has endured these eighteen hundred years because it meets the wants of the human nature. In the struggle for existence that every creed and every idea must pass through, it has stood the test of time and acted as a potent force in civilization, because it alone, along the line of sufficiency and adequacy, meets and satisfies the requirements of hungry, thirsty souls." The student concluded by comparing Christ's "manly" character to the national popularity of George Washington. After all, she or he said, "every body believes that 'an honest man is the noblest work of God.'"

---

136. Gregory, "Christian Elements of Character."

137. Illinois Industrial University, *The Illini* 4/5 (February 1875) 136–38. Gregory uses imagery from the book of Revelation here.

138. Illinois Industrial University, *The Illini* 5/3 (December 1875) 63–64.

Although student authors do not necessarily opine the official policy of the University and its leaders, their views demonstrate the larger world view of a significant sector of the I.I.U. community. In an article entitled "Character," for example, an I.I.U. student, encouraging his or her peers to "weed out our bad habits," said "We have a beautiful example" of "be[ing] obedient to all laws" in "Christ. Look at the sacrifices he had to make, the sufferings he endured, and then think, think I say, how little is required of us, in return for the many blessings we receive from his hands."[139] One character trait required in return, it appears, was charitable service. In an article called "One of Our Western Charitable Institutions," Carrie Gregory lauded the virtues of the "Ohio Asylum," a community she said made one feel "that mankind has taken another step towards the Kingdom of Heaven."[140] Another student writer described a "Visit to the Orfans' [sic] Home" in Normal, Illinois.[141] Still another said that through "Charity, the angel pure and holy," along with duty, one could become a better person, since

> "The path of duty is the way to glory."
> Through mountain passes, over rugged sod,
> From fresh, fair youth to wrinkled age so hoary,
> The path of duty is the way to God.[142]

In the same article, the "nobility of silence," was commended, saying that "silence often hides a hero." A person expressing Christian virtues should be revered, since "if a man is not rising, he is falling. If he never rises, he is soon below the beast. If he never falls he will soon be pure enough to consort with angels."

A similar view of spiritual progress is presented in the last two stanzas of this poem featured in the "Young Ladies' Department" section of the student paper:

> There is no sin repented and forgiven,
> Which does not higher lead the erring one;
> There is no heart with evil torn and riven,
> Which, conquering the wrong, is not God's own.

---

139. Illinois Industrial University, *The Illini* 8/8 (May 1879) 231.

140. Illinois Industrial University, *The Illini* 7/6 (March 1878) 227.

141. Illinois Industrial University, *The Illini* 9/1 (October 1879) 7–9.

142. Students of the Senior Class, *The Student (Illinois Industrial University)* 1/2 (December 1871) 5.

> There is no woe or trial as by fire,
> Which may not bring its own and full reward;
> There is no sorrow which may not lead higher
> The soul it fills, toward the Father, God.[143]

"Virtue," a different article said, "is the highest, purest thing upon God's footstool."[144] Another student's poem, entitled "Strength in Silence," written for the Alethenai literary society, praised the virtue of a Christian woman's purity:

> Then "to be," Alethenai,
> Of woman so nobly crowned;
> Her heart *must* be strong and pure,
> To help heal the world's deep wound.
>
> Love's still power is dwelling there,
> A woman's life within;
> Pure in heart the only cure,
> For all with the taint of sin.[145]

Yet another proverb printed in the school paper said, "Love of God and love of neighbor, Sweetens duty, lightens labor."[146]

In continuity with Christian tradition, some students believed that suffering and punishment were self-improving means of character building, too. One student said "we thank God that He has so constituted us that we *cannot* remain always in the gloom and the shadow. But, most of all, we thank Him that, in all sorrow and tribulation, He leads us to the 'Rock' which is higher than we."[147] Not only was suffering at the hand of others considered salvific, but God's judgment was, as well: "God renders earth desolate to induce you to seek a better country. He strikes away every human prop, and puts failure and vexation into every worldly scheme, that you may turn from your idols unto Him."[148]

---

143. Students of the Senior Class, *The Student (Illinois Industrial University)* 2/7 (July 1873) 83.

144. Students of the Senior Class, *The Student (Illinois Industrial University)* 1/3 (January 1872) 9–10.

145. Illinois Industrial University, *The Illini* 3/4 (April 1874) 97.

146. Students of the Senior Class, *The Student (Illinois Industrial University)* 1/3 (January, 1872) 13.

147. Students of the Senior Class, *The Student (Illinois Industrial University)* 2/8 (August 1873) 95.

148. Students of the Senior Class, *The Student (Illinois Industrial University)* 2/11

Another student writer, "G. F. K.," composed an allegory about God's judgment called "The Oaks and the Grapevine." One oak, he said, rejected the vine, growing away from it, and its twin oak brother.[149] It eventually died, while the other oak flourished. "The moral is plain," said the author. "Do not the two oaks in their careers and fates resemble two nations, one of which despised Christ and his religion, both apparently of humble birth?" Jesus, after all, called himself a vine. "Or, do they not equally show forth the direct influence of the tendencies of the heart to decide its fate even in this life; for, 'Virtue brings its own reward,' but Hate and Selfishness, only disgrace. Incivility toward those below us may bring us beneath them. Truly, the giver receives more than is given and in the end receives the crown." Live according to God's ways, the student preached, or reap what you sow.

As the I.I.U.'s Christian students saw judgment and suffering as redemptive opportunities, at least one said he or she admired patient, compassionate forgiveness as a virtue. In an article called "Mutual Forbearance," the student wrote:

> God has mysteriously linked us together by this curious fact of mutual dependence, and the wonderful possibility of mutual help. The poor may be relieved, the sick visited, the sorrowing may receive sympathy, the inexperienced may be counseled, and the faint-hearted encouraged. All these in turn may give help to the hand that gives help to them, for God has so ordered it that we are not absolutely independent of each other.[150]

Since God had arranged things in this way, the author concluded, "we ought not to be perpetually obtruding our evil tempers before our friends, imposing upon their christian [sic] forbearance, and excuse ourselves by saying *'it is my way.'*" One should do unto others as they would like to be treated themselves. Courteous gentility, the student said, demonstrated a noble and righteous character.

Temperance

One of the most addressed ethical issues at the I.I.U.—and among the era's Protestants generally—was the consumption of alcoholic beverages.

(November 1873) 132.
    149. Illinois Industrial University, *The Illini* 4/1 (October 1874) 7–9.
    150. Illinois Industrial University, *The Illini* 3/4 (April 1874) 98.

Wisconsin's John Bascom eventually published an influential pamphlet calling for the public to take temperance from the voluntary society to enforcement at the hands of the state.[151] Jonathan Baldwin Turner was a teetotaler and strong temperance advocate. When, at age eighty-nine, a physician prescribed him a case of beer as a "tonic," Turner refused to drink it, saying, "All my life I have struggled against the temptation to drink; and now, at this late day, I will not begin muddling my brain."[152] When Champaign County sent a contingent to Springfield to woo legislators to grant them the University, a journalist reported that "For the evangelical and temperance portion of 'the ring' and their friends we had a quiet room set apart provided only with a bible, a pitcher of cold water, and a bottle of bay rum (for the hair); and here your correspondent spent most of his time."[153] A public vote soon after Champaign's incorporation in 1857 favored the illegalization of liquor sales, though the village board issued licenses any way. A strong temperance society lobby kept the issue at the forefront of local politics well into the 1860s.[154] Temperance advocates throughout Illinois sought to legislate against the sale and use of liquor during the 1850s, but failed.[155] A revival occurred during the 1870s, with state Republicans favoring temperance, including governors Palmer and Beveridge.[156]

John Gregory's president and mentor at Union College, Eliphalet Nott, was a typical Protestant reformer, an immediate abolitionist, revivalist, patriot, and public school supporter. A temperance advocate, he had done much Biblical scholarship on alcoholic beverages, claiming that, as historian Harry Kersey put it,

> nine words in the Hebrew of the Old Testament had been translated into English by the single word *wine* but that their various meanings in the text could not be the same. Some meant a harmless drink, while others made wine a "mocker," or a "serpent's bite," or an "adder's sting." Therefore, he inferred, the Bible approved only unfermented fruit juices, and he answered

151. Hoeveler, "University and the Social Gospel," 290.

152. Carriel, *Life of Jonathan Baldwin Turner*. Carriel says he recovered his health without the aid of beer.

153. "History of the Champaign 'Elephant,'" in Powell, *Semi-Centennial History*, 510.

154. McCollum, "ETC," 9.

155. Howard, *Illinois: A History*, 281–83.

156. Ibid., 367.

the troublesome questions about Christ's first miracle by insisting that the wine served at the marriage feast in Cana was unfermented.[157]

Nott wrote many temperance tracts, and his 1847 *Lectures on Bible Temperance* was a key text in the movement. He frequently preached against liquor's evils in public lectures of all kinds. Nott's fervent temperance stance was rooted in his revivalistic theory of education, where one taught for moral character, gaining holiness as a result. John Gregory would share this stance at the I.I.U.[158] Himself a teetotaler, Gregory supported temperance since at least his college days, when he belonged to Equitable Union (later Delta Upsilon) secret society, which forbade alcohol consumption.[159] In 1852, while serving as an Ohio Baptist pastor, he wrote passionately about the subject, encouraging readers to pass a prohibition law similar to Maine's.[160] After moving to Michigan, where, besides teaching full-time, he was a supply preacher and Sunday School speaker, Gregory continued the crusade against liquor, publishing in that same year an article entitled "An Appeal for the Maine Law" in the Baptist's *Michigan Christian Herald*. Like many temperance reformers, he was concerned that families suffered when working men drank, fearing for "the wail of wives and the moan of little children" if partisanism in the coming election watered down the cause.[161] His article in the Detroit press called "The Maine Law the Greatest Want of the State" shrewdly claimed that prohibition would lower law enforcement and welfare costs, help alcoholics' children find useful employment, and protect the citizenry from what he deemed a social evil inherited from European immigration.[162]

In 1870 the I.I.U. trustees asked their Executive Committee to lobby the State for a law prohibiting the sale of alcoholic beverages within a three-mile radius of the campus.[163] This was wishful thinking, of course, because the radius included both downtown Champaign and downtown Urbana. But the campus itself was dry, as the 1871–1872

157. Kersey, "John Milton Gregory as a Midwestern Educator," 21–22.
158. Ibid., 21–23.
159. Solberg, *University of Illinois*, 87.
160. Kersey, "John Milton Gregory as a Midwestern Educator," 44.
161. Kersey, "John Milton Gregory as a Midwestern Educator," 55–56.
162. Gregory, "Maine Law."
163. Board of Trustees, *Third Annual Report*, 84.

University "By-Laws" declared that "All use of alcoholic drinks, and all visiting of drinking shops or saloons, and of billiard and gambling houses, are strictly forbidden as disgraceful, and destructive to the best interests of the student and of the University."[164]

Guest lecturers, though, were allowed to dissent from advocating prohibition. During his talk in January of 1873, for example, Champaign's B. F. Johnson suggested that hops—an ingredient used to make beer—might be grown as a cash crop in order to remedy the low prices wrought by grain overproduction, and, since corn was not profitable, Illinois farmers should grow tobacco, hemp, and opium poppies instead.[165] Four years earlier "the Hon. George Husmann" traveled all the way from Hermann, Missouri, to persuade the crowd to grow grapes for producing wine. He called "the noble grape" the "healthiest and most luscious of God's fruits," and rejoiced that "where one gallon of wine was made twenty years ago, tens of thousands are made now, and we are on the road to become a temperate people."[166] Unlike nations where wine was the common drink, he reasoned, whiskey consumption in the United States, England, Scotland, and Ireland had caused "misery and degradation everywhere; the image of God transformed into a hideous mockery, family ruin and strife, neglected children, deserted wives." But in contrast "every wine maker among you is an apostle of temperance," producing "that most innocent, healthful and inspiriting of all stimulants, good pure wine, thereby supplanting those abominable poisonous compounds which are now palmed off on the public." By producing wine, he said, "you do more for the cause of true temperance than Gough and all the total abstinence lecturers in the country ... [So] do not say to the sober, industrious laborer," he concluded, "'thou shalt not refresh thyself with a glass of good wine when thy muscles relax from severe toil, when thy tongue is parched with thirst, because thy neighbor makes a beast of himself by drinking whisky and brandy to excess.'"

The looming image of a beastly drunkard was on the mind of at least one student author who published a poem in the school paper called "Don't, Father," telling the frank, chilling tale of an intoxicated parent beating and murdering his daughter, only to sober up and regret

---

164. Board of Trustees, *Fifth Annual Report*, 60.
165. Board of Trustees, *Sixth Annual Report*, 178–84, 186–89.
166. Board of Trustees, *Second Annual Report*, 258.

it later.[167] On the other hand, the following year the paper printed a blurb about a certain "Gluggity-Glug Club" comprised of University students who secretly met in downtown Champaign "in a tall house near the I. B. & W. Railway... drinking from a score of long-necked bottles" as they sat "upon a few old tobacco-stained benches."[168] Regent Gregory talked to the students directly about alcohol during an 1877 Sunday Chapel sermon, noting its social, political, and financial effects.[169] Citing recent statistics, he lamented that, during a period of economic hardship, the public thirst remained, keeping the taverns, breweries, and courthouses busy while sadly adding to poverty. Reminding the students of how the whiskey lobby controlled U.S. politics, and warning "ladies" that it was dangerous to offer wine to their "guests," he challenged the students to enlist in the fight against the alcoholism which was sending some sixty thousand Americans to early graves each year.

Apparently the students responded, because by February of 1878 a "temperance union" had been organized by University students.[170] According to the *Illini*, "Most" of the student body "signed the pledge" that "no intoxicating liquors will be drank by the signer while connected with the university as a student." The paper supported this move, since "there are many of our students who come from family influences that guarded them from all temptation," and they are therefore easy prey for liquor. Desiring "sociability . . . gayety and pleasure," the editors said, too many of "the leading members" of colleges "are doomed men before they leave the college halls," since "drinking . . . creeps in unsuspectingly and before the young man knows it people say he is a drunkard." Better to sign the pledge and abstain, they urged, than to suffer the consequences.

In the spring of 1881 both Urbana and Champaign held elections asking citizens whether or not they should outlaw saloons. The I.I.U. literary societies sponsored famous temperance lecturers John B. Gough and Frances Willard to come and speak, and the townspeople

---

167. Students of the Senior Class, *The Student* (Illinois Industrial University) 1/3 (January 1872) 9–10.

168. Students of the Senior Class, *The Student* (Illinois Industrial University) 2/2 (February 1873) 15–16.

169. Ebert, *Illini Century*, 31–32.

170. Illinois Industrial University, *The Illini* 7/5 (February 1878) 190.

voted to go dry, much to the YMCA's delight.[171] But there were still other perceived dangers to character formation which students faced, including tobacco. In 1870, Illinois produced 5,249,274 pounds of the crop, making them only eleventh overall in the U. S., and far behind the 105,305,869 pounds grown by neighbor Kentucky in that year. Furthermore, the vast majority of Illinois tobacco was raised in the southeastern part of the state, "the counties on the Wabash and Ohio slopes" which, the trustees said, grew "nearly all the filthy weed."[172] Still, though, it was readily available for I.I.U. students. Guest lecturer Elmer Baldwin warned that tobacco

> perverts the taste, beclouds the mind, taints the breath, poisons the secretions, and degrades the man in his own estimation, if not in that of others. Would that our rural population would preserve their persons free from such contamination, that a tainted breath should not mingle with the sweet odor from the flowers and fruits they rear! . . . But far different is the noble form, clear intellect, the delicate sensibilities of the hardy son of toil, who, in the words of the apostle, can present his body a pure and acceptable sacrifice, whose brain is not pickled in alcohol, lips cankerous from use of the filthy meerschaum, whose breath is not redolent of beer, alcohol, and loaded with effluvia from ulcerated lungs and diseased liver, but whose every faculty is preserved by strict temperance in the condition God gave them; whose breath is as pure as an infant's breathing on flowers, whose every taste and sensibility by appropriate use have been preserved in their pristine power and purity; gratifying every taste and passion to any extent that does not interfere with the demands and requirements of every other, he preserves his *manhood* intact.[173]

The student paper referred to nicotine as "deadly" and "poisonous," advising abstinence from its consumption.[174] Trustee Willard Flagg called tobacco a "filthy weed which tobacco haters assign to a satanic origin, and loving smokers consign to a satanic fate."[175]

    171. Solberg, *University of Illinois*, 180, 302. A statue of Willard stood at a prominent spot in downtown Urbana from 1907 to 1921; see News Gazette, *Century in Pictures*.

    172. Board of Trustees, *Sixth Annual Report*, 216.

    173. Board of Trustees, *Third Annual Report*, 397–98 (italics added); Baldwin cites Romans 12:1 here.

    174. Illinois Industrial University, *The Illini* 4/2 (November 1874) 41–42.

    175. Board of Trustees, *Sixth Annual Report*, 1872–1873, 216.

Along with encouraging restraint from alcohol and tobacco use, the faculty also tried to discourage social dancing. Alternatives like student picnics, nutting parties, sleigh rides, trips to the Sangamon River, and other such activities were heartily endorsed. Literary societies hosted "sociables" in University rooms or local churches. But, as was evident in 1878 when some Seniors tried to start a dancing club, Regent Gregory disapproved.[176] One of the era's clergyman authors, a Methodist named Jonathan T. Crane, explains in his book *Popular Amusements* that dancing too closely resembles sexual intimacy.[177] He also forbade horse racing, as did I.I.U. guest lecturer Col. N. J. Colman, who said God had given humans the capacity to enjoy horses, but not to "waste their time at the race course, or to make trotting trainers of themselves," because "the influence of the race course is bad" and "tends directly to neglect of business."[178] Perhaps trying to highlight their classmates' virtue, the I.I.U. paper reported in 1873 "that some of our students spend considerable time at the Temperance Billiard Room in town, where not even the smell of tobacco-smoke is allowed to permeate."[179] But billiards, too, were on Rev. Crane's forbidden list, as were theaters, professional baseball, cards, chess, and novels.[180] Like fellow evangelical leaders of his day, Crane advocated recreations which would build character by focusing on God and his values as expressed in the Bible. There was no room for frivolity at the I.I.U., as the Illinois General Assembly had ruled that "no student shall at any time be allowed to remain in or about the University in idleness, or without full mental or industrial occupation."[181] Although in about 1880 character development began to yield to self-actualization through personality construction as the American educational goal,[182] during Gregory's tenure the I.I.U. leaders encouraged their students to refrain from character-destroying activities which they saw as a detriment to their "man"hood. As Kersey puts it, John Gregory's "career as an

---

176. Solberg, *University of Illinois*, 309–10.

177. Crane, *Popular Amusements*, 89–103. Crane was the father of American novelist Stephen Crane.

178. Board of Trustees, *Second Annual Report*, 285.

179. Ebert, *Illini Century*, 3–4.

180. Crane, *Popular Amusements*, 3–8.

181. Illinois General Assembly, "An Act to Provide," 593.

182. Harrold, *Place Somewhat Apart*, 55.

educator is a study in single-minded devotion to developing Christian character" in his students.[183]

"Monks" No More

Regent Gregory and his colleagues intentionally sought to establish a new type of university which would expand higher education to professions beyond those schooled in a traditional American college. And yet, they were explicit about their desire to yield moral and *Christian* graduates. Their new type of university meant that they needed a new type of spirituality and ethics: of being "men" rather than "monks." Their proposed model was an interesting mix of Protestant theology and American political philosophy. Some innovations came from Turner's, Gregory's, and the trustees' theologizing, while others were prompted by Morrill Act stipulations. And some of the most fruitful arenas for religious activity and reflection, like chapel talks and literary societies, were not innovative at all, but instead continuities of an inherited American collegiate tradition.

During the Gregory years, was the I.I.U.'s culture actually "Christian"? They claimed it was. And in so doing, their story illustrates a significant transition time in American higher education, a period which educational historian Julie Reuben calls a unique "unity of truth" between Christianity and collegiate life.[184] Historian Edward Eddy once said that among the greatest contributions of the land grant movement was that "each man was worth educating as a person and as a citizen in keeping with the Judeo-Christian and democratic belief in his dignity and worth."[185] Although the I.I.U.'s architects well knew they were beginning a new chapter in the history of collegiate life, they still saw themselves within that tradition's continuity, as stewards of the long Protestant legacy of Christian moral formation. They believed that, even in a state-sponsored, non-sectarian university, they could do a new thing for God's Kingdom: to somehow, in a public way transcending the boundaries of the institutional church, promote "Christian culture," educating virtuous men and women—trained in body, mind, and soul— for service to the State of Illinois, and wherever they were called to go.

---

183. Kersey, "John Milton Gregory as a Midwestern Educator," 169–70.

184. Reuben, *Making of the Modern University*, 17–35; Hawkins, *Emerging University*.

185. Eddy, *Colleges for Our Land*, 285.

4

Liturgies for "Learning and Labor"

THE ORGANIZATION OF THE ANTEBELLUM AMERICAN COLLEGE followed, for the most part, the Reformed and Congregationalist norm established during the colonial era, where presidents functioned similarly to pastor-overseers, trustees and faculty like elders, and students as the congregation.[1] Although technically not churches themselves, the colleges were self-consciously extensions of the churches' ministry. Even though the Illinois Industrial University was supported by public funds, Rev. Gregory and his colleagues continued this church-state cooperative tradition, adding innovations like the pan-Protestant non-sectarianism now deemed appropriate for a land-grant institution. At the trustees' first meeting, they unanimously passed the following resolution: "*Resolved*, That sensible of our dependence on the Divine blessing in the great work in which we are engaged, it should be a standing order of this board to commence each day's proceedings by reading of the Word of God and prayer."[2] Trustee Mahan followed by voicing a "prayer to Almighty God, in the name of His Son, Jesus Christ, invoking His blessing upon the [twenty-eight board] members individually."[3] At least ten of the trustees were Baptists, four of whom were still actively

---

1. Harrison, *Authority and Power*; Vesey, *Emergence of the American University*; Cremin, *American Education: The Colonial Experience*; *American Education: The National Experience*; Brubacher and Rudy, *Higher Education in Transition*; Miller, *Life of the Mind in America*. Harrison demonstrates the promise and peril of congregational polity, while the others concur that nineteenth-century American intellectual life was profoundly influenced by Calvinism and evangelical churches.

2. Board of Trustees, *First Annual Report*, 16.

3. Board of Trustees, *First Annual Report*, 76; Board of Trustees, *Tenth Report*, 244. During their first year, the trustees formally ratified the opening of meetings with Scripture readings and prayer into their bylaws, but in 1880, the end of J. M. Gregory's tenure, the practice was abandoned.

Figure 9: The I. I. U. seal, featuring the motto "Learning and Labor," with an illumined, open book containing the words "science, agriculture, and art," above images of a plow, an anvil, and a steam engine.

preaching, with at least two more having prior pulpit experience.[4] The I.I.U. sometimes cooperated with Champaign-Urbana and its churches directly. After the University's inauguration, for example, we find the trustees thanking "the ladies and citizens of the two cities of Urbana and Champaign and their vicinities" for "the sumptuous collation provided to-day for this Board and its guests."[5] Local churches donated their buildings and pastors for I.I.U. functions and public prayers. Likewise, the participation of students in church socials and other events indicates a strong relationship between the churches and the University.

During the early years of American land-grant education, visible on-campus religious activities were commonplace. Normally, attendance at daily and Sunday chapel services were required, and voluntary participation in campus prayer meetings, Bible studies, local church ministries, and YMCA activities were encouraged. Faculty cooperation ensured that philosophy course topics and discussions frequently coincided with chapel themes. Even religious revivals, which were characteristic at church-related schools, were welcome. An 1875 official report

---

4. Powell, *Semi-Centennial History*, 272–73, 339–40, 343–46.
5. Board of Trustees, *First Annual Report*, 133.

from Penn State, for example, cited a campus revival as being a key event that year, while a camp meeting at Iowa State temporarily competed with students' interest in their coursework.[6] Within this framework, traditional moral norms and religious practices, inherited from evangelical Christianity's pervasive influence, were upheld and taught.[7] Clerical presidents and professors insured that a moderate, non-sectarian and orthodox sanity would neutralize assaults from either perceived extreme, be it from free-thinking religionists or scientists on the one hand, or denominational partisans on the other.

The values of the I.I.U.'s leaders—concepts like labor's millennium, reversing the curse, and being "men" rather than "monks"—needed to be clearly articulated to the community, while the community, in turn, needed to internalize them and act upon them. In order to teach and live these values, the I.I.U. faithful ritualized them into a unique mix of the secular and the sacred, the public and the private, the pious and the patriotic. Americans, perhaps more than any other nation, had developed an individualized form of Christian faith which, while abandoning European forms of institutionalism, still celebrated their perception of the U.S. being a Christian country.[8] An American civil religion had developed, featuring a unique mix of Protestant Christianity and republican democracy which comprised an overarching American vision and piety.[9] During the 1860s and 1870s public religious expression and participation was commonplace in the United States, a means by which its citizens drew together, hoping to find a unity and shared identity that brought meaning to their society. Public worship in a Protestant sanctuary would have been a familiar experience for the I.I.U. community. The pulpit-centered services of Illinois' revivalistic Methodists, Baptists, Presbyterians, and other evangelicals were frequent, visible, and influential during the I.I.U.'s formative years.[10] Though the University was conceived in Chicago and Springfield, and many competing interests vied for its cultural influence, local religious mores tended to usurp those

---

6. Ross, *Democracy's College*, 132, 217; Eddy, *Colleges for Our Land*, 65–71.

7. Noll, *America's God*, persuasively demonstrates the theological and intellectual homogeneity of American culture prior to the Civil War.

8. Hatch, *Democratization of American Christianity*.

9. Albanese, *America, Religions and Religion*, 432–62.

10. Andreasen, "Proscribed Preachers," 194–212.

imposed by outsiders.[11] As Regent Gregory's successor, fellow Baptist Selim Peabody, would say: "That the people of the State of Illinois ever dreamed that . . . Christianity, the God of Heaven and Earth, and the Bible as His written word could be ruled out of its State University, so that it should be unlawful to read the Scriptures, or to pray to Him, within its walls, is a conclusion too monstrous to be entertained."[12]

Since perceived standards of public decency hinged upon appropriate liturgical behavior as deemed by the rituals of revivalistic evangelicalism and patriotic militarism, when the time came to open the new University, the inaugural exercises—and subsequent liturgical events—had a flavor much like the austere pomp of local Sunday morning gatherings or holiday parades. The I.I.U., like colleges before it, observed regular public rituals, arranged according to the academic calendar. Anniversary Day, Class Day, and Commencement became fixed and revered occasions. Beginning in 1874, Anniversary Day in March featured a chapel service, with orations and music by students and an address by the Regent. Class Day, which also started in 1874, occurred the Monday before graduation. Class members would speak original orations, sing their class song, and give a gift to the University. Unlike traditional colleges, the I.I.U.'s commencement lacked Latin and academic regalia. But they did feature the familiar baccalaureate sermon on the prior Sunday, with a midweek commencement ceremony.[13] In order to show how the I.I.U. ritualized their shared values and goals, this chapter looks more closely at these events, beginning with Inauguration Day, then daily and Sunday chapels, followed by two dedication ceremonies for the new University Hall, and finally Anniversary and Commencement days.

Inauguration Day

On the morning of Wednesday, March 11, 1868, as many as two thousand people made their way to the I.I.U. campus for a ceremony to be held in the University Building. Built a few years earlier as an unsuccessful boarding school, the brick structure was a notable regional land-

---

11. Ross, "Religious Influences." Ross argues that local religious customs were adopted by post-Civil War colleges and universities throughout the Midwest.
12. Board of Trustees, *Thirteenth Report*, 69.
13. Solberg, *University of Illinois*, 198.

mark, rising five stories above the prairie. Before, it had been a reminder of a failed educational project in a newly-settled area of the state. Now, though, with the University's arrival, it stood as a symbol of pride and hope. Only a few hundred could actually fit in the third-floor chapel room where the services were to be held. The chapel itself was a plain meeting room, constructed for school assemblies and lectures generally rather than specifically for Christian worship. Such a design was not unusual for evangelical Protestants in the United States, as revivalism had transformed worship toward a more performance oriented event occurring anywhere, not limited to the sacred space of ornate chapels.[14] Illumined by simple sunlight and gas lamps, the I.I.U. auditorium's wooden paneling was decorated especially for the occasion, draped with flags and banners in the nation's familiar red, white, and blue, making the stars and stripes visible to all present. A lithograph of George Washington—whom the trustees called "the great Farmer of the Revolutionary period"—hung at the front of the room, above and behind the chancel, where the lectern stood.[15] Beneath President Washington's iconic image—in a way reminiscent of the cherubim beside the ark's mercy seat located beneath Israel's God[16]—was the strong, winged American eagle. Above Washington's likeness, in bold, evergreen letters, the motto, "Learning and Labor," was pinned to the wall as a reminder of the University's creed. It was now time to offer, as the trustees put it, "prayers for the continued blessing of God upon the school which we here consecrate."[17]

Just before nine o'clock in the morning, the trustees, state officials, and various other dignitaries filed in to assume their places on the chancel. Chicago's celebrated composer, George Root, had been selected to direct the music for the day, and he led a choir of fifty members with two pianists. As the last of the noted guests were seated, the inaugural ceremonies began, with the choir singing "How Good Is He the Giver," a piece from Root's own *Cantata of the Haymakers*. Describing the event three days later, the *Champaign Democrat* said "the music—ah, the glorious delicious music! The enchanting harmony, the inspiring

14. Kilde, *When Church Became Theatre*; Moore, "Constructions of Religion," 59–65; Nelson, "'Building Confessions,'" 11–26.

15. Board of Trustees, *First Annual Report*, 149.

16. See Exodus 25:17–22, 26:34, and Numbers 7:89.

17. Board of Trustees, *First Annual Report*, 158.

melody, the very soul of sound grandly swelling or sweetly dying away like 'angels' [sic] whispers."[18] When the music ended, Rev. C. D. Nott of Urbana read selections from the Bible, followed with a prayer given by Rev. J. H. Noble of Champaign. With the "Giver's" blessing invoked, W. S. Moulton, President of the State Board of Education, welcomed those assembled, reminding them of the long overdue need for the great educational experiment about to be undertaken. After a quartet sang "Lord, Forever at Thy Side," letters from dignitaries like Governor Oglesby, Illinois' legislators in Washington, and college administrators from other schools throughout the nation were read.[19] When these readings were finished, the choir began to sing the University Anthem, with music composed by George Root and lyrics written by Regent Gregory. (The lyrics are printed in their entirety in "The Community Concurs" section of chapter two.) The people joined in with the choir and they sang the anthem together.[20]

When the song ended the day's featured speaker, State Superintendent of Public Instruction Newton Bateman, delivered an approximately two-hour address called "Educating the Lord's Redeemed and Anointed."[21] He began by placing the I.I.U.'s Inauguration Day as a culmination of the American republic and land grant movement, an "era" which "deserves to be called *sublime*."[22] The American Romantic literary and philosophical movement often referred to the "sublime" when speaking of the ethereal and eternal, and Bateman was setting a religious tone by invoking millennial imagery.[23] He paid homage to J. B. Turner's prophetic function as the catalyst for agricultural and mechanical education in the Midwest, and praised Turner for nudging the Illinois General Assembly and United States Congress into actions which allowed for the I.I.U. to exist. Providing a philosophical and theoretical backdrop for the University's purpose, Bateman lauded the great and even divine possibilities of scientific agriculture toward the improvement of humanity, the necessity of the I.I.U.'s proposed curriculum, and the congruence between America's collegiate "old order

18. Powell, *Semi-Centennial History*, 304.
19. Board of Trustees, *First Annual Report*, 150–54.
20. Ibid., 154–55.
21. Behle, "Educating 'The Lord's Redeemed and Anointed.'"
22. Board of Trustees, *First Annual Report*, 155.
23. Miller, *Life of the Mind in America*.

of liberal culture"[24] with the dawning day of the industrial university movement. Point by point, he painstakingly reviewed the struggles leading to, at last, this long-awaited day of the University's founding. He granted them benediction:

> May the God of light and knowledge and love smile upon the transactions of this day . . . Let this University catch here, and feel forever, the inspiration of this ennobling conception of the surely coming American democracy—let it join with the ten thousand public schools of the State, and with the ten times ten thousand public schools of the Union, in voicing down to coming generations the incarnate truth of the age and of God, that culture, as well as liberty, is the everlasting heritage of the race, and that whoso would restrict to the few what belongs to all, is a traitor to the people. Glory be to God in the highest, and on earth, peace, good will to men.[25]

When Bateman finished his speech, the choir and audience sang a petitional prayer in the form of an "original ode, written by a lady":

> God of wisdom! with thy favor,
> Bless this fane, by human hand[26]
> Reared to Science, Art, Industry,
> For the sons of our great land.
>
> Thanks we give for institutions
> Shedding light, benign and strong,
> Beaming forth like suns, dispelling
> Mists of ignorance and wrong.
>
> Bless this sun, in hope arising,
> O'er the plains of Illinois;
> Arm its splendors with thy power,
> Make its fame our pride and joy.
>
> Clear and bright, for aye, its shining,
> Far and wide its beams extend,
> Making love of useful labor
> With the love of learning blend.
>
> Give to science grander power
> Truth from every field to glean;

---

24. Board of Trustees, *First Annual Report*, 169.
25. Board of Trustees, *First Annual Report*, 172.
26. A "fane" is a temple or a church building.

> Till its light and warmth and beauty
> O'er the earth are felt and seen.[27]

Such hymn singing was common and important for mid-nineteenth-century evangelical Protestants. Popularized by revivalists like John and Charles Wesley and Charles Finney—and contemporized by Fanny Crosby and others—singing together during worship gave the people of the era a millennialistic foretaste of upcoming heavenly praise as foretold in scripture.[28] Although the I.I.U. inauguration ceremonies were different than a Sunday morning church service, the familiar genre of hymn singing allowed the participants to engage in a shared liturgical activity which they understood and affirmed as a means of dedication to action, and in which they felt inclusion and corporate solidarity.

After the sung prayer ended, in the governor's absence, General S. A. Hurlbut, on behalf of the trustees, presented Regent Gregory the keys to the University, making a brief speech emphasizing the right and necessity of education in a democratic republic. He then welcomed Gregory to the lectern to deliver the "Inaugural Address." The length of Bateman's speech forced the Regent, out of consideration for the audience, to alter his prepared manuscript so the ceremonies would not last too long. Gregory's mentor at Union College, Eliphalet Nott, favored *ex tempore* speaking, and Gregory was generally more likely to talk from a handful of notes rather than a lengthy manuscript.[29] Despite the need to ad lib, the Regent was still effectively able to explain his dream: establishing a university that would help working people build a better and more healthful society. Theirs, he exclaimed, was a special mission, where art and science would work together, hand in hand, toward the mental and moral formation of the individual. And furthermore, they were called to create a school sought by "the popular will."[30] Only then could they produce "clear-headed, broad-breasted scholars, men of fully developed minds—fit leaders of those great productive arts by which the world's civilization is fed and nourished." In summarizing his speech, he left his audience with these stirring lines:

---

27. Board of Trustees, *First Annual Report*, 173.
28. Brown, *Word in the World*, 194–96.
29. Kersey, "John Milton Gregory as a Midwestern Educator," 25.
30. Board of Trustees, *First Annual Report*, 176, 180.

> Let us but demonstrate that the highest culture is compatible with the active pursuit of industry, and that the richest learning will pay in a corn field or a carpenter's shop, and we have made universal education not only a possible possession, but a fated necessity of the race . . . The light which has heretofore fallen through occasional rifts, and on scattered hill tops, will henceforward flood field and valley with the splendors of a noon time sun, and the quickened intellect of the race will bloom with new beauty and burst into a richer fruitage of industrial arts.[31]

As Regent Gregory left the lectern, Mr. Root's choir began to sing "America." The congregation joined in, and together, finishing the hymn, they received the blessing of benediction from "the Rev. Mr. Riley, of Urbana." When the ceremony was over, they "repaired to the University dining hall below, where a plentiful and elegant repast had been provided by the ladies of Champaign and Urbana."[32] There they feasted together, celebrating the blessing which had come their way in the form of the new University. The *Champaign Democrat* summarized the Inauguration Day festivities by saying: "This may be justly called a magnificent affair throughout; happy in its conception and successful and harmonious in its execution. The substantial feast prepared for the occasion was highly creditable to our citizens, and was destroyed with a relish."

The *Chicago Evening Post*, however, was less euphemistic, saying the "banquet" was "gotten up in the highest style of Central Illinois, hog and hominy."[33] Remembering the event thirteen years later, though, the trustees said the inauguration

> was a gala day for the friends of the new educational enterprise, and especially for the citizens of the county. The attendance upon the exercises was very great, and cordial interest and hearty enthusiasm enlivened and made memorable the day. A banquet, prepared by the citizens, was served in the building, and after dinner speeches and applause continued to testify to the high anticipation and hopeful appreciation of the institution that day inaugurated.[34]

---

31. Board of Trustees, *First Annual Report*, 180.
32. Ibid., 182.
33. Powell, *Semi-Centennial History*, 304.
34. Board of Trustees, *Tenth Report*, 14.

With the day's rituals now completed, the task remaining before the I.I.U. community was to actually live what had been symbolically enacted. As the first class of students would soon find, one way to remain focused upon that shared goal would be through the discipline of daily and Sunday chapel services.

Daily and Sunday Chapels

When state officials first announced that Rev. John Milton Gregory would be the new industrial university's first Regent, Jonathan Baldwin Turner reportedly exclaimed, "'O Lord, how long, how long? . . . an ex-superintendent of public instruction and a Baptist preacher! Could anything be worse?'"[35] As early as his 1860 address to the State Agricultural Society convention in Bloomington, Turner had argued that having a clergyman leading an agricultural institution would be as big of a mistake as placing an army general in charge of a theological seminary.[36] Turner's opinion, though understandable, was too radical for his time, because until this period of American higher education it was customary to have a clergyman president who, along with educational and administrative duties, provided spiritual leadership as well. Christian educators of the day tried to cultivate what Laurence Vesey calls "mental discipline" in their students, striving for human growth and formation, especially in terms of vital piety. Around 1870, though, Vesey says this theoretical hegemony began to yield in favor of utilitarian educational goals.[37] John Gregory led a new university during a time of major pedagogical upheaval in the United States.

Although it sounds strange today that public universities would sponsor required chapel services, daily and Sunday non-sectarian chapels were normative and compulsory at land grants during the early period, as were voluntary Bible classes, prayer meetings, Young Men's Christian Association (Y.M.C.A.) activities, and even revivals.[38] In their 1883 faculty minutes, for example, regarding the topic of "Public Worship," Iowa State's professors said "The object of [chapel] sermons

---

35. Solberg, "Religion and Secularism," 186.
36. Powell, *Semi-Centennial History*, 121.
37. Vesey, *Emergence of the American University*, 1, 21.
38. Eddy, *Colleges for Our Land*, 65–66; Edmond, *Magnificent Charter*, 164; Ross, *Democracy's College*, 132; Behle, "Educating 'The Lord's Redeemed and Anointed,'" 57.

is to emphasize the principles of the Christian religion..."[39] Penn State initially held two daily chapels, and Michigan State had a daily chapel led by faculty, a Sunday chapel led by local clergy, and a strong Y.M.C.A. presence doing various campus ministries.[40] The I.I.U. hosted daily and Sunday chapel services and encouraged its students to worship with local churches.[41] But not every school followed this practice. Especially after 1870, one by one, colleges and universities, both public and private, began to drop chapel from their campus routine.[42] Benjamin Ide Wheeler of California argued against chapels at land grants because the state "had to avoid entanglements with dogma."[43] Despite its citizens' Midwestern religious ethos, Ohio State did not hold chapel services during its founding decade of the 1870s, perhaps because its president was against it. Their situation was rare, with only one of the nineteen founding trustees—and one of its original seven faculty—being clergymen.[44] But the University of Minnesota, which began focusing on agriculture in 1868, started holding morning chapel and moral philosophy classes in the 1870s.[45] Lauding his university's pious atmosphere, Minnesota's president once said, "If students...are liable to be led astray at a University within sight of twenty church spires it is a sign that something is radically wrong with the influences that surround them at home..."[46] Although not a land-grant, a neighboring public university in Wisconsin had, in 1859, a faculty chaplain and daily and Sunday chapel services, with at least one professor holding public prayer meetings in his lecture room and the preceptress accompanying students to Sunday worship, Bible lessons, and kneeling prayer services.[47]

39. Ross, *Democracy's College*, 132, 217.
40. Bezilla, *Penn State*, 9; Widder, *Michigan Agricultural College*, 325–26.
41. Behle, "Educating."
42. Patton and Field, *Eight O'Clock Chapel*.
43. Nevins, *State Universities and Democracy*, 82.
44. Cope, *History of Ohio State University*, 25–30, 64–73, 76–77. The succeeding clergyman president whom the trustees elected in hopes of establishing "religious exercises" on campus failed to accomplish it (pp. 77–83). Penn State did not have a clergyman president from its origin in 1855 until 1871 (Bezilla, *Penn State*, 8, 20).
45. Gray, *University of Minnesota*, 13–35, 47–48.
46. Ibid., 69.
47. Curti and Carstensen, *University of Wisconsin*, 176, 407. Wisconsin alumnus and famous naturalist John Muir recalled that he and other peers began and ended the day with prayer, attending Sunday morning and evening services at local churches,

Unlike the denominational schools, however, state universities favored a new type of Protestantism which, says historian Bradley Longfield, "functioned as propagators ... of a broad sectarian evangelicalism[, and] became ... unofficial nurseries of liberal Christianity and the Social Gospel."[48] Explaining what would constitute appropriate content for their chapel sermons, the leaders at Iowa Agricultural College, for example, said "in a State institution like this, it would be manifestly improper to teach or controvert the tenets of sectarianism."[49] The president of one state university tried to solve this problem by making sure he had all of the large denominations represented on his faculty. While all of the I.I.U.'s early professors were members of Protestant churches, and Regent Gregory served in various Baptist leadership positions both locally and nationally, the University favored the nonsectarian approach, seeking to "educate for life" instead of the more specific tenets of a particular doctrinal viewpoint.[50] This did not mean, though, that religious instruction was forbidden. The standard college curriculum in the antebellum United States featured a class for seniors in "Moral Philosophy" which was usually taught by the president. As was discussed in the prior chapter, Regent Gregory taught that course at the I.I.U., and his chapel talks extended his opportunity for moral teaching, dispensing the Regent's wise counsel for the entire student body, the faculty, and even townspeople who would come to listen on Sunday afternoons. Chapel sermons coordinated, clarified, and capped all of the other influences that contributed to a university education and therefore, in Gregory's mind, human formation. He once said "The general discipline of the University depends largely upon ... daily [chapel] assembly," which was in his "estimation one of the most important educational influences of a general character among us," providing for the moral and "character" formation of students.[51] In such a closely knit living and learning environment, with the community living and work-

and university chapels on Sunday afternoons (190). Wisconsin's chapels became voluntary in 1868–1869, and, after dwindling attendance since 1874, were abolished in 1885 (409–10). Voluntary groups like the Christian Association (in 1871) and the YMCA (in 1881) filled in the gap (411–12). By the 1880s, the only university-sponsored influence left was prayer at commencement (412).

48. Longfield, "From Evangelicalism to Liberalism," 46.
49. Ross, *Democracy's College*, 217, note 65.
50. Kersey, *John Milton Gregory and the University of Illinois*, 71, 70.
51. Board of Trustees, *Ninth Report*, 10.

ing in the same building, Regent Gregory's role in such an atmosphere was pastoral and even parental. Even more than its peers, says historian Winton Solberg, the I.I.U. featured a vital Christian spirituality because "Gregory was clearly more evangelical than contemporaries who led the revolution in higher education."[52] By and large, the students welcomed and respected his religious leadership, as almost all of them were from Illinois and had grown up in Methodist, Presbyterian, Baptist, or Congregational churches.

Students were required to worship with a church in town on Sunday mornings, and also had to attend chapel at the University on Sunday afternoons.[53] Initially, daily chapel lasted fifteen minutes, starting after breakfast each morning at 8: 15, but it was extended to thirty minutes in the fall of 1868. Each term thereafter, morning chapel time and length would frequently change, according to the schedule of a particular semester.[54] For daily chapels, male students quickly formed into military rank when a bugle was blown. "Hall sergeants" were in charge of assembling residents of their floor, after which they would march to the chapel. An alumni poem, "The Retrospect of Seventy-Four," said

> We'd march most willingly to chapel now
> Nor grudge the moments spent
> In song and prayer with lecture how
> Withal to live content."[55]

Female students assembled in a group as well, and then all would proceed into the auditorium. The same ritual may have been used for entry on Sunday afternoons as well, although the tone of the daily chapels differed greatly from the Sabbath-day service.[56] As the students gazed about the room, they would see on a wall an inscription that read, "There is nothing so kingly as kindness; There is nothing so royal as truth."[57] Services would begin, and they would sing familiar hymns, hear the Scriptures read, and prayers recited. Often, local or visiting clergy would participate. Regent Gregory frequently led prayers, a re-

---

52. Solberg, "Religion and Secularism," 186, 188.
53. Behle, "Educating 'The Lord's Redeemed and Anointed'" 62–63.
54. Ibid., 64–65.
55. Ibid., 63.
56. Kersey, *John Milton Gregory*, 164.
57. Solberg, "Conflict between Religion and Secularism," 189.

sponsive New Testament reading, and a recitation of the Lord's Prayer.[58] Along with these religious activities, chapel services provided an opportunity to talk about business affecting the entire campus, things like student conduct, academics, and the threat of fraternal secret societies.[59] Faculty members kept student attendance and functioned as additional chapel speakers.[60] The faculty records do not discuss chapel content or events, other than the monitoring of student excuses.[61]

From the students' perspective, it appears some monitoring of the faculty was in order as well. An 1873 advertisement in the student paper said "WANTED—The presence of our faculty at chapel exercise in the morning."[62] Some mock concern was expressed in the April, 1876 *Illini* regarding "the system of rapid distribution of testaments in chapel," since "the appearance of half a dozen or so of Belia's comets rushing relentlessly towards the cranium of some innocent victim, is not a very agreeable spectacle . . . "[63] With similar jest, the October, 1877 *Illini* reported that "the choir has been removed from the south end of the Chapel to a position near the door . . ." What necessitated this move? So "the bashful ones will not be compelled to walk the entire length of the platform with all of those boys looking at them."[64] Chapel, at times, even provided some campus humor, as this piece from the October, 1877 *Illini* attests: "Scene in Chapel.—Prof. Crawford, librarian, on behalf of certain books in the library appeals to the class in English Literature to keep their hands clean. Prof. of English Literature indignantly examines his hands. Exit Prof. Crawford. Curtain drops. Profound cheering by preps."[65]

It appears that chapel was not always a stimulating time of worship, though, and by the end of Regent Gregory's tenure, the students were openly questioning the hypocrisy of mandatory chapel attendance for

---

58. Solberg, *University of Illinois*, 178.
59. Behle, "Educating," 64; Kersey, *John Milton Gregory*, 162.
60. Behle, "Educating," 63–64.
61. Ibid., 65.
62. Students of the Senior Class, *The Student (Illinois Industrial University)* 2/2 (February 1873) 9.
63. Ebert, *An Illini Century*, 6.
64. Ibid.
65. Ibid., 36.

students when only half the faculty were attending any given session.⁶⁶ But despite some student dissent, historians Patton and Field said of the era, "Chapel more than any other spot, *was* the college," since it promoted unity, passed on traditions, enabled students and faculty to interact, identified emerging student leaders, and grounded the day's beginning with "a common center."⁶⁷ Whether the students realized it or not, chapel was a key ingredient of the shared life of the I.I.U. community.

The great statesman Bob LaFollette said that John Bascom's Sunday afternoon chapel talks at Wisconsin were among the most important influences of his life. He recalls the President speaking on such varied topics as the endorsement of trade unions and strikes, Richard Ely's support of European socialism, the equitable distribution of wealth, and prohibition.⁶⁸ Regent Gregory's influence was at least as great at the I.I.U.⁶⁹ Students loved to hear him preach, and raved about his elegant, *ex tempore*, pacing style of course lecturing as well.⁷⁰ Despite the downsides of the chapel experience, alumnus Lorado Taft recalled that, because of Gregory's rhetorical skill, chapel attendance "was always large and eager. How eloquently that rich voice used to ring in our ears! The very reading of the Scripture was impressive...I recall some of the texts and the very intonation with which they were spoken: 'Vanity, vanity: all is vanity—' and 'Though I speak with the tongues of men and angels and have not charity...'"⁷¹

Student recollections from other alumni indicate that his personality and rhetoric strongly impacted his hearers.⁷² An alumnus who would later became Mayor of Kansas City said "It will never be known how far-reaching was the effect of these chapel talks."⁷³ Alumnus John Ockerson said that "Every University of Illinois student of the '70s will tell you of Dr. Gregory's morning chapel talks, those earnest, kindly ap-

---

66. Illinois Industrial University, *The Illini* 10/1 (October 1880) 4; Illinois Industrial University, *The Illini* 10/3 (December 1880) 8.

67. Behle, "Educating 'The Lord's Redeemed and Anointed,'" 72–73. The quotation is from Patton and Field, *Eight O'Clock Chapel*, 201.

68. Curti and Carstensen, *University of Wisconsin*, 288–89.

69. Kersey, *John Milton Gregory and the University of Illinois*, 165.

70. Ibid., 173–74.

71. Powell, *Semi-Centennial History*, 315–16.

72. Gregory, *John Milton Gregory: A Biography*.

73. Powell, *Semi-Centennial History*, 315.

peals with their almost personal challenge to each one of us."[74] In 1898, Charles G. Neely of the class of 1880 said

> No single thing in my college days so deeply impressed me as Dr. Gregory's chapel talks. Politics, religion, social conditions, were his themes. He would take some living question of the day and present it in a manner so attractive and forceful that it became a possession of the hearer ... I heard him declare that every man's life is like some great wheel in the factory, a segment of which is at one time down in the foundation; then again that same segment sweeps upward to its highest arc until it catches the full sunlight. Again he said: "It makes little difference what a man thinks provided he will be sincere and think long enough. If he does this he will think to a right conclusion." Once, rising to the occasion of his speech, with silver tongue, he proclaimed truth and justice God's two vicegerents [sic] upon earth, and that it was man's duty to manifest the one and strive after the other ... At another time in a burst of eloquence, he said: "Some men build of blocks of marble; others there are who build in immortal thought." He was an orator in every sense of the word, and easily held and convinced men by the pure diction of his thought and eloquence."[75]

Twenty years after Neely's remarks, alumnus Franklin W. Scott attested that "Dr. Gregory had a gift for speaking that enabled him to supplement the influence of class work with a series of chapel talks which impressed the youth of that day to an extent hard, if not impossible, now to realize."[76] Speaking at Gregory's funeral, colleague Thomas J. Burrill said,

> above all this, he was capable upon short notice of masterly efforts upon the platform. If he was not an orator, he had a wonderful gift of utterance, and had the power of lucid presentation of ideas so that audiences large and small, upon common or upon exalted themes, were held in rapt attention and tireless mental following. His chapel talks were gems of diction and models of stirring helpfulness. In his efforts before agricultural societies, at the county fairs, in the country school houses, in teachers' assemblies, before the learned and before those of little scholastic attainment, he was ever the forceful, the instructive,

---

74. Scott, *Semi-Centennial Alumni Record*, xi.
75. University of Illinois, *Memorial Convocation*, 24.
76. Behle, "Educating 'The Lord's Redeemed and Anointed,'" 59–60.

the convincing, and the inspiring master of the hour. In the pulpit his power was none the less, for the plain truths of a practical and consoling Christianity came from his lips in rare sweetness and in hope-inspiring power.[77]

Late in his own life, Taft would say: "Proud as we are today of the giant institution which we claim as Alma Mater, with its army of teachers and its cityful of pupils, one must acknowledge that something very precious has been lost in the passing of these intimate chapel meetings."[78] Using his extraordinary rhetorical ability, Gregory provided the theological vision which unified and solidified the I.I.U. community. When the Regent left for a sabbatical in Europe in 1873, a student wrote in the campus paper: "We will miss the kindly advice which [Gregory] was wont to give from time to time, to stimulate us to new efforts. We will miss the Sabbath lectures, in which he pointed out to us so clearly the ways of truth, and especially will the graduating class of '73 miss those words of encouragement, and that friendly counsel which he knew so well how to give."[79]

Gregory wisely chose themes which resonated with the concerns of young adults living in east central Illinois during the 1870s. When he returned from Europe for the 1873 autumn term, he organized his Sunday chapel talks in a series called "The Temptations of Young Men."[80] The first sermon spoke against the procurement of wealth, which would not, Gregory said, satisfy spiritual needs. The second spoke against gambling, calling it a theft of another's money. The third decried drinking alcohol, warning students "not to disappoint the hopes of their friends and of the State by allowing themselves to become victims" of intoxicating drinks. A fourth and fifth talk, both "of great interest and value" according to the school paper, featured "idleness" and an address "especially to the young ladies."[81] Summarizing the series' content for the school paper, a student reporter said "we are sorry to learn that on account of his pressing cares, the Doctor will be unable to lecture every Sabbath,

77. University of Illinois, *Memorial Convocation*, 17.

78. Powell, *Semi-Centennial History*, 315.

79. Students of the Senior Class, *The Student* (Illinois Industrial University) 2/4 (April 1873) 37–48.

80. Students of the Senior Class, *The Student (Illinois Industrial University)* 2/11 (November 1873) 127.

81. Ibid., 128.

but only occasionally."[82] A later article regretted that the Regent was still "unable to give his regular lecture every Sabbath afternoon" during the autumn of 1874."[83] He did speak at least once that term, in November, on "The Authenticity of the Bible." Back in form for an 1875 series of chapel talks, his topics, as advertised in the student newspaper, included attention-getters like: "Is there a God?"; "Is the human soul immortal?"; "Is the Bible of divine authority?"; "Was Jesus of Nazareth more than a mere man?"; "Is Christianity true?"; and "Is religion necessary?"[84]

The content and method of Gregory's preaching will be explored more fully in the next chapter. At this point, suffice it to say that, like the chapel talks of American college presidents before him, Gregory's pulpit persona highly influenced belief and practice at the I.I.U. Through the vehicle of daily and Sunday chapels, Gregory offered the religious instruction so vital to his own experience at Union College, but in ways appropriate for a new generation of students in an industrial university setting.

Commemorating the New University Hall

September 13, 1872, was a special day for the I.I.U. community. At just after three o'clock in the afternoon, a ceremony celebrating the new "Drill Hall" and "Mechanical Shops" began, capped by the laying of the new University Building's cornerstone.[85] A "procession" formed on the campus grounds, led by uniformed and armed students, followed by one hundred and twenty-five freshmen; the faculty, trustees, and state officials; and community residents who had come for the festivities. They walked to the construction site, where an audience of over a thousand people was waiting. Regent Gregory told the crowd that Governor Palmer sent a telegram explaining that he and his staff had missed the train, so the governor would not be able to speak as planned. With that disappointing news, the ceremony began, with the University Band launching into Schubert's *Parade March*. When they finished, Jonathan B. Turner stepped forward and ceremonially laid the cornerstone. "The Rev. Mr. Frame then followed," the trustees' minutes record, "in a short

- 82. Ebert, *Illini Century*, 5–6.
- 83. Illinois Industrial University, *The Illini* 4/2 (November 1874) 54.
- 84. Solberg, "Conflict between Religion and Secularism," 190.
- 85. Board of Trustees, *Fourth Annual Report*, 352–53.

but impressive prayer; and, after a statement by the Regent of the dimensions of the new building, the procession reformed and marched to the new Mechanical Shops, with the band playing *Hail Columbia.*"

When they arrived there, Regent Gregory told the crowd the building was probably the first of its kind in the United States. He heartily thanked all who had contributed to its completion, and then announced the day's featured speaker, who needed no introduction, he said, since "his name, if not so long as the State, is as broad as the Continent." J. B. Turner had unexpectedly been asked to speak due to Governor Palmer's absence. But he was always ready to talk at length about his lifelong passion. Turner began by recounting his understanding of agricultural education's evolution in Illinois, a movement, he said, which was started by "a little band of brothers" who had agitated "for more than twenty years." Initially, he said, the agriculturists had been disappointed with the I.I.U., but had come around into believing in what Gregory and the other leaders were doing. The I.I.U., he affirmed, would form "true sons of the Republic, and true sons of God," since they would be educated in a "broad, scientific, catholic, American and truly christian [sic] spirit," unsullied by "the narrow and scholastic spirit of caste and sect."[86] As usual, he finished his speech with a millennial flourish, prophesying that a blessed, agricultural, prairie civilization would result. On cue, the University Band played "Prof. Colberg's 'Industrial University March.'" When the song ended, State Superintendent Newton Bateman delivered his scheduled address.

Reminding his listeners that "just three and a half years" earlier they had spoken "words of gratitude and of hope" in a similar ceremony, Bateman recalled that "the benedictions of Almighty God were solemnly invoked upon this new child of humanity and of civilization, as, in weakness, yet in faith, it stepped into line, and entered upon its work."[87] Asking them if their University had been just one more failed attempt in agricultural and industrial education, he answered emphatically that no, it had flourished, and cited the increasing campus enrollment and building construction as proof. Bateman attributed this success to the trustees' and faculty's choice to take the moral, political, and pedagogical high ground, even though their plan was "to some . . . a stumbling block,

---

86. Board of Trustees, *Fourth Annual Report,* 354.
87. Ibid., 355.

FIGURE 10: The auditorium of University Hall, where chapel services were held

to others foolishness."[88] But "the most potential cause of the triumphant success of the Illinois Industrial University," he said, was "that its work [was] in harmony with and demanded by the *pressing needs of the living present*; that it [was] moving in the line of the ocean-currents of modern thought—in the direction of the paramount interests and necessities of humanity."[89] In other words, the I.I.U.'s utilitarian and pragmatic focus was cooperating with the invisible hand of God, making God's will known for humanity according to that which was revealed in the course of history. The I.I.U., he implied, was an agent of public ministry, blessing society by its presence and its work. To poetically make his point, he said "The cry of the disappointed and tired world is 'Give us the true bread and water of life.'"[90] God would meet those needs through the blessing of industrial education. This new "movement," he said, "is from the few toward the many—through the abstract to the concrete—from books to nature—from sect and caste and party, to humanity." Truly, this was a revolution indeed. The "trumpet voices," he said, "seem[ed] to ring

---

88. Ibid., 357. Here Bateman makes in implied literary reference to the Apostle Paul's description of the Christian message as recorded in 1 Corinthians 1:23.

89. Ibid., 358.

90. Ibid.

out from these rising walls and foundation stones, sounding upwards to God and grandly echoing onwards into the stillness and silence of the waiting future."[91] Their enterprise was "the *new departure* in education . . . uplifting the gorgeous banner of Nature, written all over with symbols of matchless wisdom, and flashing with the ineffable glory of God . . . " Calling like the Sirens, the trumpet voices of Divine Nature were "seeking to attract to it and to gather about it the devotion and love and joyful service of those whom philosophy and learning have made keen-sighted strong." In closing, Bateman told them he had traveled to celebrate the cornerstone's laying because it and the I.I.U. were "linked with the future well-being and glory of Illinois, and with these brighter hopes for the on-coming ages of culture and humanity . . ."[92] He finished by praying, with millennial faith: "God grant that the dawn of a long career of great usefulness and prosperity; of liberal provision and fostering care; of public respect, confidence and affection, which to-day seems breaking along the horizon of this Institution, may shine on, brighter and brighter, until the perfect day."[93] A "Rev. Riley" said a prayer, followed by various trustees and public officials saying a few words in support of the University. When they were done, the band played a final song, "and then the audience adjourned," the trustees said, "to meet next year, Providence permitting, to dedicate the main building."

That event did in fact happen, at one in the afternoon on December 10, 1873, when the I.I.U. held their "Dedicatory Exercises" for the new University Hall. The school band played as the audience filed in to the new and larger auditorium, which even had the luxury of an organ, funded primarily through Regent Gregory's personal efforts.[94] A prayer was given, and the collegiate choir sang the "University Anthem" composed for the 1868 Inauguration. Regent Gregory then rose to deliver an "Historical Address—1867–1873" entitled "The University."[95] "At the dawn of each new epoch," the Regent said, "there comes the demand for the historian and the prophet—the one to record the past, the other to forecast the future."[96] Noting that he had been assigned to recount the

91. Ibid., 359.
92. Ibid., 360.
93. Ibid.
94. Board of Trustees, *Eighth Report*, 193.
95. Board of Trustees, *Seventh Annual Report*, 62–87.
96. Ibid., 63.

school's history, he added, "since we have no inspired prophets in these days, it may be allowed me to show the trend of the history . . . and thus give to all the means to forecast for themselves the probable future which lies yet veiled before us." He recounted the ideological events leading to the I.I.U., quoting Newton Bateman's inaugural address, lauding J. B. Turner and the 1851 Granville convention, thanking the state legislature and the Morrill Act, the agricultural press, and the like. Next, Gregory began interpreting the signs of the times. Noting that Princeton University's president, the "learned [Presbyterian] Scotchman . . . Dr. McCosh," had labeled European agricultural colleges "very feeble institutions," Gregory called that "bold and baseless assertion . . . false . . . illiberal and mean," asking, "can it be that the President of Princeton fears the rivalry of these new and growing institutions?"[97] McCosh, Gregory said, was trying to prevent Congress from giving any more public land to support industrial schools, and therefore deserved "the severest reprobation" for his "deplorable" and "unpatriotic" words and deeds. Furthermore, said Gregory, the burgeoning enrollments of public universities were rapidly catching the old colleges, whose "schools of theology and law" were not sought by the public as much as industrial programs were. Regarding the fear at the I.I.U. that, if literary courses were offered along with scientific ones, that students would prefer the old learning, Gregory said he was "firm in [his] own faith," and had "proved that [he] was no false prophet" by declaring, in his Inaugural Address, that the two could exist together without threat.[98]

Next, the Regent reminded his hearers of the chronological scheme of building the University's structures. He referred admiringly to J. B. Turner again, and his address at the cornerstone's laying a year ago. Recalling the struggles of completing the new University Building— including the setback of public monies caused by restoration after the Chicago fire—he thanked the state and its legislature for funding public higher education. Finally, Gregory said, the most important thing about a university is its "general bent . . . the life and spirit and breath . . . the organized temper, tone and trend of the University itself."[99] For him, that ethos was "Learning and Labor," the new learning, the accomplishments of the nineteenth century, "around whose brow lies as a coronal

97. Ibid., 68–69.
98. Ibid., 70.
99. Ibid., 74.

[sic] of light the magnificent circle of sciences . . ." The benevolence of "all the power that science, conspiring with the forces of nature and of man" extended "for the good of mankind" was the motto's "central thought—the pulse-beating heart, the very brain center of this institution of learning."[100] He closed by invoking God's blessing upon their enterprise, and predicted that, years later, everyone would clearly see that their university was a manifestation of labor's millennium.[101] When he had finished speaking, the University Choir sang a "dedication ode" called "Learning and Labor," the lyrics of which are printed in their entirety in chapter two of this book.[102] This "ode" became known and frequently used as the I.I.U.'s "University Hymn."[103]

As the hymn pays homage to "Labor," it is worth noting that ancient Greek craftsmen worshiped a goddess named "Industry"—called *Ergánēn* by Plutarch in *De Fortunata* 99a—who is probably synonymous with the goddess Athena.[104] The orthodox Christian apologist Clement of Alexandria mocks this goddess in his "Exhortation to the Greeks," quoting Sophocles, who refers to divine "Industry" too. While the I.I.U.'s liturgies make no specific reference to this classical deity, when Gregory's student, Lorado Taft, class of 1879, designed his "Alma Mater" statue for the I.I.U. in the 1920s, he included three persons: a peaceful mother, quoting Proverbs 31:28, with outstretched arms; "Labor," a bare-chested farmer or mechanic who is presumably a prototype of the ideal Illinois "man"; and "Learning," who is "a classic figure, the head suggested by the Lemnian Athena," shaking hands with "Labor."[105] At the 1873 "Dedicatory Exercises" it is unlikely, yet possible, that Regent Gregory or his audience would consciously have these concepts in mind. As the lyrics attest, however, they did revere the twin virtues of learning and labor.

100. Ibid., 75.

101. Ibid., 74–76.

102. Ibid., 62; Kammen, *Cornell: Glorious to View*, vi.

103. Unknown, "Decennial Anniversary."

104. Plutarch, *De Fortunata*, 99 A. As referenced in Butterworth, *Clement of Alexandria*, 212–13.

105. McCauley, "Taft Completes on Alma Mater Group," *Chicago Post*, 6 June 1922. The statue still stands prominently as a well-known University of Illinois campus landmark.

When the choir had finished, "his excellency," Gov. J. L. Beveridge, gave an address. He began by saying that the I.I.U. "is not Harvard nor Yale," or "Cambridge nor Oxford," since it was new and therefore "has not the glow of sunset, but . . . is encircled with the radiance of the rising God of day."[106] Beveridge said "I wish to-day I might speak with the spirit of prophesy . . . that the Illinois Industrial University, with . . . its new temple . . . blest with the care of a wise and judicious Board of Trustees; cherished by an intelligent and christian [sic] Faculty . . . may grow in power and widen in influence," and thus surpass the older collegiate institutions.[107] Beveridge claimed that if his words "were prophecy," the only thing "in the way of its fulfillment" was the stinginess of Champaign county, which was "*morally* . . . bound to pay [their] bonds." Suggesting that the I.I.U. might fail financially if their obligation went unmet, the governor urged "the good people" of the county to replace their board of supervisors "at the ballot-box," and thus remedy the situation, which was the "honorable" thing to do.

When Beveridge had finished, "Miss M. E. Stewart" sang a solo, followed by another speech by "Gen. John Eaton, of Washington, U. S. Commissioner of Education." Eaton said, "Of the thirty-seven state institutions benefited by what is known as the National Agricultural Grant I consider this among the most successful in its administration."[108] Noting that a university's architecture reflects its ethos, and describing various European campuses, he mused about "the far future" and "what pilgrimages are to be made hither" to the I.I.U.[109] He lauded their democratic system of public education, noting that "in religion the culture now to be imparted here, is non-sectarian, but not unchristian . . . a part of the civil organization, it is not in antagonism with institutions of any grade that may be established and conducted by the different branches of the church."[110] This arrangement, Eaton said, provided a uniquely American "harmony of educational forces," the best arrangement humankind had yet produced, since Eaton "should become uneasy if there was such action by the civil organization as to preclude the free action of the church, and should be equally alarmed to see such exclusive con-

---

106. Board of Trustees, *Seventh Annual Report*, 76.
107. Ibid., 77.
108. University of Illinois, *Memorial Convocation*, 20.
109. Board of Trustees, *Seventh Annual Report*, 79.
110. Ibid., 80.

trol by the church as to forbid this action by the State."¹¹¹ This system, Eaton said, ensured an educated public, enabling them to usher in a millennial "age of pre-eminent excellence in virtue—an age surpassing all past ages in progress ... leading the world in the application of equity and reason ... ."¹¹² "God speed your efforts," he concluded, encouraging them to bring light and prosperity to their culture through the Illinois Industrial University.

After "Miss Kincaid" sang a solo, even more addresses were given, by "Prof. J. B. Turner, Dr. Rich'd Edwards, Gen. M. Brayman, and others," including a "Mr. Fellows," who, though not listed in the program, was "called upon" to speak. He began by saying he knew that the crowd "wanted the benediction and the amen," but needed, as "a friend of industrial education," to "bid [the I.I.U.] God-speed."¹¹³ He said that the history of western civilization showed a record of "learning *or* labor" or "learning *above* labor," but the true way was learning *and* labor, "the motto which the ever living God teaches to his children upon earth, and what God hath joined together let no man—no Board of Trustees—put asunder." Encouraging the "young ladies" and "young men" present to be proud of their farming heritage as the backbone of their nation, he closed by saying, "God bless you in your efforts to realize the ends at which you are aiming." When Mr. Fellows had finished, "Mr. Wines, Secretary of the State Board of Charities," chimed in. Noting that "Dr. Fellows," when beginning his comments, had told a joke about a "clergyman," Wines could not be topped. So he told one about "a sermon once delivered by an eloquent Baptist preacher, upon the text "Adam, where art thou?" He divided his subject as follows: *First*, All men are somewhere. *Second*, Some men are where they hadn't oughter be. *Third*, Some men, if they don't look out, will be where they will not want to be; and *Fourth*, A few remarks, by way of exhortation, upon infant baptism."¹¹⁴

The minutes do not record the amount of laughter evoked by such wit. It must have been sizable, because Wines told yet another joke. Finally, he lauded a noteworthy Baptist preacher in attendance named John Milton Gregory, and closed his speech by saying, "I hope

---

111. Curiously, the word "State" is capitalized in this sentence, while the word "church" is not.

112. Board of Trustees, *Seventh Annual Report*, 82–84.

113. Ibid., 85–86.

114. Ibid., 86.

the Industrial University will go onward and upward, conquering and to conquer." With that, the University Band played a final song, a benediction was given, and the day's ceremony was completed, the building having been, according to their custom, properly dedicated to God and the mission before them.

Commencement Week and Anniversary Day

The spring term's conclusion prompted the I.I.U. community to commemorate the end of an academic year by celebrating the achievements of students and graduates via commencement ceremonies. The first commencement week was observed in 1871, when four days' worth of activities lauded the founding class of students to graduate from the University. On Sunday, June 4, at four in the afternoon, Regent Gregory delivered a "Baccalaureate Address" in the University Chapel. Former governor Richard Oglesby spoke to the Industrial Society the following night, and, on Tuesday night, "J. Mahoney, Esq.," of Chicago, spoke to the literary societies. On the morning of Wednesday, June 7, the third year students did their "exercises," consisting of a time of music, prayer, and speeches. The first oration after the prayer was called "God in Nature," by Charles W. Rolfe, of Montgomery, Illinois. Of the fifteen student speeches that followed, two addressed the topic of education, and the rest touched upon history, progress, and civil religion. One student, for example, gave a talk about "Columbia's Heroes."[115] When all the speeches were done, Regent Gregory presented the students their certificates, and then gave a speech for the class. "President Erastus O. Haven, Doctor of Divinity," was scheduled to speak to the University at two in the afternoon, but was unable to attend. The University Battalion finished the day by drilling at 3:30.

Roughly the same format was followed in 1872, with "Professor Rodney Welch, of the *Prairie Farmer*" speaking to the graduates and "Dr. Edwards, President of Normal University" talking to the literary societies. The seven student orations delivered that year had patriotic and utilitarian titles like "Progress," "American Peculiarities," and "The Practical." After certificates were presented, the Regent gave an address, the University Band played, and student militias drilled, ending the

---

115. Board of Trustees, *Fourth Annual Report*, 57–58.

week's festivities.[116] 1873's edition featured Rev. W. G. Pierce preaching the Sunday afternoon Baccalaureate Sermon in the University Chapel, with Cornell's President A. D. White speaking on "The Battle Fields of Science" the following Thursday afternoon. As was the case in the prior year, none of the student orations had explicitly religious titles—although one, by Charles P. Graham, was curiously called "Man's True Greatness"—and the week ended, once again, with the band playing and a military drill.[117]

The 1872–1873 University Catalogue's calendar for the following school year lists a "Baccalaureate Sermon in University Chapel" on Sunday, June 7, 1874, indicating the rite's solidity as a fixture of the school's annual routine. Likewise, it was scheduled in the Chapel for every commencement week from 1876–1878.[118] For the 1874 "Baccalaureate Sermon," Regent Gregory preached on Luke 18:8, "Nevertheless when the Son of Man cometh shall he find faith on the earth."[119] A student observer said "the chapel was full, about a thousand persons being present." Gregory, the student writer said, talked about "faith," by which he meant "trust in God ... more than belief" but also "confidence and conviction." The Regent's sermon had three points: "Shall Faith fail on the earth?; Faith has obstacles and opposition; [and] Faith is useful." The student writer called the sermon "the best and most appropriate baccalaureate we ever heard ..." attesting once more to Gregory's homiletical skills.

Commencement week 1874 added a new event, "Senior Class Day," featuring speeches and music.[120] On Wednesday, June 10, 1874, the "Exercises of Commencement Day" were attended by an "overflowing" crowd in a chapel hall "tastefully decorated with wreath and festoons of evergreen boughs, and over the speakers' stand was an ambitious arch with the words and figures 'Class of '74.'" A procession of dignitaries was followed by "Rev. Dr. Cleghorn"'s prayer and a hymn from a fifty-voice choir. Events included music by the University and nine-piece String Bands; a vocal solo, duet, quartet, and opera chorus; student orations on "Language," "Friendship," "Success," "The Farmers' Movement," "Despotism of Ideas," "Farming," "Community of Nations," and "Self

116. Board of Trustees, *Fifth Annual Report*, 63–64.
117. Board of Trustees, *Sixth Annual Report*, 65.
118. Board of Trustees, *Eighth Report*, 74–75.
119. Illinois Industrial University, *The Illini* 3/6 (June 1874) 164.
120. Ibid., 165–69.

Superintendence"; theses on engineering and biological topics; the presentation of certificates; Dr. Gregory's instructions to remember "Alma Mater" and "God's choicest blessings"; Governor Beveridge's speech; and, finally, the big finale: a "Parting Class Song" and benediction. The closing act featured "the batalion [sic] drill," which "brought all the male students together and a host of spectators." Aided by the band, the trustees said, military tactics professor "Col. Snyder and his Captains were in their glory."[121]

After 1874 the trustees' records are less specific regarding the details of Commencement Week celebrations, although a few facts are still listed. In 1878, for example, Edward Orton, President of the Ohio State University, spoke on "The Liberal Education of the Industrial Classes."[122] The speech echoed the themes proposed for years by Jonathan Baldwin Turner and John Milton Gregory, with a muted though still audible millennial ring. And then there was Regent Gregory's final Baccalaureate Sermon, on June 7, 1880, which was remembered and recounted by alumnus W. L. Pillsbury: "[Gregory] said, 'My text is from St. James: "What is your life?"'—The question came home to each of us, bringing us face to face with the future that lay before us, out in the big, round world, when we should go there to assume duty."[123] Gregory challenged the students to a life of Christian public service, a recurring theme which will be demonstrated more fully in the following chapter.

Despite the relative pomp and significant effort afforded to the I.I.U.'s commencement events, at least some students who attended the 1873 "Commencement week" at Northwestern University in Evanston decided "the exercises were all quite interesting, and we think that Commencement week at the N. W. U. excelled in interest Commencement week at the I.I.U."[124] This comment is especially intriguing when considering that, from the description of the week's sermons by noteworthy clergy with their academic processions, the commencement at Northwestern more closely resembled the formal, "monkish" collegiate liturgies so loathed by the agricultural visionaries advancing the cause of labor's millennium. But the I.I.U. continued to

121. Board of Trustees, *Seventh Annual Report*, 53.
122. Board of Trustees, *Ninth Report*, 1878, 193–204.
123. Gregory, *John Milton Gregory: A Biography*, 372.
124. Students of the Senior Class, *The Student (Illinois Industrial University)* 2/7 (July 1873) 80.

celebrate commencement in its own way, as they did its Anniversary Day. On March 11, 1877, for example, the University marked its tenth anniversary with the following events:

> Saturday morning the reception committee with the university band went to Tolono where they met the special train from Springfield bearing our expected guests [from the State Legislature]. The train reached the Doane House about noon where a party stepped into the dining room and partook of a bounteous repast, and the remainder were taken to the Griggs House, Urbana, and there similarly served. At a little after one o'clock, the Battalion headed by the band appeared at the Doane House to act as escort to the visitors. The Battalion made a very creditable appearance and was admired by all for its orderly movements and military bearing. Having arrived at the drill hall, the sixth regiment was ready to show its guests what excellent military discipline is given at this institution. All the spare room was soon filled by spectators ...
>
> The visitors were then requested to fall into line with the band and march to the Auditorium of the University where the anniversary exercises proper would take place. The Urbana cornet band was waiting in front of the building and discoursed good music. Ushers were present at the Auditorium doing their duties well and soon the room was filled to its utmost capacity. The Rossini club opened the exercises with well executed instrumental music. After a prayer by Rev. Mr. Evans, of Urbana, the choir sang the University hymn. The addresses of Dr. Gregory, Gov. Cullom, Judge Smith and Speaker Shaw were universally admired ... After the close of the exercises the guests were invited to the formal opening of the [art] museum and were there addressed by Professor Taft ...
>
> After a hurried visit to witness the exercises of the Calisthenic class, the audience betook themselves to the Physical lecture room where the ladies of Champaign and Urbana had spread a feast fit even for legislators ...[125]

Like other significant events, this occasion was ritualized, forming a tradition of memory and belonging. Events like Anniversary Day, Commencement Week, Sunday and daily chapels, dedicatory ceremonies for buildings, and Inauguration Day enabled the I.I.U. community to unite in the expression of their values, achievements, and goals. As we have seen, sometimes they even incorporated traditional elements of

125. Ebert, *Illini Century*, 24–25. The quotation is from the April 1877 *Illini*.

Christian worship. Regent Gregory's preaching, for example, was central to many of the ceremonies, when he spoke from a Bible text about God, and humanity's response to God's desires and actions. The next chapter examines in detail the content of Gregory's sermons, and the way in which he communicated to the I.I.U. community.

5

Preaching Labor's Millennium

WHEN ONE THINKS TODAY OF THE SKILLS REQUIRED FOR THE LEADER of a public university, Christian preaching does not come to mind. In the case of the Illinois Industrial University, however, preaching and other forms of public speaking were among the more prominent and effective tasks in which John M. Gregory engaged. This made sense during an era when preachers were among the most respected and influential public leaders in the nation.[1] During his thirteen years at the I.I.U. Gregory literally gave hundreds of addresses to various conventions, institutes, societies, and high schools, often traveling at night so he could be at his I.I.U. desk the next morning.[2] Already a well respected leader in an era when a fine line existed between pastoral and educational leadership, Gregory's regency allowed him to continue his life-long preaching ministry, functioning much as it would in a church or church-related college, but now *beyond* the church in a land grant university. This was new in the history of higher education, illustrating a transition time between the practices of church-related colleges and the church-state separation of large public universities. This chapter will demonstrate that John Gregory's preaching ministry at the I.I.U. enabled him to continue and expand his sense of divine calling by allowing him to express the I.I.U.'s vision, rally the community around it, and integrate it into the overall educational experience.[3] To do so, it will first consider Gregory's Baptist roots and personal calling; second, discuss his preaching methods and style; third, examine the content of his mission-empowering sermons; and fourth, conclude by showing how Gregory's understanding of the

---

1. Howden, "'Pulpit Leads the World,'" 169–72.
2. Nevins, *Illinois,* 66.
3. Vasquez, "'Correctly Forming Public Opinion,'" 173–92.

Kingdom of God prompted him to encourage I.I.U. students to engage in public service. Several selected passages from his sermons will be quoted at length in order to get a first-hand feel for the stylistic and doctrinal content of his work. One's understanding may be enhanced by slowly reading these quoted passages aloud, as they were originally intended to be audibly spoken rather than silently read.

Called to Preach

In order to understand the importance of preaching to John Gregory, one must remember his biography, his personal understanding of the Christian faith, and his own religious calling. He was influenced by revivalistic theology from an early age, being born into a prominent Baptist family in Sand Lake, New York, just east of Albany. This was an area well-known for revivals and conversionistic Christianity. His farmer father, known as "Deacon Josie" to the public, was a state representative, and an active layman in his Baptist church, as were many of his relatives.[4] The piety of his Baptist upbringing manifested itself with some typical spiritual benchmarks common to like-minded evangelicals of his day. For example, as a child, on the banks of Sand Lake, John had a vision of Jesus calling him by name, much like Jesus called the disciples by the Sea of Galilee.[5] Some time after, at the age of twelve, Gregory sought baptism and church membership, which is a common age for these rites to occur in Baptist life.[6]

While a student at Union College, President Eliphalet Nott influenced young Gregory greatly.[7] An antebellum college president typically functioned much like a pastor for a congregation. John Gregory experienced no better example of this pastoral presidential model than his own "Dr. Nott." An ordained Presbyterian minister, Nott became President of Union in 1805 when he was only thirty-one years old. He remained in that office for an astounding sixty-two years, while Union gained the stature of its rivals Harvard, Yale, and Princeton. Nott was a typical Protestant reformer—an immediate abolitionist, temperance

---

4. Gregory, *John Milton Gregory and the University of Illinois*, 2–9.
5. Ibid., 33–34.
6. Ibid., 5.
7. Gregory, "Dr. Nott," 155–62; Kersey, "John Milton Gregory as a Midwestern Educator," 9–15; 24.

advocate, revivalist, patriot, and public school supporter. His zeal for public service was rooted in his revivalistic theory of education, where one taught to help form moral character, a stance which, as chapter three demonstrated, Gregory would later share at the I.I.U.[8] Nott's was a pastoral vision, where, as he put it, the "college is a family, and its government should be paternal. These young students are my children. I am to them in place of a father." Nott's pedagogy anticipated the developmentalism of Horace Bushnell as expressed in his classic *Christian Nurture*. Like other presidents of his day, Nott valued the educational opportunity provided by the Moral Philosophy course, where he used Lord Kames' famous 1761 *Elements of Criticism* as his text, and the Bible as a point of departure for virtually any topic, integrating and synthesizing the college experience in an interdisciplinary way. John Gregory, too, would use Lord Kames along with the Bible for his first Moral Philosophy course at the I.I.U.[9]

During college, Gregory planned on a legal career, but soon after leaving Union he sensed a call to a higher Christian commitment, including preaching.[10] His struggles—which again are common among evangelicals of this era—are well documented in his diary. He complained, for example, of his "coldness of heart . . . vanity" and "pride."[11] Reminiscent of a young John Wesley, Gregory practiced an ascetic and sometimes severe piety, attempting to submit control of his life completely to the will of God.[12] He adopted, for example, a precise and detailed set of resolutions to aid his faith and ministry.[13] Ordained at twenty-five, John and Julia Gregory were so committed to the church that they honeymooned on a revivalistic preaching tour through upstate New York.[14] Even after leaving pastoral ministry John continued to serve in various Baptist leadership posts, including Kalamazoo's presidency. A frequent guest preacher and prolific popular author, he published articles in Baptist magazines on topics like Sunday Schools

---

8. Kersey, "John Milton Gregory as a Midwestern Educator," 21–23.
9. Ibid., 15–20.
10. Ibid., 35.
11. Gregory, *John Milton Gregory and the University of Illinois*, 37.
12. Ibid., 38–44.
13. Kersey, "John Milton Gregory as a Midwestern Educator," 40.
14. Gregory, *John Milton Gregory: A Biography*, 51–53.

and temperance.[15] One article for *The National Baptist* laments the affect of scientific skepticism on the Christian faith.[16] In the December 15th, 1881 issue, *The Standard* published "Christ the Answer to Doubt," Gregory's second lecture for the First Baptist Church of Chicago in a series called "The Attitude of Christianity Toward Modern Doubt."[17] Another article called "Jesus and Gautama" for *The National Baptist* argues for the inferiority of both the Buddha and Buddhism when compared to Christ and the church.[18] According to the *Decatur Republican*, one Sunday morning Gregory spoke to the Baptist church there for an hour and ten minutes on "What I have thought on Jesus, Gautama, and Confucius," saying that, although the other two taught and did good things, they never reached the stature of Jesus.[19] After leaving the I.I.U., Gregory served as "Superintendent of the Educational Work carried on for the colored people by the American Baptist Home Mission Society," overseeing the founding of the "Nashville Institute," which became "Roger Williams University."[20] It is difficult if not impossible to separate Gregory the educator from Gregory the Christian missionary. His church, First Baptist of Champaign, eventually honored him by placing a stained glass portrait of him in their sanctuary window.[21]

Clergy were evidently respected by the I.I.U. community. For example, one student wrote an article for the University paper in which she described her embarrassment, while teaching at a local school, that her students misspelled "gospel" and "preacher" the day a local pastor "called" on the teacher and school during a class session.[22] In another

---

15. For example, Gregory published what would become his famous book *The Seven Laws of Teaching* as a series in *The Sunday School Teacher*, a monthly headquartered in Chicago. He also published "The Aims of the Sunday School" in the May 1867 edition (Vol. 2, No. 5, pp. 129–32), saying the three "main aims of the Sunday School work are . . . The Conversion of the Pupils . . . The Formation of Christian Character . . . [and] Christian or Bible Scholarship" (129).

16. Gregory, "The Loss of Faith," 40–42.

17. Gregory, "Christ the Answer to Doubt," 13.

18. Gregory, "Jesus and Gautama," 11–12.

19. Gregory, "Religious News and Notes," 24.

20. Gregory, "From Nashville," 32.

21. Though since removed from the sanctuary, the circular window remains on the church's campus, which is now in Savoy, Illinois.

22. Students of the Senior Class, *The Student (Illinois Industrial University)* 2/8 (August 1873) 96.

article, one of the people featured during a series on "great" Americans was T. DeWitt Talmage, "One of the most celebrated preachers in America" whose "sermons" as published in New York newspapers were "among the finest we have ever read."[23] British Baptist preaching luminary Charles Haddon Spurgeon is quoted on the following page of the same copy. And, in a later issue, the great American pulpiteer Henry Ward Beecher is defended, canonized, and even compared to various holy persons named in the Bible.[24] It was considered a boon to the I.I.U. that Regent Gregory, too, was an extraordinarily effective preacher who was active in churches and the affairs of religious organizations. During his I.I.U. career, he said, he had "visited and addressed ... religious and social gatherings," and had "preached sermons" and "met the people in their homes, schools, churches, and other assemblies" on behalf of the University.[25] He officiated at least one student wedding ceremony, which was held on the I.I.U. grounds.[26] He tried to know each student by name, hoping to be able to have a personal impact, visiting the homesick in their rooms, hosting class parties in his home, attending virtually all student extracurricular activities, and even offering financial assistance when needed.[27] Students sensed that he cared, and they reciprocated, establishing the necessary prior relationship which made his preaching so effective. At the beginning of his June 4, 1871 baccalaureate address, Gregory said,

> I fancy myself a father standing in the midst of his family, and uttering his parting words of counsel to some of the older sons who are about to leave the home circle with its cherishing love and its protecting power, and to go forth to the encounter with the magnificint [sic] but stormy and struggling world without. And if you too ... shall imagine yourselves as sons and daughters listening to the voice of a father, the counsels addressed you may perhaps come home to your hearts with a more impressive force and pathos."[28]

23. Students of the Senior Class, *The Student (Illinois Industrial University)* 2/4 (April 1873) 37.

24. Illinois Industrial University, *The Illini* 7/5 (February 1878) 181–83.

25. Board of Trustees, *Eighth Report*, 193–94.

26. Illinois Industrial University, *The Illini* 3/6 (June 1874) 161; Kersey, *John Milton Gregory and the University of Illinois*, 192.

27. Kersey, *John Milton Gregory and the University of Illinois*, 163–64.

28. Gregory, "Baccalaureate Address, University Chapel."

One receptive student, James Matthews, literally called him "Father Gregory" in a letter home to his own father.[29] In an earlier letter, Matthews had said to his dad, "Dr. Gregory is gone with his wife to Saratoga and I know not when they will return. Dr. is missed around the University, by the boys and every body else."[30] Matthews had "been waiting for an opportunity for consulting Dr. Gregory in regard to [his] decision" to drop out of school.[31] As this and other student accounts attest, John Gregory had a vital and effective pastoral ministry while at the I.I.U., which was enhanced by the quality of his preaching.

Methods and Style

Thirty-six remaining handwritten sermon manuscripts composed by Gregory for the I.I.U. between 1867 and 1878 are stored among his personal papers in the University of Illinois archives. They are written longhand in pen or pencil, in a beautiful, flowing cursive script with barely a correction, despite an occasional feel of being rushed. Both the language and sentence structure are elegant and impressive. Most of the sermons are brief, around five or ten minutes in length, probably written for the daily chapels. Some are longer, probably twenty to thirty minutes long, as appropriate for Sunday and Baccalaureate sermons. Other than the aforementioned Dr. Nott, Gregory's preaching influences are hard to know, but an article attests that, while visiting London in 1873, he was impressed with "Canon Liddon's Good Friday sermon in St. Paul's cathedral." On the same trip he heard C. H. Spurgeon preach in his Tabernacle. The two even visited afterward, with Gregory recording the topic of their conversation for *The National Baptist*.[32]

The Regent employed a variety of homiletical methods. Most often, he preached from a scripture text, and only occasionally was a sermon topical. He demonstrates a keen familiarity with the content and language of scripture, as his sermons are full of references to, and illustrations from, various passages in the Bible. "Rev. W. H. Stedman, D.D.," First Baptist of Champaign's pastor, said Gregory once told him:

---

29. Matthews, Papers, letter October 7, 1871.
30. Matthews, Papers, letter October 3, 1868.
31. Matthews, Papers, letter March 4, 1870.
32. Gregory, "London Preachers and Churches," 8–9.

> Do you know, I have found a new use of the Bible. I have been for many years troubled with insomnia. I have gotten into the habit of taking up some portion of Christ's sayings. I have committed to memory whole chapters of the Gospels and the writings of St. Paul, and have sought to go to the bottom of them. I have turned them over and over. I have looked at them from every point of view until my soul was aglow with light. My brother, I no longer dread sleepless hours. I rather rejoice in them. They are the most blessed of my life."[33]

Gregory's close relationship with the biblical text enabled him to frequently and effectively compose and speak symbolically and even poetically, as in, for example, a sermon called "To What Shall I Liken This Generation?": "It was a foolish generation. Like children at play;—[sic] not like men in earnest. The mightiest doings of Providence were passing around them; yet they did not awake from their dreams. The grandest visions of the prophets were about to be fulfilled; all things pointed to the near approach of the long expected Messiah . . ."[34]

During a Christmas sermon Gregory eloquently painted a word picture by saying, "Judea the small and solitary home of the true faith was trodden down under the iron heel of a lordly paganism."[35] In a chapel talk, he prompted an emotive response, saying, "For six thousand years the world has been trying to find happiness in sinful pursuits and indulgences, and the very dust is ready to shriek with the long and mortal agonies of the millions of wretched sinners who have been buried in it."[36] On another occasion he said that in Romans 8 "the apostle sends his raptured and far reaching glance abroad into the glories of that great landscape of divine love revealed in the gospel."[37] Or consider the poetic tone—and intentional repetition and cadence—in the following passage:

> now the swelling notes of joyous angels chanting the high praises of the glorious God; now the stern note of alarm arousing the slumbering and guilty to a sharp sense of danger and damnation; now a prophetic strain coming from the far future like the echoes of that martial music which is guiding the advancery

33. University of Illinois, *Memorial Convocation*, 9.
34. Gregory, "Sermon on Malachi 11:16–19."
35. Gregory, "Sermon on Luke 2: 10–11."
36. Gregory, "Lectures to Young Men."
37. Gregory, "Sermon on Romans 8:38–39."

march of the millions whose distant tramping grows louder and louder along the line of passing centuries. now [sic] the loud stern voice of justice calling to judgment; now the calm tones of wisdom instructing her children; now as in our text the winning pleading sweetness of mercy inviting to pardon and promising peace[.]³⁸

The building of momentum accomplished in sermons like this one, where the word "now" is repeated by a phrase, is a familiar rhetorical device which Gregory used elsewhere, as in his 1872 baccalaureate sermon, which was inspired by Psalm 3:

> Trust in him as your Maker who cares for His Creations. as [sic] your King who regards kingly His subjects. as [sic] your Father who loves His children. Trust in His tremendous power which supports unwearied the vast universe of being. Trust in His sublime wisdom which marks with its unerring prescience the infinite cycles of an all embracing history. Trust in His unchanging, undying love & goodness, which leaves no spot unvisited with beauty & good and no being unfurnished with its share of light and joy. Trust Him when you suffer that you may not despair. Trust him when you toil that you may be full of courage & strength. <u>Trust in the Lord</u> and <u>do good</u>.³⁹

Repeated use of the word "trust" not only gives the listener a rhythmic benchmark for communicating a new idea, but leads to and reinforces the theme of the sermon itself, which is captured in its title: "Trust in the Lord, and Do Good."

Stylistically, Gregory wisely used illustrations and images which were appropriate for his audience's era and age. Responding, for example, to St. Paul's famous "If God be for us who can be against us" in Romans 8, the Regent—though not a veteran himself—used a Civil War image, saying the Apostle's summons sounds like "the tramp and battle calls of myriads and millions of souls, bursting up the heights of some Lookout Mountain combat . . . there is charging cry of splendid squadrons, confident in the unmeasured might and the unerring tactics of their great leader. 'Tis the 'Rally round the flag, Boys,' of a diviner host than ever came at their country's call."⁴⁰ This device enabled the stu-

---

38. Gregory, "Sermon on Matthew 11."
39. Gregory, "'Trust in the Lord,'" 3–4.
40. Gregory, "'Providence.'"

dents to make the connection, based upon a recent and familiar news event which was significant for their generation. Perhaps appealing to the number of veterans in the I.I.U. student body and their families, he also used a war image in his 1871 baccalaureate address, which was itself poetic in tone:

> I cannot claim to speak to you with the wisdom of a patriarch looking back upon life from the calm of the evening time, and seeing the obverse of your young hopes as they will show in the clear light of the setting sun but my words may still be of worth as the utterances of one who in the high noon of his hardest and bravest toil, tells you from amid the dust and smoke, how the work goes on, and how the battle of the world swells and sways as fresh columns enter the field, and new batteries open fire.[41]

Despite his eloquence with this genre, though, Gregory did not limit himself to only dramatic and symbolic language in his I.I.U. preaching. Sometimes his analytical and rhetorical strategy was more expository and didactic. For example, in a sermon on the Lord's Prayer he breaks down the prayer's petitions into two themes, saying the audience can learn both "lessons of duty" and "hopeful promises."[42] Then, he adds two application points which one can glean and attempt personally, those being "the submission of our own souls" and "seek[ing] to extend God's reign." A similar organizational scheme may be found in an 1872 chapel lecture which elaborated on the three "lessons" of spring: its opportunities, its "great miracle of the year" of rebirth, and finally, "the most important and useful of all lessons, the great goodness of God."[43] This familiar three point paradigm was used again in his sermon from Matthew 13:45–46, where, in the introduction, he informs the audience of his three points: "1st, Religion is of great value—a pearl of great price. 2nd, It is to be sought for diligently. 3rd, It is to be purchased at the sacrifice of all other good." The sermon progresses with three sections— one for each of the points—in which he elaborated to make his case and persuade the listener.[44]

---

41. Gregory, "Baccalaureate Address. University Chapel."
42. Gregory, Sermon on Matthew 6:10. The sermon's title, handwritten in Greek letters, is "Elthetōē Basileíason."
43. Gregory, "Lessons of the Springtime."
44. Gregory, "Sermon on Matthew 13:45–46."

Another of his homiletical tactics was to create a logical sequence which would draw listeners from generalities to the specificities of their own real life situation. To illustrate, once, while preaching from Isaiah 40:30–31, Gregory begins by asking the audience if "faint" and "weary" describe the human condition generally. Then, he talks about the average working person, who tires of "employments" and "struggles" and "even of their pleasures!" Then, he says, "Nor is this confined to the laborer or business man. The student often grows weary with his long pursuit of learning and as he compares the little progress made, with the vast fields before him he often says to himself 'why should I undergo this long wearisome labor, while others eat, drink & enjoy as much as I.'" Then, Gregory applies his touché, making the link between the text and personal faith: "So too the Christian laborer looking on the hardly diminished mass of iniquity and vice, and the slow progress of the truth, grows weary through the long week of his care and labor intervening between the sabbath of religious rest."[45]

Elsewhere in his preaching Gregory uses deductive logic and disputation as rhetorical devices. For example, in an 1875 chapel talk called "Was Jesus of Nazareth More Than a Mere Man?" he lists three perspectives about Jesus which are held by those who claim to be Christians, followed by a presentation of the arguments backing each of the three views. Next, he lists "two classes of opponents"—the "rationalists" and "mythists"—followed by his critique of their claims.[46] In another sermon he follows a similar reasoned tack by laying out a series of five "proofs" regarding the unsurpassed excellence of God's love. In his first proof, he claims that divine love "is the only rational notion of God," raising four possible assumptions: "that [God] is entirely indifferent to the well being of his creatures. 2nd that he is a malevolent being. 3d that He is a being of mixed character and 4th that he is infinitely benevolent." Gregory says the first three are logically impossible, leaving, therefore, the fourth assumption "that <u>God</u> is <u>Love</u>" as the only rational choice. From there, he claims his second proof indisputably shows God's benevolence through history's progress. His third proof involves "human consciousness," that "We instinctively admire and involuntarily approve a God of Infinite Benevolence." His fourth proof is that "His <u>word</u> is full of explicit declarations of His love. [sic] and mercy and goodness."

45. Gregory, "Sermon on Isaiah 40:30–31."
46. Gregory, "'Was Jesus of Nazareth More Than a Mere Man?'" 3–5.

The fifth proof is that "Christian experience is an ever fresh proof of the love of God." Then, he offers another objection: "that there is evil in the world." To this question, he argues that God's allowing humankind to exercise "free powers" was a better choice on God's part than making people "mere machines," although Gregory says such reasoning is only speculation, and therefore not indisputable. Finally, he concludes with two characteristics of God's love: "It is all comprehending," with examples from nature, and "It's eternity," arguing again for the benevolence shown in history.[47] Obviously, this was a structurally detailed and didactic sermon, quite different from the word pictures uttered by the Regent in some of the passages cited earlier.

As these examples illustrate, then, John Gregory showed much diversity and creativity in the style and method of his I.I.U. preaching. Let's now consider how his sermons' contents reflect his and the I.I.U.'s educational vision and goals, and the impact they had upon his hearers.

Doctrinal Content

Even to a twenty-first century reader Gregory's sermons have a surprisingly timeless quality. Some of his works could even be effectively preached and received in Baptist and other churches today. Doctrinally, the content of his sermons could be classified as that of a moderate evangelical.[48] Given his closely-knit campus context, he was amazingly able to not repeat himself, covering a wide range of scripture texts and theological topics. Time and space prohibit covering them all, so this section will focus around four of his more prominent themes: his understanding of the person and work of Jesus Christ; his views on human knowledge and how God communicates with persons; his understanding of the human condition and the relationship between people and God; and the biblical concept of the Kingdom of God, and what it meant to a mid-nineteenth century American evangelical.

John Gregory's understanding of Jesus Christ is consistent with the predominant Protestant theology of his day. He frequently mentions Jesus in his sermons, where the Christ is repeatedly called a "Savior" and

---

47. Gregory, "God Is Love."

48. Marsden, *Fundamentalism and American Culture*, 11–32; Noll, *America's God*, 170–74.

"Divine." During a Christmas sermon, for example, Gregory called the birth of Jesus "the great gift of God to Men—the gift of a Savior."[49] On another occasion, he said "The gospel story" of Christ's crucifixion and resurrection "is the grandest <u>love tale</u> ever told on earth. Love stooping to Earth, leaving riches and glory behind, toiling, suffering and dying for the beloved ones; and these unworthy of it."[50] To such an unworthy individual—"to the <u>Soul</u> tossed with doubts and fears. racked [sic] with sin and pain how … perfect the peace in Jesus, the intellect rests in him as the solution of all its difficulties—the heart rests in him as a fullness of love & joy."[51] In a sermon called "Glory to God in he highest, and on earth peace, good will toward men," Gregory said "The wonderful and glorious revealings of His matchless love and holiness in the gift of his Son, [sic] must have grown clearer and grander with every fresh soul saved from sin & death." According to the Regent, since the time of Christ, he says, the knowledge of God has been increasing throughout the world. The church started as a very small group, while "all else was one wide mass of Heathenism." Gregory calculates that only "1/160 of the inhabitants of the Earth knew of the God whom we adore." By the 1870s, though, he said more than a fifth of humanity "believe in one, almighty God, the God of the Bible, and reject all heathen Gods … " The rise and spread of this faith not only "lies linked with all science and all civilization," but Jesus Christ, Gregory said, "has through the Gospel written His name and grace upon multitudes of redeemed & converted souls."[52] As a result, we find that "The Christians [sic] love for his Savior—the love of the church for Christ—is one of the most incomprehensible to the world, of all religious feelings."[53]

Gregory believed that Christ's divinity was evident and indisputable. Paul's writing, he said, shows that "if any difference in the greatness and divineness still exists between the <u>father</u> & the <u>son</u> it lies in a region too remote and too infinite for us to see it."[54] "The Jews," he said, "awaited his coming as the advent of the great descendant of David and the restorer of David's monarchy. How can he be a mere human descendant

49. Gregory, "Sermon on Luke 2:10–11."
50. Gregory, "God Is Love."
51. Gregory, "Sermon on Luke 2:14."
52. Ibid.
53. Gregory, "Sermon on Song of Solomon 5:9."
54. Gregory, "Sermon on Philippians 2:9–10."

whom David, a 1,000 years before, called <u>Lord</u>?"⁵⁵ Yet even though "The Divinity of Christ is generally believed fundamental to Christianity," it is admittedly mysterious, but "Its incomprehensibility ought not to stagger us any more than the incomprehensibility of any other <u>infinite problem</u> . . ."⁵⁶ Besides, he said on another occasion, "<u>Divine</u> is like every other notion involving the infinite, a word into which no two minds probably puts the same amount of meaning . . . So with God, so with Christ."⁵⁷ A further proof in Gregory's mind of Christ's divinity involves his perceived influence over human history, which "implies some profound and vital sympathy between Jesus and Mankind—some deep and fundamental adaptations of his character and doctrines to human needs and human beliefs . . . [His power is explained] by the silent, persuasive force of its own deep truthfulness—leaven slowly working its way from particle to particle, from soul to soul, by the resistless power of those great natural affinities which lie hidden in the very constitution of mind—has it made its way."⁵⁸

"Jesus," he said in reference to 1 Corinthians 1:23–24, "stands forth <u>singular</u> and <u>alone</u> in the world's history—to the philosopher a marvel. to [sic] the sceptic a stumbling block[.] to [sic] the Greek foolishness—to the Believer the Power of God & the Wisdom of God . . . He cannot be denied as a fact. There, in the field of History, he stands as undeniable as he was wonderful and inexplicable." Gregory then gave his University audience this clever thought: "To deny his existence is to suppose the greater marvel. [sic] that a few poor illiterate men should have each accomplished what the worlds [sic] greatest geniuses have attempted in vain.—the description of a model character.—a perfect man."⁵⁹ And along with his noble presence in history, the Regent explained, Jesus' existence was evident by the testimony of "the four distinct histories, and the apostolic letters" of scripture, "[plus] Josephus, Pliny & Tacitus . . ." In ancient times, Gregory said, "no one then questioned his existence, nor his pretended character."⁶⁰ Jesus is "prominent in history" because "his recorded words & deeds present a character of such matchless ex-

55. Gregory, "Sermon on Matthew 22."
56. Ibid.
57. Gregory, "'Was Jesus of Nazareth More Than a Mere Man?'" preliminary page.
58. Gregory, "Sermon on Philippians 2:9–10."
59. Ibid.
60. Gregory, "'Was Jesus of Nazareth More Than a Mere Man?'" 1.

cellence and moral grandeur that he compels the admiration of all right thinking men," and that is why his religion has flourished throughout the world.[61]

Unfortunately, though, Gregory said, some wrongly thinking people have misunderstood Jesus. While preaching from the prophet Malachi, the Regent warned the I.I.U. that even though Jesus and John the Baptist were daily among the people "in a fellowship the most winning and sacred that ever dwelt in a human heart," the crowd eventually "rejected John as one who was the victim of an unwholesome melancholly [sic]" and "turned from Jesus as a convivialist and wine bibber, a friend of publicans & sinners."[62] In a sermon from Philippians 2:9–10, though, the Regent told his community how they could be sure not to miss God in their midst: "In his stoop of mercy we see [Jesus] coming down from the "equality["] with God successively to the disrobing himself of his divine "reputation"—to servile position. to [sic] humanlikeness. to obedience to death. to the Cross [.] But thence he is lifted by equally grand steps to exaltation. to universal dominion and honor. to divine honor and worship."[63] Paradoxically, Gregory believed, Christ's glory came through his humiliation. In another sermon he explained that Jesus left "the glory and bliss of heaven . . . bowing to a lowly life and a miserable death to gain [the Kingdom] for us. He descended to the infinite deep to bring up this pearl of great price."[64] And "so far as God is concerned," the pearl "is free. 'Without money and without price.' He gives it royally to all who will receive it. But man must relinquish all other wealth, must take his heart off from all other good before he can receive this. The honor and glory of God require that His grace & salvation shall not be held subordinate to any earthly good. So also the whole heart must be roused to its mightiest efforts of love, to grasp and enjoy this infinite blessing."[65] Christ's work in this paradigm invites people into a covenant relationship with God. As this and Gregory's other sermonic utterances indicate, his understanding of the person and work of Christ is consistent with the normative evangelical doctrine of his era.

61. Gregory, "'Was Jesus of Nazareth More Than a Mere Man?'" 2.
62. Gregory, "Sermon on Malachi 11:16–19."
63. Gregory, "Sermon on Philippians 2:9–10."
64. Gregory, "Sermon on Matthew 13:45–46."
65. Ibid.

Along with the centrality of Christ in his thinking, Gregory also had a high view of scripture. "No profounder, no more instructive utterances are to be found in human language than those of our Lord's Prayer," he said.[66] "The Bible is one of these bulwarks of the church," he told a chapel audience. "It is a power in the earth. Triumphing over ages of opposition, outliving every argument framed against it, it still stands a monument of the divine power and mercy of God."[67] In a sermon called "Is the Bible of Divine Authority?" he answered by saying scripture's inspiration is evident in "its unity in variety—its responsiveness to the human consciousness[,] its utility as shown in personal life & history, & its endurance against all assaults & corruptions."[68] Furthermore, he explained in three points, we can conclude that God wrote the Bible because of "1. The superior character of the truths taught, above mere human wisdom[;] 2. The truthfulness of these truths, 3[.] The Beneficence of these truths, the character they produce[,] then all the historic evidence," which he called the success of "Christian civilization."[69] He concluded that "The Bible is to be regarded in the general scope and meaning of its teachings." Encouraging his I.I.U. audience, he suggested, "If you can only accept the New Testament take that. If others find inspiration in the Old they will take that also."[70]

Like other Christian leaders of his era, Gregory believed that God not only communicated to humankind through scripture, but also through nature.[71] "Springtime," he told a chapel audience, "has lessons of all sorts ... the Christian believes it a very word of God for him."[72] At the 1874 Baccalaureate service, he said "Natural law necessarily implies God if men have the courage or candor to look to the end."[73] He believed that God's existence may be known by both "a priori" (philosophical)

66. Gregory, "Sermon on Matthew 6:10."
67. Gregory, "Sermon on Luke 12:32."
68. Gregory, "'Is the Bible of Divine Authority?'" 1.
69. Ibid., 3.
70. Ibid.
71. Edwards, "Preaching of Romanticism in America," 297–312. Gregory's and the other I.I.U. leaders' rhetoric sometimes takes a popular Romantic tone when talking about nature and human possibility, but this is not necessarily inconsistent with Calvinism's high view of gracious justification and natural revelation through creation—see Noll, *America's God*, 28.
72. Gregory, "Lessons of the Springtime," 1.
73. Gregory, "Baccalaureate Sermon on Luke 18:8," 2.

and "a posteriori" ("arguments from design") means.[74] This assumption allowed him and peer educators to welcome science as a means of great societal blessing, a place for people of faith and virtue to accomplish much good,[75] and not something to be feared by Christians.[76] He said "every advance in knowledge shows more magnificent verities, more wide reaching harmonies more convincing proofs of a Divine wisdom, power and goodness."[77] Claiming no quarrel with Darwin, Gregory said that "a single universal intelligence" was indeed necessary to explain "the harmony & agreement of the entire kosmos.[sic]"[78] But in 1872 he did tell the Chicago Theological Union that

> Science threatens religion. It discredits its doctrines as not susceptible of scientific proof. It denies God as knowable, or dispenses with Him as unnecessary. It fastens man by physiological ties to the brutes with whom he must share a common fate. It seeks a natural origin for his soul, and thus ties it to a natural rather than a supernatural destiny. It digs for the foundations of Nature & thus purposely or without thought undermines religion. If Darwinism is true Christianity as far as regards another world, [sic] is without proof . . .

Atheistic science was one of what Gregory called many "Satanic agencies" which he claimed threatened Christian belief. Despite this challenge, though, he encouraged the listeners to fear not, that objections to the faith occured "in Paul's day," and science, being intrinsically limited to the material realm, only deals with "the objective" and "matter," but not with "the subjective" and "mind."[79] About three years later he told the I.I.U.: "The serious affirmation that there is no Creator, no over-ruling intelligence who has watched over and planned and effected this beautiful kosmic [sic] harmony is to most minds so repulsive, so shocking & monstrous that it cannot be soberly entertained. But there are others to whom the progressive discoveries of science seem to

---

74. Gregory, "'Is There a God?'" 2–3. This belief is consistent with the highly influential William Paley's *View of the Evidences of Christianity* (1794) and *Natural Theology* (1802); see Noll, *America's God*, 234.

75. Gregory, "'Trust in the Lord,'" 5.

76. Gregory, "'Christianity and Civilization.'"

77. Gregory, "Baccalaureate Sermon on Luke 18:8," 2.

78. Gregory, "'Is There a God?'" 6.

79. Gregory, "'Religion of the Future.'"

render 'God an unnecessary hypothesis' as one of them has said."[80] Yes, Darwinism is helpful in some ways, he assured these agricultural and mechanical scholars, because it explains "many of the forms of animals & plants and some of the phenomena of life . . ."[81] But to promote atheism merely due to the cause and effect of "matter and force"—in ["] the survival of the fittest"—he deemed "perfectly incredible, and utterly repugnant to the simplest dictates of consciousness," because in such a scheme "no such thing as intelligence properly exists . . . Closely considered, this theory is only a scientific version of the old theory of <u>Chance</u> so often rejected by the common sense of mankind."[82] Gregory, though, did not underestimate the power of the intellectual currents of his day. He told the 1874 Baccalaureate audience "The times tend to doubt. This is not strange. It is a regularly recurring phenomenon of history."[83] Since, he told his students in August of 1875, they live "in these times of scientific inquiry & research," where the doubts expressed in literature and the press would "assail" them, his Sunday chapel series would address "six of those great fundamental questions which are almost perpetually in debate among men" like the existence of God, the immortality of the soul, the authority of scripture, and the divinity of Christ.[84] He believed there was much at stake, because regarding "God" and "the Soul of man," he said, "around these two the forces of doubt always and almost instinctively gather."[85] He began an 1872 Sunday afternoon chapel talk by reading from Matthew's Sermon on the Mount, and then saying that, though he himself was a believer, he understood that some of them might themselves have doubts. Specifically, he addressed the assertion that Christianity had borrowed ideas from other prior religions, assuring them that this was no reason to disbelieve.[86] In fact, he said on another occasion,

> it is through doubts and questionings that the mind comes to its truest beliefs. True doubt knocks at the door to gain admission for truth. It is only false doubt—doubt that hates truth instead

80. Gregory, "'Is There a God?'" 3–4.
81. Ibid., 5.
82. Ibid., 4–5.
83. Gregory, "Baccalaureate Sermon on Luke 18:8," 1.
84. Gregory, "'Chapel Talks.'"
85. Gregory, "Baccalaureate Address, University Chapel," 3.
86. Gregory, "Lecture, Sunday Sep. 22," 1, 8.

of loving it—destructive doubt which delights itself in tearing down belief and not in building it up—that I would warn you against as being both bad and harmful. The doubter who honestly waits for light, earnest to learn & obey the truth, is worthy of our highest regard. But the Skeptic who continues to question out of mere wantoness & to show his skill in criticism, is both an unhappy & a dangerous man.[87]

A university scholar need not fear any information, Gregory believed, because all truth comes from God. What did matter, though, was how one processed that information, via the spiritual condition of one's heart. "A man's habits of thinking constitute his character," he once said. "As he thinketh so is he."[88] And empirical ways of knowing were limited, he told his 1872 Baccalaureate audience. He praised "science and learning," stressing their importance, and reminded the students of the long hours they had spent together in teaching and study at the I.I.U. "But above them," he said, " ... we would mount now to that realm of grander, diviner truth—the science of the immortal, the spiritual[,] the divine."[89] He would later say that "All thinking whether in morals or science, leads finally to the idea of a God—a Divine Ruler and Creator."[90] But even such lofty thoughts are limited, he said, because "reason alone can not prove," for example, "the immortality of the soul."[91] Regarding his own theological speculation on the existence of evil and the merits of "free choice" over predeterminism, he hedged that "all these are mere suppositions and will not silence or satisfy always. Then let us take the fact, and dismiss all efforts to explain it, as we <u>must</u> dismiss all questions when they pass over the bounds which limit thought—scientific as well as theological[.]"[92] At some point, he believed, all that is left is "faith," which is nothing for a scholar to be ashamed of, since it is "the <u>Intellect</u> of <u>Man</u> in its proudest and highest action."[93] He defined faith as "<u>trust</u>

---

87. Gregory, "'Chapel Talks,'" 2.

88. Gregory, "Untitled Document," John Milton Gregory Papers, 1839–1898, Series No. 2/1/1, Box 2 (University of Illinois Archives, Urbana, IL, 1870 folder).

89. Gregory, "'Trust in the Lord,'" 1–2.

90. Gregory, "Untitled Document," John Milton Gregory Papers, 1839–1898, Series No. 2/1/1, Box 3 (University of Illinois Archives, Urbana, IL, 1875 folder).

91. Gregory, "'Is the Bible of Divine Authority?'" 3.

92. Gregory, "God Is Love."

93. Gregory, "Sermon on 1 Corinthians 13:13."

in God ... <u>belief plus confidence</u> plus <u>conviction</u>."⁹⁴ And it is "needful" for human beings to have "peace of mind, the practice of virtue, the common affairs of business, and even to the existence of society. Not doubt but a firm, trusting faith is the cornerstone of a grand character and a noble & pure life."⁹⁵

Gregory and other evangelicals of the day believed that faith in Christ enabled human beings to attain salvation. In one chapel sermon from Isaiah 40:30–31, Gregory focused in on the line "But they that wait upon the Lord shall renew their strength." He said "<u>Waiting upon God</u> means specifically worshiping Him both in private and in public worship—prayer and praise. The word <u>wait</u>" meant "not a momentary act but an abiding attendance upon God—a dwelling of the thoughts and heart in His presence." It was through this type of faith that strength came.⁹⁶ Because "Christian experience," he said, "is essentially a life of love, and [sic] its love mounts highest and flows freest when in closest communion with God."⁹⁷ One's relationship with God, though, has been threatened and even broken by the problem of sin. For Gregory, Paul's Epistle to the Romans showed "the inexcusable sinfulness and pitiable helplessness of all mankind Jew as well as Gentile."⁹⁸ He defined sin as "an excess—a transgression, a going beyond what is lawful and right—and like all excesses it tends to more & more ungodliness. How should that which is itself <u>immoderate</u> ever exist in <u>moderation</u>?"⁹⁹ Sin was ever threatening to his students. In one of his "Lectures to Young Men," Gregory preached: "'<u>We have only one life to live</u>'—So says the advocate of sensual pleasure. The folly of the sentiment is only equalled by its falsity. 'Only one life' [?] Where then is that eternal existence lying beyond the grave? But even if we had only one life to live, how egregious the folly of devoting it to sin!"¹⁰⁰ "The prisons of the world," he said, are "filled with tens of thousands of the victims of vice [and] are gloomy monuments of the unhappy results of a life of sin."¹⁰¹ "So unsubstantial

---

94. Gregory, "Baccalaureate Sermon on Luke 18:8," 2.
95. Gregory, "Baccalaureate Sermon on 1 Corinthians 13," 1.
96. Gregory, "Sermon on Isaiah 40:30–31."
97. Gregory, "God Is Love."
98. Gregory, "Sermon on Romans 8:38–39."
99. Gregory, "Lectures to Young Men," Lecture 1.
100. Ibid.
101. Ibid.

and unsatisfying are the objects of earthly pursuit and enjoyment that even the youth faints and grows weary . . . "[102] Even "the body suffers" from "the robbery of health and joy and life . . . Almost every death is a suicide or a murder, ignorantly but not innocently committed."[103]

Gregory believed that people were created for immortality, calling his students "incarnate souls."[104] Even though, he told them, the research of his era's physicists and physiologists had caused some to question the existence of the soul—and neither the Bible nor the church have indisputably defined its nature—"the showings of Science do not disprove the existence of the Soul . . . They touch its processes or phenomena, but say nothing of its origin, its essential nature or its destiny . . . Science throws no light on the question of immortality, either for or against it" because it deals only with what is presently observed.[105] So, given the immortality of the soul, and sin's threat to alienate a person from God forever, Gregory deemed Paul's Epistle to the Romans a "powerful and resplendent argumentation to the necessity and certainty and power of salvation by faith."[106] "Faith in the Divine," he said, "in religion, God & heaven this is the condition of a grand, strong, effective life."[107] Through faith in Christ, salvation occurs:

> In the secret soul of man. in [sic] the very center of consciousness and life. the [sic] name of Jesus has come and asserted its superhuman and kingly power[.] To the intellect it has offered the solution of its grandest problems of thought and will always do so more and more . . . To the Sensibilities it has afforded the sweetest comforts and the highest joys. To the will and desire it has offered the noblest laws of action and the strongest motives of effort . . . Jesus reenacts his incarnation in the soul.[108]

Once this regeneration takes place, one is free from sin and empowered to do good works, a theology consistent with the mid-nineteenth century "holiness movement" popular among English-speaking

---

102. Gregory, "Sermon on Isaiah 40:30–31."
103. Gregory, "'Trust in the Lord,'" 7.
104. Gregory, "Baccalaureate Address, University Chapel."
105. Gregory, "'Is the Bible of Divine Authority?'" 1–2.
106. Gregory, "Sermon on Romans 8:38–39."
107. Gregory, "Baccalaureate Sermon on Luke 18:8," 4.
108. Gregory, "Sermon on Philippians 2:9–10."

evangelicals worldwide.[109] In his 1872 baccalaureate sermon, Gregory told the crowd that good works depend on faith in God, and differed from their counterfeits. "Skepticism," he said, "may have its humane hearts, and its men of pure impulse. Even atheism may live in a soul full of kindly feeling, and prudent morality, but these exist in spite of their creed, not as the natural fruit or logical consequence of it."[110] Too often, he said, there is "correct belief or at least correct understanding of God, united with gross selfishness and with even low sensuality and sin, but all the world sees how illogical such a life from such a creed, and is unsparing in its denunciation of the inexcusable guilt or hypocrisy of the life so false to its beliefs."[111] The secret to victorious living and a life of good works is for people to "work out their salvation with fear and trembling and only succeed at last because <u>God works in them</u>, both to <u>will</u> and to <u>do</u> . . . " He elaborates:

> The <u>salvation</u> of a soul consists not merely in its conversion and pardon, but in its entire sanctification. The entire nature is to be renovated and made spotless. The whole soul is to be made saintly & angelic. Selfishness is to be entirely replaced by the love of God—Self will is to be entirely lost in the hearty choice of God's will [.] Christian life and duty are to absorb the whole powers of soul and body. The Body is to be offered a "living sacrifice." And all this is to be done in this life, for there is no change in the grave to which we hasten."[112]

Personal surrender is necessary for this to happen:

> I must give myself up to the power and the luxury of the conviction that God's love cannot be alienated from us . . . God's love begets ours. 'We love him because he first loved us.' <u>His love</u> furnished the attracting <u>motive</u> and provides the <u>means</u> for <u>our love</u>. The same light that bears the image of your face to the glass brings back the reflected image to your eye. The same rays of God's love which fall upon the mirroring soul return to Him

---

109. Noll, *History of Christianity in the United Sates and Canada,* 181–87, 235, 378–81.
110. Gregory, "'Trust in the Lord,'" 2–3.
111. Ibid., 3.
112. Gregory, "Sermon on 1 Peter 4:18." "Living sacrifice" is a reference to Romans 12:1.

from where they emanated becoming the reflected image of His own love."[113]

This work of the Holy Spirit is "The first and foremost of the sentiments which Ch'ty[114] proposes to implant in us," nothing less than "the love of God—a supreme, unselfish affection for the infinite one—the Maker, Father & Friend."[115] All of this grace, he believed and taught, is available to any one who comes to Christ in faith.

To emphasize his belief in the necessity of the Holy Spirit's work in people both individually and collectively, Regent Gregory preached an I.I.U. chapel sermon based on "Zechariah. IV. 6" entitled "Not by might nor by power, but by my Spirit, saith the Lord of Hosts." After beginning with a brief contextual explanation of the scripture text, he opines that "The <u>Safety</u> and <u>Success</u> of <u>God's church lies not in</u> the inherent <u>might</u> of its <u>membership nor in the power they may exert</u> or call to <u>to</u> [sic] <u>their aid from earthly friends</u> but <u>in the Spirit</u> of <u>God working in them and through them</u>."[116] From there, he uses historical examples of "various and wonderful revivals of religion the world has beheld," such as "Luther's reformation," where the era's "impiety" and the church's "sensualism" hindered faith; "Whitefield's revivals," where faith flourished despite the cold, deadening arrogance of the Enlightenment; and "Edwards' revival at Northhampton" which unexpectedly and ironically "broke out by the sudden conviction of a young woman noted as a ringleader in gayety." Gregory concludes: "So with all recorded revivals. They have arisen under circumstances so unlikely and by agencies so simple and have reached results so mighty as clearly to mark them the manifestations of a divine power." And as the Spirit worked in those movements, he said, so we should "seek by our daily endeavor . . . to bring souls through Christ into the love & service of Heaven . . . "[117]

The love of God, he believed, was irresistibly attractive. All people will agree, he told a chapel audience, in the "excellence of a kind and loving temper, an affectionate spirit and of a pure and sincere affection for all worthy whether man or God. On the doctrine and duty of

---

113. Gregory, "Sermon on Romans 8:38–39."
114. This is Gregory's shorthand for "Christianity."
115. Gregory, "Christian Elements of Character" (chapel sermon).
116. Gregory, "Sermon on Zechariah 14:6."
117. Gregory, "Sermon on Matthew 6:10."

being deeply and sincerely <u>charitable</u>, that is kindly, loving, just, we are all orthodox. The deep inward light teaches us all this truth."[118] Here, he asserts belief in the universality of God's love, and the possibility of charity to be exhibited through natural means, of familial and neighborly love, across cultures and religious beliefs, to be praised by all, as music and literature show worldwide.[119] But charity is not simply "that mere gushing feeling . . . even to ecstasy or delirium without moving the hand to one benevolent deed . . . nor is it that beautiful poetic sentimentalism which praises itself by painting some picturesque but wholly unreal view of some person, or people, or cause, and then falling down to worship this golden calf which thus imaginations have wrought."[120] No, charity is defined by action. And to be a person who cares enough to act, one must attain, as was discussed in chapter three, "character," which is synonymous with holiness. In a Sabbath lecture, Gregory told his students "The formation of character then is the greatest need in education . . ."[121] This talk began a series for the autumn term of 1872 called "The Christian Elements of Character."[122] In order to attain such "moral character" one must have "faith," because character "can have no adequate support without faith in the Divine moral gov. [sic]. Neither man nor nations will fight the battle against vice & sin without faith."[123] Gregory defined the good as what is "right in moral character," "pure in moral purpose," and "benevolent" according to "divine law." Its "law" is "rectitude" and its "end" is "well being."[124] To attain character takes intentional effort, because "all excellencies and virtues are growths[.] Would you have in your character all manly virtues you must sow the seed. In the small beginnings are laid the foundations of future power."[125]

As discussed in chapter three, Gregory and the I.I.U. leaders believed there were divinely-created differences between men and wom-

---

118. Gregory, "Baccalaureate Sermon on 1 Corinthians 13," 3.

119. Ibid.

120. Ibid., 5.

121. Gregory, "Lecture, Sunday Sep. 22," 4.

122. Gregory, "Untitled Document," John Milton Gregory Papers, 1839–1898, Series No. 2/1/1, Box 3 (University of Illinois Archives, Urbana, IL, 1872 folder).

123. Gregory, "Baccalaureate Sermon on Luke 18:8," 4.

124. Gregory, "Trust in the Lord," 6.

125. Gregory, "Lessons of the Springtime," 2.

en.¹²⁶ But "all broad and universal principles of Character," he claimed, are "both womanly and manly, feminine in its delicacy, tenderness and beauty but masculine in its power."¹²⁷ This type of virtue—what J. B. Turner envisioned as true Christian manhood—would necessarily lead to good works, including righteous labor, which Gregory said, in an 1874 chapel sermon, has four virtues: it "Educates . . . Gives Health . . . is Honorable . . . and is Essential to Success."¹²⁸ Although a fallen world will resist such virtue, "Victory lies in our surmounting the world not in surrendering to it.—surmounting it by the aid of another world[.]"¹²⁹ The renunciation of the selfish will must give way to God's sovereign control, resulting in nothing less than "the unreserved consecration of each man's whole self, his talents & possessions, to the eternal service of Heaven."¹³⁰ "Had man 'only one life to live,'" he told the young people entrusted to his care, "it were wise to make that life radiant with an angel's purity rather than waste it in riotous living."¹³¹ "But to the Christian how much higher is the interest attaching to the young! He sees them entering upon an existence wonderful and everlasting and whose weal or woe is to be decided during the first few years of its progress."¹³²

John Gregory's leadership at the I.I.U. was inseparable from his identity as a Christian educator. Out of concern for his students, he continually stressed the need for them to have good character and to do charitable works, which leads to a fourth major theme in his preaching: his focus on building the Kingdom of God. "The Kingdom of Heaven is to be within us as well as without," he said.¹³³ There was both a personal and a societal dimension in his preaching. He said the Kingdom was both present and coming. And it was larger than the Christian and the church—it affected all the earth: all people, all governments, all affairs. So when Gregory spoke of reversing the curse and labor's millennium, he was expressing his understanding of the Biblical vision of God's Kingdom. The role of the I.I.U. and its graduates, he preached, was to

126. Gregory, "Address to Young Ladies."
127. Gregory, "Baccalaureate Sermon on 1 Corinthians 13," 6–7.
128. Gregory, "Labor," *The Illini* 4/2 (November 1874) 33–36.
129. Gregory, "Baccalaureate Address," 5.
130. Gregory, Sermon on Matthew 6:10.
131. Gregory, "Lectures to Young Men," Lecture 1.
132. Ibid.
133. Gregory, "Sermon on Matthew 6:10."

have the Christian faith and resulting character to take the blessing of science into the world and—as he repeatedly said in his 1872 baccalaureate sermon on Psalm 3—"do good."[134]

Gregory was not alone in emphasizing God's Kingdom as a rationale for public service. Fellow Baptist and university president John Bascom taught an expanded form of moral philosophy using his textbook *Ethics: Or Science of Duty* (New York, 1879), including expanded sections on government and politics. He also published one of if not the first academic sociology textbooks in America, advocating temperance, feminism, and organized labor, rooting them in a quest for God's Kingdom being realized on earth.[135] Bascom once said, "We seem to see the Kingdom of Heaven coming along these very lines of union between scientific research and religious insight." He told an 1880 baccalaureate audience that in the era's new and emerging academic disciplines—political science, economics, sociology, and the like—"moral truths have their seat."[136] In his 1887 and final baccalaureate address in Madison, called "A Christian State," he critiqued unbridled capitalism and wanton greed, not from the perspective of a yet fully developed socialism, but from that of crusading progressive evangelicalism. Oil magnate John Rockefeller—a fellow Baptist—was a frequent target of Bascom's ire on this topic.[137] For evangelical progressives like Bascom and Gregory, God's unfolding Kingdom meant social improvements hastening the millennium. And higher education, for them, was an important and expanding way for such improvements to happen.

The Kingdom was perceived as something to desire and anticipate. "It is an impressive and inspiring thought," Gregory said about the Lord's Prayer, "that millions are daily uttering this prayer, in all languages and lands."[138] He told the I.I.U. community "It is no light or idle thing to pray for the coming of God's Kingdom, the setting up of Gods [sic] reign & authority on the Earth. Let us seek to know the full import of the words we use."[139] The Kingdom might even mean sacrifice, "as the Royalists of England were ready to give and suffer all things to bring

134. Gregory, "'Trust in the Lord.'"
135. Hoeveler, "University and the Social Gospel," 286.
136. Ibid., 293.
137. Ibid., 291–92.
138. Gregory, "Sermon on Matthew 6:10."
139. Ibid.

back their expelled King, Charles II, so we should be ready to give property or life even to bring back God to his throne over Earth."[140] To attain it, I.I.U. students and staff should submit their souls to God's control and guidance, he said, "for the Kingdom of Heaven is to be within us as well as without, the renunciation of our own selfish wills & plans …"[141] Through this covenant between God and his people, the Kingdom will be realized, as "The character and grandeur of a kingdom are to be estimated partly by its dominion and its long endurance, but chiefly by its <u>Citizens</u> & its <u>King</u>."[142] No mere hope in a future event, when Jesus likened the Kingdom to a "pearl of great price," he wasn't only referring to "the <u>far off</u>, <u>future</u> kingdom," Gregory said, "but the present reign of Christ in and over the soul—this is the infinite blessedness which the text and the whole Bible presents to the sinner as the grandest good."[143]

Once the Kingdom of God was properly cultivated within the I.I.U.'s people, they could join in with others actively engaged in the unstoppable progress of labor's millennium. "The kingdom shall finally belong to the church[,] the kingdom of a redeemed earth. Christian Principles must ultimately triumph."[144] Not even the "Satanic agencies" of proud, sinful humanity or perverted and fractious Christianity could stop the Kingdom, which was driven by scriptural truth, the needs of humanity, and most importantly "Jesus Christ … with his superhuman purity, wisdom, goodness and grandeur, as a unique and inexplicable fact of History …"[145] In a Christmas sermon he reminded his audience that once "Judea the small and solitary home of the true faith was trodden down under the iron heel of a lordly paganism. Every where else was the thick darkness of heathenism. Eighteen centuries have passed and the <u>good tidings</u> have spread till Christianity is the dominant religion of the world … It is sure promise of good to any land when Christianity enters it."[146] In fact, he said, civic virtues like "liberty, fraternity, equality, Arts, education, wealth, all have come from Christianity."[147] Demonstrating

---

140. Ibid.
141. Ibid.
142. Ibid.
143. Gregory, "Sermon on Matthew 13:45–46."
144. Gregory, "Sermon on Luke 12:32."
145. Gregory, "'Religion of the Future.'"
146. Gregory, "Sermon on Luke 2:10–11."
147. Gregory, "Sermon on Luke 2:14."

a firm belief in millenarian progress, Gregory believed that "history in its shorter reaches is full of acknowledged evils and wo[e], but in the longer sweep of centuries and ages it tends ever towards higher grounds of <u>truth</u> and <u>good</u>. The great leader of the march of humanity has most evidently in view an end full of glory and immortal good."[148] The "name" of Jesus "has come down along the track of History and still abides in civilization an element of most plastic force. It has led every great reform. It has commenced and crowned every triumph of <u>right</u> & <u>truth</u> over tyranny and error[.]"[149] Matthew 6: 33, he said, teaches three things about the Kingdom of God: that there is an "essential unity of human life—all its manifold aims and interests are virtually one"; that "this final all-comprehending, all-subordinating aim" of seeking the Kingdom "is at one with God's aim in His creations & government"; and third, "the success in this grand central aim carries success in all the others."[150] So Gregory summoned the I.I.U. community to join in with God's movement in history, because in the "great peopled world of the XIX century," among its "states and empires," "<u>learning</u> and <u>labor</u> are striking hands in the mightiest league for power mankind has yet seen."[151] At the 1876 baccalaureate he said "his heart is weighed down with a deeper solicitude as he recognizes their relations to the divine Being, to the Kingdom of God, to religion, to eternity and the judgments of heaven."[152] This was serious business. And so his parting Sabbath words to his 1876 graduates were, "<u>Seek ye first the Kingdom of God, and His righteousness, and all these things shall be added unto you.</u>"[153]

Public Service

It was precisely through this belief in God's unfolding Kingdom that Gregory and his peers advocated public service, both for the church and wider society. One of John Bascom's most noteworthy students, Robert M. La Follette, would later recall that, for Bascom, there was no higher calling. "He was forever telling us," La Follette said, "what the

---

148. Gregory, "God Is Love."
149. Gregory, "Sermon on Philippians 2:9–10."
150. Gregory, "Baccalaureate Address on Matthew 6:33," 3.
151. Gregory, "Baccalaureate Address, University Chapel."
152. Gregory, "Baccalaureate Address on Matthew 6:33," 2.
153. Ibid., 3.

state was doing for us and urging our return obligation not . . . for our own selfish benefit, but to return some service to the state."[154] Similarly, the problem of selfishness was a major theme in Gregory's preaching. In his 1870 baccalaureate sermon he begins by saying "The great uses of our education are social, not selfish. A man is educated only in some little part for himself. The main aim of his education is that he may do society service."[155] Reminding both students and parents that the state had paid for their education, he painstakingly showed how many different people and institutions have contributed for their education from childhood through college. Since theirs and others' welfare hinges upon the health of the society in which they live, he said "you owe it to God and humanity to take upon you all the education you can get . . . Society stands ready, sphinx like, to devour those who cannot solve its riddles. She enslaves those who cannot lead her."[156]

An experienced collegiate educator, Gregory well understood the choices young people faced. As he told the class of 1871, "with your keen appetites and passions, urging you to haste, almost to recklessness, in the grapple for wealth or fame or power," one would do better to deny the self and instead act upon "your yet unwasted generosity ready to feel the impulse to a noble life . . ."[157] There would be temptations to neglect this responsibility, as "The world is the natural foe of the church. Her whole gravitating power is downward and away from God, whether she meets the people of God in conflict or drags them down in the embrace of pretended friendship."[158] By "world," Gregory refers to the Christian concept of human collectives and systems which are antithetical to God's intended Kingdom purposes, and therefore detrimental to believers. But he encouraged his students by reminding them that "You and the World were made by the same divine hand . . . you are mysterious correlatives of the same living essence . . . yours are responsive powers coworking in the same universal history . . . You are in its powerful em-

154. Hoeveler, "University and the Social Gospel," 293.
155. Gregory, "Baccalaureate Sermon, University Chapel."
156. Ibid.
157. Gregory, "Baccalaureate Address, University Chapel."
158. Gregory, "Sermon on Luke 12:32." In an earlier draft for an August 7, 1870, sermon at the Second Baptist Church of Chicago, he added: "Just now the enemies of our Christianity exult in the hopes of our defeat," namely "Sabbath desecration" and "scientific scepticism."

brace, and by a machinery of law as cunningly contrived as Omniscience can make it, and as irresistable as Omnipotence, it weaves the threads of your life with its own."[159] While living cooperatively with the rebellious and fallen world, Jesus gives believers peace, which Gregory defines as "security" and "rest," and good will as "benevolence" and "well being."[160] He speaks of peace on two levels, for both the individual and for "society." Regarding society, "the principles of religion alone promise peace," because they cure "antagonisms" between "nations and races." The Holy Spirit is at work in the "<u>individual soul</u> in its personal and private life" and in the larger society where "Jesus still proves the needed panacea and king & crown[.]"[161] Yet these two dimensions are related: "Your interests and those of the world without if not identical, are so intimately involved and interwoven that the one cannot be separated from the other."[162]

Given this reality, then, Gregory asked the 1872 graduating class to obey God and fulfill their mission, as the call to

> do good ... comes as a deep groan, shaping itself as into an unfortunate cry from the depths of ignorance & poverty and sin where so many millions of our wretched race, [sic] writhe or revel in the muck and mire of deep and almost unnamerbable [sic] degradation, starvation, and sin, bidding you in God's name and of theirs and their children's sake to <u>do good</u> ... It comes from the angel host who bend in loving interest from the battlements of heaven, and measure with clearer than mortal vision the needs and the woes of our race, and the possibilities of a higher destiny—a splendid and eternal victory over sin.[163]

Join in, he said, with "all the host of earnest men and women who are struggling to establish right and disestablish wrong, whether in society, or science, in church or school or state. Their battle cry appealing to you from the thick fight is to fall in, somewhere in the line of true and working souls, and <u>do good</u>."[164] This, above all, was what he wanted them to remember from the finale "of these last sabbath counsels."

---

159. Gregory, "Baccalaureate Address, University Chapel."
160. Gregory, "Sermon on Luke 2:14."
161. Gregory, "Sermon on Philippians 2:9–10."
162. Gregory, "Baccalaureate Address, University Chapel."
163. Gregory, "'Trust in the Lord,'" 4–5.
164. Ibid., 4.

In 1877 he told a chapel audience, "There are two words whose import ... you ought thoroughly to learn. These are <u>Duty</u> and <u>Destiny</u>."[165] On another occasion he said, "Whatever of learning you may carry forth from these halls, if you go forth with no high purpose to bear some noble part in the world's great struggle for right and good—for the beautiful and the true—your education will be contemptible ... The aim that should inspire and guide you is the <u>Good</u> of <u>Mankind</u> and the <u>Glory of God</u>."[166] He concluded his 1870 baccalaureate sermon with this challenge:

> The world doubtless wants true scholars—men of thought and men of science—who with clear and uncompromising fidelity shall set themselves to the great work of gaining truth, truth in all fields—and for all arts. But with a still more vital want, it needs great hearted men—philanthropists, patriots, Christians—scholars of the Good—who shall discover and reveal with the splendid argument of a great example, how life itself can be purged of its darkness, drudgery and doubt, and made blessed with knowledge and cheerful effort and high faith.[167]

Such "faith and hope in action," including its application in the "secular" realm, was his definition of charity,[168] which he also called "the benevolent feeling[,] the genuine affection—the love from which all alms-giving all generous and kindly actions spring," a virtue even greater than faith and hope.[169] "In its broadest sense it is the passion for universal well being—for the greatest good of all being, God's angels or men. It loathes only evil, and wrong & wretchedness."[170] He ended his 1875 Baccalaureate sermon by pointing to Jesus as the ultimate example of charity, saying,

> His was a life of love. He was still a young man, only a scarcely [sic] older than some of you, when he began that career so short, so sublime, so seemingly sad but so grandly beautiful, beneficent and blessed, so childlike in its simplicity, so manful

---

165. Gregory, "Chapel Sermon: 'Duty & Destiny.'"
166. Gregory, "Baccalaureate Sermon."
167. Gregory, "Baccalaureate Sermon, University Chapel."
168. Gregory, "Sermon on 1 Corinthians 13:13."
169. Ibid., 2.
170. Ibid., 6.

in its patient toil, its steady courage and its unwavering devotion to principle, so divine in its even handed justice, kindness and self sacrifice for friends and foes. What is that one central attribute of the character of Jesus around which were grouped all the rest, and whose controlling power gave its beautiful symmetry & consistency of his life, and makes that life still to stand forth above the field of human history with an aspect at once so majestic and winning?[171]

Gregory's unspoken answer was the theme of his sermon: charity, which meant public service, out of love for God.

Speaking at John Gregory's memorial service, I.I.U. alumnus Charles G. Neely said:

> On the 7th day of June, 1880, Dr. Gregory delivered the baccalaureate sermon to our class. We were his audience, though this hall was crowded. He said: 'My text is from St. James: "What is your life?"' The question came home to each of us, bringing us face to face with the future that lay before us, out in the big, round world, when we should go there to assume duty. Many, many times that question has arisen. What my life is today, or may be is largely due to his teaching and example. I stand here loving him for what he did for me and for others. I know he loved me. This sweet child of God drew men unto him. He was known and loved and honored on two continents.[172]

After leaving the I.I.U., Gregory continued in public service, being elected President of the state Board of Health in 1881. In 1882 he became General Secretary of the American Baptist Home Mission Society, through which he worked for the improvement of freed slaves and their families.[173] That same year he published *The Political Economy*, and his Union classmate, President Chester A. Arthur, commissioned him and two others to work on the Civil Service Act of 1883. This led to other forms of government service on a second continent, Europe, where Gregory served as an ambassador, returning to spend his remaining years mostly in the Washington, D.C. area.

The Regent's homiletical emphasis on public service proved to be effective for his graduates, who practiced a variety of professions. It is interesting that in a student's article in the I.I.U. paper entitled "Where

---

171. Ibid., 8.
172. University of Illinois, *Memorial Convocation*, 25–26.
173. Johnson and Malone, *Dictionary of American Biography*, 603.

Should Our Best Men Be" clergy were not mentioned, while lawyers, doctors, and "mechanics"—that is, engineers—were.[174] By 1885, only two alumni reported having become clergymen, representing only about one half of one percent of the alumni population.[175] This is not surprising given that they had been educated in an industrial university, and had consistently been told that they could serve the Lord in ways outside of the church and beyond a traditional religious vocation. According to historian James Dombrowski, by the 1870s a realized eschatology was developing in mainstream churches which focused on God's immanence, "destroy[ing] the distinction between the secular and the religious world," an outgrowth, he says, of Calvinism, "a reaffirmation of the Puritan ideal of theocracy" which set the stage for the full-fledged Social Gospel.[176] By the early twentieth century, says educational historian David Setran, a "conservative social gospel" was evident on American campuses, emphasizing public service in a way distinctive from the English "cultured gentleman" and the German "scholar" ideals.[177] John M. Gregory's belief in—and preaching on—the need for his students to engage in public service provides one example of this transition. His own Christian and, more precisely, Baptist theology informed his public educational vision and practice. His thought demonstrates a balance between the individual and collective dimensions of God's Kingdom, stressing salvation as simultaneously personal and communal. His teaching did not privatize faith, nor did it advocate a social gospel devoid of the necessity of a personal relationship with God.

John M. Gregory expressed these beliefs to the I.I.U. community and others primarily through the vehicle of preaching. In his sermons, he communicated the University's vision of "Learning and Labor," and encouraged its mission of public service in agriculture and industry. Through this homiletical ministry, and the other means by which the University taught, Gregory and the I.I.U.'s leaders sought to send forth graduates who would rely upon God as they worked to hasten labor's

---

174. Students of the Senior Class, *The Student (Illinois Industrial University)* II, no. 11 (November 1873) 125–26.

175. Behle, "Educating 'The Lord's Redeemed and Anointed,'" 61, note 32.

176. Dombrowski, *Christian Socialism*, 14–15.

177. Setran, *The College "Y,"* 141.

millennium, hoping and striving—as Gregory said in a chapel sermon—for God's will to be done, on earth as it is in heaven.[178]

---

178. Gregory, "Sermon on Matthew 6:10."

Conclusion

ON DECEMBER 11, 1970, IN OSLO, NORWAY, NOBEL PEACE PRIZE recipient Norman Borlaug—whom Senator Charles Grassley of Iowa called the "father of the green movement"—delivered his Nobel Lecture.[1] He told the audience that, since the time of Adam and Eve, humans have struggled to grow enough good food to feed themselves. Citing scriptural examples of agricultural challenges mentioned in Genesis 41:54, Amos 4:9, Joel 1:17–20, and Isaiah 8:21, he argued for the ongoing implementation of a science-driven "Green Revolution."[2] He concluded his speech saying, "[By] developing and applying the scientific and technological skills of the twentieth century for 'the well-being of humankind throughout the world,' [we] may still see Isaiah's prophecies come true [chapter 35, verses 1 and 7]: '. . . And the desert shall rejoice, and blossom as the rose . . . And the parched ground shall become a pool, and the thirsty land springs of water.' . . . May these words come true!"[3]

A child of Norwegian Lutherans living in rural Cresco, Iowa, Borlaug learned from his Grandfather Nels that "Some people look up to the sky in search of God. I say, look at the soil and the growing things. That's where you'll find God."[4] Borlaug's high school principal—and former Olympian wrestling coach—told young Norman to "Give the best that God gave you. If you won't do that, don't bother to compete," advice his biographer calls "a code for life."[5] After wrestling for the University of Minnesota and earning a PhD there, Borlaug spent his professional life outside of the U.S., working to help nations around the world grow grain more efficiently. Reflecting on his career while speaking at Ohio State's commencement ceremony in 1981, he said "we live a longer and better life than all previous generations. Remember that constructive

---

1. Dil, *Norman Borlaug*; Grassley, "Public Policy and Feeding a Hungry World."
2. Dil, *Norman Borlaug*, 60–61.
3. Ibid., 77.
4. Hesser, *Man Who Fed the World*, 5, 8.
5 Ibid., 12.

work is the best medicine God ever gave to man," reminding them of Thomas Jefferson's warning that "ease and security" could sadly result in "decadence."[6] As the keynote at a 1996 international symposium in Brazil, he said that "small-scale" farmers tend to favor the newer, scientific methods, because older technologies—like those used by the organic movement—"tend to perpetuate human drudgery and misery and the risk of hunger and famine."[7] Until his death in 2009, Borlaug continued to say that material prosperity wrought by scientific research has created a better society around the globe.[8]

Obviously, religious reflection of various kinds and in different places could be brought to bear upon life's necessities, including the production of food. For example, Jewish agricultural utopias sprung up in the U.S. at the end of the nineteenth century to correct a perceived imbalance of wealth and give the poor a chance to prosper.[9] Or, in another case, in early twentieth century Oklahoma an agrarian religious socialism formed through a congenial mix of evangelical Christianity, Jeffersonian rural romanticism, and the labor movement.[10] Although Norman Borlaug was not directly influenced by either of these communities, and earned his Minnesota degrees decades after the Illinois Industrial University got its start, one curiously hears him proposing religious ideas regarding progressive agriculture with which J. B. Turner and J. M. Gregory would wholeheartedly agree. To be clear, this book in no way claims to speak for the U.S. agricultural and industrial university movement as a whole. That would be far too broad of a topic, with too much regional and cultural diversity, to be encompassed in one small volume.[11] But while this book does not claim to speak for the whole, by providing one case study in the larger context of American higher education, it hints at the possibility that popular theology may

---

6 Dil, *Norman Borlaug*, 234.

7 Ibid., 479–80.

8 Ibid., 490. Throughout his later years, Borlaug consistently warned of two dangers: population growth and the shortage of arable land, and affluence's moral dangers as a threat to U.S. security and prominence (Dil, *Norman Borlaug*, 233, 354).

9. Herscher, *Jewish Agricultural Utopias in America*.

10. Bissett, *Agrarian Socialism in America*.

11 For example, the situation of the southern U.S. during the I.I.U. era, having until recently relied upon slave labor, may have impacted the new agricultural education differently than in the Midwest or other regions.

have been more influential in the theory and practice of the early land-grant leaders than has traditionally been stated.

As a theological history, this book has shown that the I.I.U.'s founders, most of whom had been trained within the worldview of evangelical Christianity, believed that agricultural and mechanical education would result in a divinely-ordained blessing for the larger society, an outpouring of God's Kingdom on earth which J. B. Turner conceived of as labor's millennium. As a missionary to Illinois, Turner, in collaboration with others of like mind, saw agricultural improvement as a way to help the western peoples. Working hard to organize and mobilize agricultural workers, he and his friends successfully lobbied the state to establish and fund an industrial university. Once it commenced its operations, the expectations and surrounding rhetoric were high, claiming that toiling humankind were about to be elevated by eliminating the need for degrading and inefficient modes of labor, reversing Adam's curse of having to sweat to earn a living.

Having established the campus facilities and curriculum, and rallying around the motto "Learning and Labor," the Illinois Industrial University soon began, under the leadership of John Gregory, to adopt its own particular practices, seeking to create ideal human beings through the attainment of Christian culture. This meant, among other qualities, character formation, gentility, military and domestic prowess, physical fitness, and abstinence from liquor, tobacco, and idle amusements. An interesting figure bridging a significant educational transition in the U.S., Gregory was, for the most part, an educational conservative, never wavering from what I.I.U. historian Harry Kersey calls the "two pillars of education" Gregory learned from Eliphalet Nott at Union College: "the overall religious orientation of the educational enterprise, and the epistemology of commonsense realism upon which it was based."[12] At the same time, though, Gregory was an innovator, as proven by his prior leadership in Michigan and the respect shown to him by his land-grant presidential peers. Along with a new and developing curriculum both nationally and locally, the I.I.U., with Gregory at the helm, taught through extracurricular groups like literary societies, the campus Y.M.C.A., and the student newspaper. It also communicated and committed through a vital and active liturgical life, as evidenced by its compulsory daily and Sunday chapels, as well as special

---

12. Kersey, *John Milton Gregory and the University of Illinois*, 169.

occasions like Inauguration Day, Commencement, Anniversary Day, and the dedication of new buildings. While many of these events were ceremoniously akin to secular collegiate and other forms of public ritual, a vestige of the Protestant tradition remained, with some explicit forms of civil religion intact. As Regent Gregory's preaching ministry at the I.I.U. demonstrates, the traditional language of evangelical Christianity remained a part of their public rhetoric, which student compositions for the school paper and oratorical contests attest. Through his public speaking, Gregory was able to confirm a pastoral relationship with the student body, and communicate the curse reversing, "men, not monks," labor's millennium vision of the University. As informed by his own Christian faith he motivated students into pious living and public service, bridging, along with his presidential peers, antebellum evangelical education with an emerging Protestant liberalism which was beginning to be expressed through the new and rising public universities.

What has yet to be discussed, though, is that, while these things were occurring at the I.I.U., the United States and Illinois were beginning to experience some demographic shifts which would impact the reception and effectiveness of the I.I.U.'s founding vision. In 1850, over eighty-four percent of Americans lived in rural areas, with almost fifty-five percent working in agriculture and forty-four percent living on farms.[13] Another scholar reports almost a third of Americans doing so in 1862, with a whopping eighty-five percent of Illinoisans residing on farms when the I.I.U. was founded in 1867.[14] But according to the 1890 census thirty-one Illinois counties lost population in the prior decade.[15] Most of these counties were in the top agricultural regions. Historian Robert Howard explains that, since increased mechanization enabled farm work to be accomplished with less manual labor, people went to cities and towns seeking employment. This industrialization and urbanization occurred most prominently in Chicago, which added almost six hundred thousand residents between 1890 and 1900. While over sixty-nine percent of Illinois' residents were considered "rural" in 1880, only fifty-five percent would be so by 1890, decreasing another ten percent by 1900, at which time Chicago accounted for a full third of Illinois' population.

13. Widder, *Michigan Agricultural College*, 3.
14. Moores, *Fields of Rich Toil*, vii, 13.
15. Howard, *Illinois: A History*, 392.

This emerging trend toward urbanization may help account for why, despite the curse-reversing vision painted by the I.I.U.'s energetic and vocal emphasis on agriculture's inevitable millennium, student participation in agricultural study was quite dismal. By 1879, only seventeen scholars were agriculture majors, down from a high water mark of seventy-nine in 1871.[16] While agriculture majors dropped from over twenty percent to only six percent of the student body when Regent Gregory left office, engineering majors held steady at about twenty percent per year. The new field of architecture continued to grow, and general literature and science course majors became the largest group, accounting for fully half the student body between 1874 and 1876.[17] Granted, it did not help that the I.I.U. was unable to maintain a competent, long-term agriculture professor until the arrival of George Morrow in 1876, almost a full decade after classes began.[18] Plus, the University had an ongoing public relations issue with rural residents, who, despite the motivational rhetoric of Turner, Gregory, Bateman, and the rest, simply could not justify paying tuition for students to travel to Champaign to study what they thought could be apprenticed at home. Consider, for example, this sarcastic quip from the Hillsboro *Journal*:

> They take the young men out in the spring of the year and compel them to sit on the fence with kid gloves in their hands, umbrellas over their heads and fifteen cent cigars in their mouths, and there watch the men who are employed to do the work ... This is hard on the young gentlemen but they learn to farm, you know, and that is what the institution is for.[19]

Meanwhile, while still an I.I.U. student, future architecture professor Nathan Ricker and classmate M. F. Hatch wrote an article for the school paper about "The Architect, Engineer, and Inventor's Calling," trumpeting God's new machine age which had surpassed "the age of arms, of poetry, [or] theology."[20] Since student interest in agriculture declined while engineering and architecture blossomed, it may be that the era's young adults saw more career potential in cities like Chicago than

16. Solberg, *University of Illinois*, 132–34.
17. DeMartini, "Student Protest," Table 16.
18. Moores, *Fields of Rich Toil*, 48–82.
19. Illinois Industrial University, *The Illini* IV, no. 5 (February 1875): 154.
20. Students of the Senior Class, *The Student (Illinois Industrial University)* 1, no. 2 (December 1871) 6.

on the sacred farms from which they came, as an engineering graduate was likely to earn more than four times the pay of an agriculture major.[21] Recognizing this possibility led I.I.U. researcher Joseph DeMartini to conclude that labor's millennium was a failed attempt "to socialize a people to values and norms unrelated to what these people saw as their real necessities."[22]

Illinois was not the only new agricultural and mechanical university to struggle. Prior to 1880 Penn State, for example, was not only unable to establish a successful agricultural program, they had no engineering course at all.[23] Cornell only had three agriculture students in 1874, Wisconsin graduated only one before 1880, and Minnesota had none until 1899.[24] At the I.I.U., it was not only the students who were beginning to question the efficacy of labor's millennium. In its Decennial year of 1877 the University faced financial shortages, prompting the trustees to consider reducing faculty salaries. Regent Gregory told them he would rather take a personal pay cut of twenty or twenty-five percent "rather than see the already too meager compensation of his associates lessened."[25] The trustees did just that, initially docking his pay "as he requests" by four hundred dollars, and then cutting the Regent's and full Professors' salaries by ten percent.[26] Granted, the concept of sacrificial service among Baptist ministers—even to the point of damaging one's health—was a common enough theme in the nineteenth century. Gregory had told the trustees earlier that year that the quarter's end

> closes the fifth biennial term of my service as regent of the University. Amidst my many difficulties, and with such light and strength as God has given me, I have tried to do my duty. I leave to posterity to judge of the wisdom of my administration of the affairs of the University. Removed, at an important juncture, from my seat in the board, I have owed to the courtesy of the trustees, the opportunities to mingle still in your counsels and to aid in shaping the policy of the institution. I hoped a year ago to be released from my labors, but yielded to the judgment of others in consenting to fill out my term of service. I find the

21. Moores, *Fields of Rich Toil*, 59.
22. DeMartini, "Student Protest," 138.
23. Bezilla, *Penn State*, 1–24.
24. Moores, *Fields of Rich Toil*, 56–57.
25. Board of Trustees, *Ninth Report*, 23.
26. Ibid., 46.

> desire for rest still haunting my mind, and while I do not absolutely decline a re-election, I do not ask it, and shall rejoice if another is chosen to the place. For the courtesy and confidence thus far extended to me, my thanks are herewith paid.[27]

Weary and seeking rest, after offering his resignation, he was elected unanimously to another two-year term.[28] He accepted, but in the following year attempted to remove the word "Industrial" from the University's name.[29] Some of his own children were enrolled in the general studies curriculum at the I.I.U., with its more classical course, and graduates and probably others among his constituency were pressuring him to expand the University's image beyond that of only an agriculture school. In 1879 he told the student paper, "I do not look for the millennium of colleges more than for the millennium of Christianity."[30] After he left office the following year, the alumni continued to lobby the trustees to appeal to the State Legislature, and they did. The name was officially changed to "The University of Illinois" on June 10, 1885.[31]

Despite the alumni's reserved embrace of the I.I.U.'s millennialistic rural vision, one wonders if there was a bit of regret. When alumnus J. N. Matthews read his poem "Nancy Jane, it Hain't no Use" for an 1874 alumni meeting, it so captivated the community that they printed it in the school paper the following autumn. The poem, told in the voice of a hardscrabble Illinois pioneer, expresses displeasure at cultural trends among the young. "This age is bound to bust itself," says the narrator, "by runnin' things too high . . . In makin' sport of holy things," he laments, "there seems to be no lack . . . " Sadly, he says to Nancy Jane, who is presumably his wife,

> The times hain't what they used to was, when you and I were young,
> When people prized their honesty as highly as their tongue;
> When everybody thought it right to give a man his due,
> And stick the stopper in the valve, if slime was flowin' through.
> We loved the Lord in them old days, and prayed our level best,
> And, like the balm of Gilead, it brought our spirits rest.
> We didn't kneel in prayin' gowns, and mix our prayers with gold,

27. Ibid., 25.
28. Ibid., 30.
29. Ibid., 107–8.
30. Ebert, *Illini Century*, 17.
31. Solberg, *University of Illinois*, 226–27.

But gave our humble hearts to God, as christians [sic] did of old.
We didn't hear of "sal'ry grabs" and "stealin' contracts" then,
For the land was ruled by patriots, and they were honest men,
What wouldn't trample honor down, and sell their souls for gain;
They wore their homespun trowsers, and we loved 'em, Nancy Jane . . .
It's jes' disgustin' I declare, to see how things is goin',
And where at last it will end, there hain't no means of knowin',
But if the Lord dont [sic] interfere, and check 'em pretty soon,
They'll go an octave higher still and strike a faster tune . . .[32]

One can imagine the mocking laughter coming from the mouths of the ambitious and upwardly-mobile alumni and students as they listened to this satire of the silly folkways they had hoped to shed by obtaining a university education. But, behind the sarcasm, perhaps a latent fear of learning, high culture, and urbanization lurked in the hearts of the prairie farmers' newly educated daughters and sons.

Much has changed, of course, since those days. Over the fourteen decades since its founding, the University of Illinois at Urbana-Champaign has evolved into the sort of large, public research university so typical in the United States. John Gregory had requested to be buried on the I.I.U. campus, a desire which was ultimately granted after his death on October 19, 1898.[33] At his Memorial Convocation, Judge Charles G. Neely, class of 1880, predicted that "Many feet in the years to come will make pilgrimages here to lay softly on the grassy mound that holds [Regent Gregory's] dust."[34] In reality, though, while thousands of feet do walk by the gravesite each day, very few stop. Even though a quotation attributed to J. B. Turner—"Industrial education prepares the way for a millennium of labor"—is engraved on a prominent building nearby, and a University lecture hall and scholarship are named for him, few in Urbana-Champaign are aware of the school's formative theological vision, or even know who he and Gregory are.[35] In 1852 Turner was a household name among agriculturalists, when Philadelphia's influential *North American* predicted that if his educational dream were realized it "cannot be doubted that with the advance of agricultural science we

32. Illinois Industrial University, *The Illini* IV, no. 1 (October 1874) 4–5.
33. University of Illinois, *Memorial Convocation*, 3, 8, 30.
34. Ibid., 26.
35. Turner's quotation is on Mumford Hall, formerly the Agriculture Building, which now houses the Department of Anthropology and faces the main quadrangle lawn in the center of the campus.

should witness an almost *incredible increase of production*."³⁶ On this point, the author, Turner, and their colleagues proved to be prophetic, as labor's millennium has in fact borne much fruit. In 1860 the average U.S. farmer produced enough food to feed about five people.³⁷ The gains made by the I.I.U. and other agricultural colleges and universities allowed producers to slowly increase the productivity of their land. U.S. agricultural research has continued to enhance growth, especially after the 1940s, when an average of one and eight tenths tons of maize was grown per hectare.³⁸ By 1970 an American farmer was feeding about sixty people—twelve times more than just over a century ago—and had increased the average yield to about eight and two tenths tons per hectare by 1992.³⁹

Despite, as Borlaug and others contend, the good that has come to the world through modern agricultural practices, though, some have questioned the social consequences wrought by what Turner called labor's millennium. Eugene V. Debs, for example, complained as early as 1900 that "the great bonanza farm is driving the small farmer to bankruptcy and ruin."⁴⁰ In 1960 Kermit Eby lamented the inability of young Hoosiers to make a living by farming, noting the period's negative economic fallout on unskilled labor as a whole.⁴¹ In 1978, the United Presbyterian Church in the USA convened a conference at Iowa State University which consisted of campus pastors and professors from ten land-grant universities.⁴² Although affirming a Turneresque and Borlaugian faith in modern agriculture's ongoing ability and duty to efficiently and inexpensively feed the world's poor, some expressed concern about the increasing environmental impact of fertilizers, herbicides, pesticides, and soil depletion caused by non-rotated crops.⁴³ Large

36. Turner, *Industrial Universities*, 49.
37. Edmond, *Magnificent Charter*, 150.
38. Dil, *Norman Borlaug*, 469.
39. Ibid., 469; Edmond, *Magnificent Charter*, 150.
40. Buckingham, *Expectations for the Millennium*, xi.
41. Eby, "Technology and Man," 46–52. A "Hoosier" is a citizen of Indiana, Illinois' neighboring state.
42. Conner and Hessel, *Agricultural Mission*.
43. Sandra Steingraber claims that agricultural and industrial pollution in Illinois has hurt its citizens' health; see her *Living Downstream*. For a brief history of activism against environmental pollution in the United States, see Epstein, "Grassroots Environmental Activism," in Conway, Keniston, and Marx, *Earth, Air, Fire, Water*.

scale farming technologies, they said, were causing the dissolution of communities and jobs, harming the quality of life of traditional farm families. As these views began to be increasingly accepted by the wider public, dozens of rock and country bands converged on the University of Illinois football field on Sunday, September 22, 1985, for the inaugural "Farm Aid" concert.[44] About seventy-eight thousand fans joined the musicians in a daylong lament over the indebtedness of farmers, the foreclosing of small farms, and a perceived loss of a wholesome, rural life enjoyed by their ancestors.[45] In 2005 a cultural critic mourned the erosion of "a world gone by," tracing U.S. agricultural market forces and concluding, in Jeffersonian fashion, that the failure of U.S. "agrarianism" has brought an "insidious cultural cost."[46] In 2009, only two percent of Americans operated farms, and forty-two percent of farmers in the Midwest earned $20,000 or less annually.[47] Contemporary "Green Christians," who contend that scientific agriculture's practices have hurt God's creation might emphasize the irony of a movement initiated by a group of pious millennialists bent on restoring Eden having instead produced "destroyers of the earth," people who—according to one possible reading of Revelation 11:18—are possibly worthy of destruction themselves.

Despite today's social realities, though, a stubborn, romantic longing for Illinois' pristine agricultural past remains in the popular consciousness of some of its downstate youths, as demonstrated by the April 21, 2000, *Daily Illini*'s two-page feature story, complete with color photographs, about a recent graduate who had taken over operations on his family's farm, telling the university paper "you don't know how good it feels to be home."[48] Although some Illinoisans today maintain a lingering desire for Eden's home on the prairie, the I.I.U.'s legacy may cause

---

44. Collins, "FarmAid Rolls On Despite Rain, Cold," *The Daily Illini*, September 23 1985, 1; Paaswell, "Performers Hope Attention on the Farmers is Profitable," *The Daily Illini*, Monday, September 23 1985, 3; Associated Press, "Group Will Grade Politicians on Efforts at Aid for Farmers," *The Daily Illini*, September 23 1985, 9.

45. For a study of an ongoing romanticism forged by the intersection of Jeffersonian idealism with "formal" and "informal" religiosity, see Brinkerhoff and Jacob, "Quasi-Religious Meaning," 63–80.

46. Hanson, "World Gone By," *Chicago Tribune*, March 11 2005, Section 1, 13.

47. Patrick J. Carr and Maria J. Kefalas, "The Rural Brain Drain," *The Chronicle Review*, September 25, 2009, B8.

48. Hendricks, "'Going Back to the Field,'" *The Daily Illini*, April 21 2000, 18–19.

one to conclude that, among John Gregory's constituents, either theory and reality were two separate things, or, over time, the University's children lost the expressed faith of their founders. Regardless, the hope of labor's millennium provided a compelling, unifying, public theological vision for the Illinois Industrial University, at least in its initial conception and first decade or so of operation.

Bibliography

Primary Sources

Associated Press. "Group Will Grade Politicians on Efforts at Aid for Farmers." *The Daily Illini*, September 23 1985.

Beverly, Robert. *History and Present State of Virginia [1705]*. Chapel Hill: University of North Carolina Press, 1947.

Board of Trustees of the Illinois Industrial University. *Seventh Annual Report of the Board of Trustees of the Illinois Industrial University*. Springfield: State Journal Printing Office, 1875.

———. *Ninth Report (Second Biennial) of the Board of Trustees of the Illinois Industrial University*. Springfield, IL: Weber & Co., 1878.

———. *Tenth Report of the Board of Trustees of the Illinois Industrial University*. Springfield, IL: H. W. Rokker, State Printer and Binder, 1881.

———. *Twelfth Report of the Board of Trustees of the Illinois Industrial University*. Springfield, IL: H. W. Rokker, State Printer and Binder, 1882.

———. *Thirteenth Report of the Board of Trustees of the Illinois Industrial University*. Springfield, IL: H. W. Rokker, State Printer and Binder, 1886.

———. *First Annual Report of the Board of Trustees of the Illinois Industrial University*. Springfield, Illinois: Baker, Bailhache & Co., 1868.

———. *Second Annual Report of the Board of Trustees of the Illinois Industrial University*. Springfield, Illinois: State Journal Printing Office, 1869.

———. *Third Annual Report of the Board of Trustees of the Illinois Industrial University*. Springfield, Illinois: State Journal Printing Office, 1870.

———. *Fourth Annual Report of the Board of Trustees of the Illinois Industrial University*. Springfield, Illinois: Illinois Journal Printing Office, 1872.

———. *Fifth Annual Report of the Board of Trustees of the Illinois Industrial University*. Springfield, Illinois: State Journal Steam Print, 1873.

———. *Sixth Annual Report of the Board of Trustees of the Illinois Industrial University*. Springfield, Illinois: State Journal Printing Office, 1874.

———. *Report of Committee on Courses of Study and Faculty for the Illinois Industrial University*. Springfield, Illinois: Baker, Bailhache & Co., Printers, 1867.

———. *Eighth Report of the Board of Trustees of the Illinois Industrial University*. Springfield: D. W. Lusk, State Printer and Binder, 1877.

Bollman, Lewis. *The Industrial Colleges: The Nature of the Education to be Given in Them; Their Several Kinds and Courses of Instruction Considered*. Washington, DC: U.S. Department of Agriculture, 10 December 1864.

Bullard, Samuel A. Papers. 41/20/20. Student Affairs Student Scrapbooks and Papers. University of Illinois. Urbana, IL, 1873–81.

Central Committee. "Address of the Central Committee to the Citizens of Morgan County Relative to the Location of the Industrial University." In Burt E. Powell, *Semi-Centennial History of the University of Illinois, Volume I: The Movement for Industrial Education and the Establishment of the University, 1840–1870*, 565–78. Urbana, IL: University of Illinois, 1918.

Collins, Lisa. "Farm Aid Rolls On Despite Rain, Cold." *The Daily Illini*, September 23, 1985.

Crane, Jonathan Townley, D. D. *Popular Amusements*. Cincinnati: Hitchcock & Walden, 1869.

Curtiss, William G. *Scrapbook*. 41/20/2. Dean of Students' Scrapbooks. University of Illinois, Urbana, IL, 1878–82.

Davenport, Eugene. "Dedication Speech for Davenport Hall." Unpublished speech. University of Illinois Archives, Urbana, IL, 1901.

Ebert, Roger, editor. *An Illini Century: One Hundred Years of Campus Life*. Urbana, IL: University of Illinois Press, 1967.

Eby, Kermit. "Technology and Man." *Religion in Life* 30 (Winter 1960–61) 46–52.

Allene Gregory, *John Milton Gregory: A Biography*. Chicago: Covici-McGee, 1923.

Gregory, Dr. J. M. "Labor." *The Illini* 4/2 (November 1874) 33–36.

Gregory, John M. "Dr. Nott." *The Michigan Teacher* 1 (May 1866) 155–62.

Gregory, John Milton. "Address to Young Ladies." John Milton Gregory Papers, 1839–1898. Series No. 2/1/1, Box 3. University of Illinois Archives, Urbana, IL, 1873, 22 November.

———. "The Sunday School." Unpublished manuscript. (2/1/1). University Archives, Urbana, IL, c. 1860.

———. Letter. Gregory papers. University of Illinois Archives, Urbana, IL, 1844.

———. "Michigan Christian Herald." Gregory papers. University of Illinois Archives, Urbana, IL, 1852.

———. "The Maine Law the Greatest Want of the State." Gregory papers. University of Illinois Archives, Urbana, IL, 1852.

———. "Christian Union I." *Michigan Christian Herald* 12 (April 1853) 2.

———. "Christian Union III." *Michigan Christian Herald* 12 (May 1853) 1.

———. "Christian Union IV." *Michigan Christian Herald* 12 (June 1853) 1.

———. "Christian Union V." *Michigan Christian Herald* 12 (June 1853) 1.

———. "The Detroit Democrat." Gregory papers. University of Illinois Archives, Urbana, IL, 1853.

———. "Christian Union VI." *Michigan Christian Herald* 12 (July 1853) 1.

———. *The Right and Duty of Christianity to Educate*. Kalamazoo, MI: Walden, Ames & Co., Printers, Herald Office, 1865.

———. Sermon on Matthew 22 [sic], "What Think ye of Christ?" John M. Gregory Papers, 1839–1898. Series No. 2/1/1, Box 2. University of Illinois Archives, Urbana, IL, 1867–1871.

———. "Sermon on Philippians 2:9–10." John M. Gregory Papers, 1839–1898. Series No. 2/1/1, Box 2. University of Illinois Archives, Urbana, IL, 1867–1871.

———. "Sermon on Luke 12:32." John M. Gregory Papers, 1839–1898. Series No. 2/1/1, Box 2. University of Illinois Archives, Urbana, IL, 1867–1871.

———. "Sermon on Isaiah 40:30–31." John M. Gregory Papers, 1839–1898. Series No. 2/1/1, Box 2. University of Illinois Archives, Urbana, IL, 1867–1871.

———. "Sermon on Matthew 13:45–46." John M. Gregory Papers, 1839–1898. Series No. 2/1/1, Box 2. University of Illinois Archives, Urbana, IL,1867–1871.

———. "Sermon on Matthew 6:10." John M. Gregory Papers, 1839–1898. Series No. 2/1/1, Box 2. University of Illinois Archives, Urbana, IL,1867–1871.

———. "Sermon on Malachi 11:16–19." John M. Gregory Papers, 1839–1898. Series No. 2/1/1, Box 2. University of Illinois Archives, Urbana, IL, 1867–1871.

———. "Sermon on 1 Peter 4:18." John M. Gregory Papers, 1839–1898. Series No. 2/1/1, Box 2. University of Illinois Archives, Urbana, IL, 1867–1871.

———. "Sermon on Song of Solomon 5:9." John M. Gregory Papers, 1839–1898. Series No. 2/1/1, Box 2. University of Illinois Archives, Urbana, IL, 1867–1871.

———. "Sermon on Luke 2:14." John M. Gregory Papers, 1839–1898. Series No. 2/1/1, Box 2. University of Illinois Archives, Urbana, IL, 1867–1871.

———. Sermon on Luke 2: 10–11. John M. Gregory Papers, 1839–1898. Series No. 2/1/1, Box 2. University of Illinois Archives, Urbana, IL, 1867–1871.

———. "Sermon on Zechariah 4:6." John M. Gregory Papers, 1839–1898. Series No. 2/1/1, Box 2. University of Illinois Archives, Urbana, IL, 1867–1871.

———. "Sermon on Song of Solomon 2:11–12." John M. Gregory Papers, 1839–1898. Series No. 2/1/1, Box 2. University of Illinois Archives, Urbana, IL, 1867–1871.

———. "Sermon on Matthew 11:28." John M. Gregory Papers, 1839–1898. Series No. 2/1/1, Box 2. University of Illinois Archives, Urbana, IL, 1867–1871.

———. "God Is Love"—sermon on 1 John 4. John M. Gregory Papers, 1839–1898. Series No. 2/1/1, Box 2. University of Illinois Archives, Urbana, IL, 1867–1871.

———. "Sermon on Romans 8:38–39." John M. Gregory Papers, 1839–1898. Series No. 2/1/1, Box 2. University of Illinois Archives, Urbana, IL, 1867–1871.

———. "Agricultural Education in France." President John M. Gregory Scrapbooks, 1849–1898. Series No. 2/1/2, Box No. 1, Volume C-2. University of Illinois Archives, Urbana, IL, 1869.

———. "Agricultural Education in Germany." President John M. Gregory Scrapbooks, 1849–1898. Series No. 2/1/2, Box No. 1, Volume C-2. University of Illinois Archives, Urbana, IL, 1869.

———. "Lectures to Young Men." Lecture 1. John M. Gregory Papers, 1839–1898. Series No. 2/1/1, Box 2. University of Illinois Archives, Urbana, IL, 1870.

———. "Untitled Document." John Milton Gregory Papers, 1839–1898. Series No. 2/1/1, Box 2, 1870 folder.University of Illinois Archives, Urbana, IL,

———. "Baccalaureate Sermon, University Chapel." John M. Gregory Papers, 1839–1898. Series No. 2/1/1, Box 2. University of Illinois Archives, Urbana, IL, 1870.

———. "Baccalaureate Address, University Chapel." John M. Gregory Papers, 1839–1898. Series No. 2/1/1, Box 2. University of Illinois Archives, Urbana, IL, 1871.

———. "The Christian Elements of Character, Lecture 4—'Love of God.'" John M. Gregory Papers, 1839–1898. Series No. 2/1/1, Box 3. University of Illinois Archives, Urbana, IL, 1872.

———. "Lecture, Sunday Sep. 22." John M. Gregory Papers, 1839–1898. Series No. 2/1/1, Box 3. University of Illinois Archives, Urbana, IL, 1872.

———. "'Providence,' a Sermon on Romans 8: 'If God be for Us Who Can be Against Us?'" John M. Gregory Papers, 1839–1898. Series No. 2/1/1, Box 3. University of Illinois Archives, Urbana, IL, 1872.

———. "Sermon on 1 Corinthians 13:13." John M. Gregory Papers, 1839–1898. Series No. 2/1/1, Box 3. University of Illinois Archives, Urbana, IL, 1872.

———. "'Trust in the Lord and Do Good'—Baccalaureate Sermon from Psalm 3." John M. Gregory Papers, 1839–1898. Series No. 2/1/1, Box 3. University of Illinois Archives, 1872.

———. Untitled Document, John Milton Gregory Papers, 1839–1898. Series No. 2/1/1, Box 3, 1872 folder, University of Illinois Archives, Urbana, IL.

———. "Lessons of the Springtime." Chapel Lecture, John M. Gregory Papers, 1839–1898. Series No. 2/1/1, Box 3. University of Illinois Archives, Urbana, IL, 1872.

———. "'Religion of the Future'—a Sermon for the Chicago Theological Union." John M. Gregory Papers, 1839–1898. Series No. 2/1/1, Box 3. University of Illinois Archives, 1872.

———. "The Christian Elements of Character." Chapel Sermon. (2/1/1). University Archives, Urbana, IL, 1872.

———. "London Preachers and Churches." President John M. Gregory Scrapbooks, 1849–1898. Series No. 2/1/2, Box No. 1, Volume C-2. University of Illinois Archives, Urbana, IL, 1873.

———. "Baccalaureate Sermon on Luke 18:8—'Nevertheless When the Son of Man Cometh Shall He Find Faith on the Earth.'" John M. Gregory Papers, 1839–1898. Series No. 2/1/1, Box 3. University of Illinois Archives, Urbana, IL, 1874.

———. "'Chapel Talks, Autumn Term 1875,'—Introduction." John M. Gregory Papers, 1839–1898. Series No. 2/1/1, Box 3. University of Illinois Archives, Urbana, IL, 1875.

———. "Untitled document" John Milton Gregory Papers, 1839–1898. Series No. 2/1/1, Box 3, folder. University of Illinois Archives, Urbana, IL, 1875,

———. "'Was Jesus of Nazareth More Than a Mere Man?'" John M. Gregory Papers, 1839–1898. Series No. 2/1/1, Box 3. University of Illinois Archives, Urbana, IL, 1875.

———. "'Christianity and Civilization'—Address Before Alumni of the Baptist Theological Seminary, Chicago." John M. Gregory Papers, 1839–1898. Series No. 2/1/1, Box 3. University of Illinois Archives, Urbana, IL, 1875.

———. "Baccalaureate Sermon on 1 Corinthians 13." John M. Gregory Papers, 1839–1898. Series No. 2/1/1, Box 3. University of Illinois Archives, Urbana, IL, 1875.

———. "'Is There a God?'" John M. Gregory Papers, 1839–1898. Series No. 2/1/1, Box 3. University of Illinois Archives, Urbana, IL, 1875.

———. "'Is the Bible of Divine Authority?,'" John M. Gregory Papers, 1839–1898. Series No. 2/1/1, Box 3. University of Illinois Archives, Urbana, IL, 1875.

———. "Women Manuscripts c. 1875." John M. Gregory Papers, 1839–1898, Series No. 2/1/1, Box 3, folder. University of Illinois Archives, Urbana, IL, 1875.

———. "Baccalaureate Address on Matthew 6:33." John M. Gregory Papers, 1839–1898. Series No. 2/1/1, Box 3. University of Illinois Archives, Urbana, IL, 1876.

———. "Chapel Sermon: 'Duty & Destiny,'" John M. Gregory Papers, 1839–1898. Series No. 2/1/1, Box 3. University of Illinois Archives, Urbana, IL, 1877.

———. "Baccalaureate Address—'God and the Soul of Man'—'Our Father.'" John M. Gregory Papers, 1839–1898. Series No. 2/1/1, Box 3. University of Illinois Archives, Urbana, IL, 1878.

———. "Religious News and Notes." President John M. Gregory Scrapbooks, 1849–1898. Series No. 2/1/2, Box No. 1, Volume C-2. University of Illinois Archives, Urbana, IL, 1880.

———. "Christ the Answer to Doubt." President John M. Gregory Scrapbooks, 1849–1898. Series No. 2/1/2, Box No. 1, Volume C-2. University of Illinois Archives, Urbana, IL, 1881.

———. *The Seven Laws of Teaching*. Grand Rapids: Baker, 1995.

———. "From Nashville." President John M. Gregory Scrapbooks, 1849–1898. Series No. 2/1/2, Box No. 1, Volume C-2. University of Illinois Archives, Urbana, IL.

———. "Industrial Education—Its Grades and Its Schools." President John M. Gregory Scrapbooks, 1849–1898. Series No. 2/1/2, Box No. 1, Volume C-2. University of Illinois Archives, Urbana, IL.

———. "Jesus and Gautama." President John M. Gregory Scrapbooks, 1849–1898. Series No. 2/1/2, Box No. 1, Volume C-2. University of Illinois Archives, Urbana, IL.

———. "The Loss of Faith." President John M. Gregory Scrapbooks, 1849–1898. Series No. 2/1/2, Box No. 1, Volume C-2. University of Illinois Archives, Urbana, IL.

Hanson, Victor Davis. "A World Gone By." *Chicago Tribune*, March 11 2005, Section 1, 13.

Hendricks, Darcy. "'Going Back to the Field.'" *The Daily Illini*, April 21 2000.

"History of the Champaign 'Elephant,' by One of the 'Ring.'" *Chicago Times*. In Burt E. Powell, *Semi-Centennial History of the University of Illinois*. Volume 1, *The Movement for Industrial Education and the Establishment of the University, 1840–1870*, 365–426. Urbana, IL: The University of Illinois, 1918.

Hovey, Alvah, and John Milton Gregory. *The Bible and How to Teach It*. Philadelphia: American Baptist Publication Society, n.d.

Illinois General Assembly. "An Act to Provide for the Organization and Maintenance of the Illinois Industrial University." In Burt E. Powell, *Semi-Centennial History of the University of Illinois*. Volume 1, *The Movement for Industrial Education and the Establishment of the University, 1840–1870*, 590–98. Urbana, IL: University of Illinois, 1918.

Illinois Industrial University. *Circular and Catalogue of the Officers and Students of the Illinois Industrial University, Urbana, Champaign County*. Chicago: Church, Goodman, and Donnelley, Printers, 1868.

———. *Third Annual Circular of the Illinois Industrial University, Urbana, Champaign County, Ills*. Champaign, IL: Unknown, 1869–1870.

———. *Catalogue and Circular of the Illinois Industrial University*. Chicago: Church, Goodman, and Donnelley, Printers, 1870–1871.

———. *Fourth Annual Circular of the Illinois Industrial University, Urbana, Champaign County, Ills*. Champaign, IL: unknown publisher, 1870–1871.

———. *Catalogue of the Illinois Industrial University*. Champaign, IL: Illinois Industrial University, 1871.

———. *Catalogue and Circular. Illinois Industrial University. Champaign, Illinois*. Champaign, IL: Illini Steam Print, 1872–1873.

———. *Illinois Industrial University. Catalogue and Circular. Urbana, Champaign County, Illinois*. Champaign, IL: Unknown, 1873.
———. *The Illini* 3/1 (January 1874) 1–28.
———. *The Illini* 3/2 (February 1874) 29–56.
———. *The Illini* 3/3 (March 1874) 57–84.
———. *The Illini* 3/4 (April 1874) 85–112.
———. *The Illini* 3/5 (May 1874) 113–41.
———. *The Illini* 3/6 (June 1874) 141–72.
———. *The Illini* 4/1 (October 1874) 1–26.
———. *The Illini* 4/2 (November 1874) 33–58.
———. *The Illini* 4/3 (December 1874) 65–96.
———. *Catalogue and Circular. Illinois Industrial University. Champaign, Illinois*. Champaign, IL: Illini Steam Print, 1875–1876.
———. *The Illini* 4/5 (February 1875) 129–61.
———. *The Illini* 5/3 (December 1875) 63–91.
———. *The Illini* 5/8 (May 1876) 200–227.
———. *The Illini* 7/1 (October 1877) 3–40.
———. *The Illini* 7/3 (December 1877) 83–120.
———. *Catalogue and Circular of the Illinois Industrial University, Urbana, Champaign County, Illinois*. Champaign, IL: George Scroggs, Printer, 1878.
———. *The Illini* 7/4 (January 1878) 121–58.
———. *The Illini* 7/5 (February 1878) 159–200.
———. *The Illini* 7/6 (March 1878) 201–38.
———. *The Illini* 7/7 (April 1878) 239–80.
———. *The Illini* 8/4 (January 1879) 98–128.
———. *The Illini* 8/7 (April 1879) 194–223.
———. *The Illini* 8/8 (May 1879) 224–54.
———. *The Illini* 9/1 (October 1879) 1–30.
———. *The Illini* 10/1 (October 1880).
———. *The Illini* 10/3 (December 1880).
Illinois Industrial University Faculty. "Faculty Record." University of Illinois Archives. Urbana, IL, 1868–1901.
Matthews, James N. Papers. 41/20/26. Student Affairs Student Scrapbooks and Papers. University of Illinois Archives. Urbana, IL, 1868–72.
Morrill, Justin S. *Speech of Hon. Justin S. Morrill of Vermont on the Bill Granting Lands for Agricultural Colleges; Delivered in the House of Representatives, April 20, 1858*. Washington, D.C.: Congressional Globe Office, 1858.
Myron C. Parsons, Ira Y. Munn, Thos. W. Baxter. "A Petition to the General Assembly of the State of Illinois." In Burt E. Powell, *Semi-Centennial History of the University of Illinois*, Volume 1, *The Movement for Industrial Education and the Establishment of the University, 1840–1870*, 599–615. University of Illinois, 1918.
Paaswell, George. "Performers Hope Attention on the Farmers is Profitable." *The Daily Illini*, September 23 1985, 3.
Periam, Jonathan. *The Groundswell. A History of the Origin, Aims, and Progress of the Farmers' Movement*. St. Louis: N. D. Thompson & Co., 1874.
Ricker, Nathan C. "The Story of a Life," Nathan C. Ricker Papers, 1875–1925. University of Illinois Archives, Urbana, IL.

Students of the Senior Class. *The Student (Illinois Industrial University)* 1/3 (January 1872) 9–13.
———. *The Student (Illinois Industrial University)* 1/11 (September 1872) 40–49.
———. *The Student (Illinois Industrial University)* 1/12 (September 1872) 70–79.
———. *The Student (Illinois Industrial University)* 2/1 (January 1873) 1–12.
———. *The Student (Illinois Industrial University)* 2/2 (February 1873) 13–24.
———. *The Student (Illinois Industrial University)* 2/4 (April 1873) 37–48.
———. *The Student (Illinois Industrial University)* 2/5 (May 1873) 49–60.
———. *The Student (Illinois Industrial University)* 2/6 (June 1873) 61–73.
———. *The Student (Illinois Industrial University)* 2/7 (July 1873) 74–84.
———. *The Student (Illinois Industrial University)* 2/8 (August 1873) 85–96.
———. *The Student (Illinois Industrial University)* 2/9 (September 1873) 97–108.
———. *The Student (Illinois Industrial University)* 2/11 (November 1873) 121–32.
———. *The Student (Illinois Industrial University)* 2/12 (December 1873) 133–36.
Students of the Senior Class, editors. "'Student's Organizations.'" *The Student (Illinois Industrial University)* 1/1 (November 1871) 1–4.
———. *The Student (Illinois Industrial University)* 1/2 (December 1871) 4–8.
Talbot, Arthur N. Diary. 11/5/29. Civil Engineering. University of Illinois. Urbana, IL, 1878.
Talmage, T. DeWitt. *The Battle for Bread. A Series of Sermons Relating to Labor and Capital.* New York: Ogilvie, 1886.
Turner, Jonathan Baldwin. "The Millenium of Labor." *Transactions of the Illinois State Agricultural Society* 1 (1855) 55–61. Springfield, IL.
———. *Industrial Universities for the People.* 2nd ed. Chicago: Robert Fergus, Printer, 1854.
———. *A Plan for an Industrial University for the State of Illinois, Submitted to the Farmers' Convention at Granville, Held Novemeber 18, 1851.* n.p. 1851.
———. "Report of Committee on Location of Industrial University." In *Semi-Centennial History of the University of Illinois, Volume I: The Movement for Industrial Education and the Establishment of the University, 1840–1870*, 365–426. Urbana, IL: The University of Illinois, 1918.
University of Illinois. *Memorial Convocation for John Milton Gregory, LL.D.* Urbana: University of Illinois, 1898.
Unknown. "Decennial Anniversary of the Illinois Industrial University." Program. Publications Scrapbook. Series 2/1/11. University of Illinois Archives, 1877.
———. Illinois Industrial University Seal, found in RS: 26/20/8, Box 1, Folder James O. Pearman Diplomas and Certificates 1878, 1881, 1885, 1938, University of Illinois Archives.

Secondary Sources

Ahlstrom, Sydney E. "The Scottish Philosophy and American Theology." *Church History* 24 (1955) 257–72.
———. *A Religious History of the American People.* New Haven: Yale University Press, 1972.
Albanese, Catherine L. *America, Religions and Religion.* 3rd ed. Belmont, CA: Wadsworth, 1992.

Bibliography

Allen, Henry E. *Religion in the State University: An Initial Exploration*. Minneapolis: Burgess, 1950.

Andreasen, Bryon C. "Proscribed Preachers, New Churches: Civil Wars in the Illinois Protestant Churches During the Civil War." *Civil War History* 44 (1998) 194–212.

Appleby, Joyce Oldham. *Thomas Jefferson*. New York: Times Books, 2003.

Artigas, Mariano, and Thomas F. Glick. *Negotiating Darwin: The Vatican Confronts Evolution, 1877–1902*. Medicine, Science, and Religion in Historical Context. Baltimore: Johns Hopkins University Press, 2006.

Barbour, John D. *Versions of Deconversion: Autobiography and the Loss of Faith*. Charlottesville: University Press of Virginia, 1994.

Bardolph, Richard. *Agricultural Literature and the Early Illinois Farmer*. Urbana: University of Illinois Press, 1948.

———. "Illinois Agriculture in Transition, 1820–1870." *Illinois State Historical Society Journal* 41 (1948) 244–64.

Beardsley, Henry M. "Dr. Gregory and the Students at Illinois." *Illinois Alumni Quarterly* 8 (1914) 162–65.

Behle, James Gregory. "Scholars from the Sod: The Social Origins and Backgrounds of Students at the University of Illinois, 1868–1894." PhD diss., University of Southern California, 1996.

Behle, J. Gregory. "Educating 'The Lord's Redeemed and Anointed': The University of Illinois Chapel Experience, 1868–1894." *The Master's Seminary Journal* 11 (2000) 53–73.

Behle, J. Gregory, and William E. Maxwell. "The Social Origins of Students at the Illinois Industrial University, 1868–1894." *History of Higher Education Annual* 18 (1998) 93–109.

Bellah, Robert. "The Triumph of Secularism." *Religion and Intellectual Life* 1 (1984) 13–26.

Bendroth, Margaret L. *Fundamentalism & Gender, 1875 to the Present*. New Haven: Yale University Press, 1993.

Bernstein, Richard B. *Thomas Jefferson*. New York: Oxford University Press, 2003.

Bezilla, Michael. *Penn State: An Illustrated History*. University Park: Pennsylvania State University Press, 1985.

Bidwell, Percy W., and J. I. Falconer. *History of Agriculture in the Northern United States, 1620–1860*. Washington, D.C.: Carnegie Institution of Washington, 1925.

Bissett, Jim. *Agrarian Socialism in America: Marx, Jefferson, and Jesus in the Oklahoma Countryside, 1904–1920*. Norman, OK: University of Oklahoma Press, 1999.

Bledstein, Burton J. *The Culture of Professionalism: The Middle Class and the Development of Higher Education in America*. New York: Norton, 1976.

Blight, David W. "The Civil War in History and Memory." *The Chronicle of Higher Education*, 12 July 2002, B7.

Bloch, Ruth H. *Gender and Morality in Anglo-American Culture, 1650–1800*. Berkeley: University of California Press, 2003.

Brinkerhoff, Merlin B., and Jeffrey C. Jacob. "Quasi-Religious Meaning Systems, Official Religion, and Quality of Life in an Alternative Lifestyle; A Survey from the Back-to-the-Land Movement." *Journal for the Scientific Study of Religion* 26 (1987) 63–80.

Brown, Candy Gunther. *The Word in the World: Evangelical Writing, Publishing, and Reading in America, 1789–1880.* Chapel Hill, NC: The University of North Carolina Press, 2004.

Brown, Donald R. "The Educational Contributions of J. B. Turner." Master's thesis, University of Illinois, 1954.

Brubacher, John S., and Willis Rudy. *Higher Education in Transition: A History of American Colleges and Universities.* 4th ed. Foundations of Higher Education. New Brunswick, CT: Transaction, 1997.

Bruce, Steve, editor. *Religion and Modernization: Sociologists and Historians Debate the Secularization Thesis.* New York: Oxford University Press, 1992.

Buckingham, Peter W. *Expectations for the Millennium: American Socialist Visions of the Future.* Contributions in American History 192. Westport, CT: Greenwood, 2002.

Buhle, Paul. *Marxism in the United States: Remapping the History of the American Left.* London: Verso, 1987.

Burtchaell, James Tunstead. *The Dying of the Light: The Disengagement of Colleges and Universities from Their Christian Churches.* Grand Rapids: Eerdmans, 1998.

Butterworth, G. W. *Clement of Alexandria.* Loeb Classical Library 92. Cambridge: Harvard University Press, 1999.

Carnes, Mark C. *Secret Ritual and Manhood in Victorian America.* New Haven: Yale University Press, 1989.

Carr, Patrick J., and Maria J. Kefalas, "The Rural Brain Drain," *The Chronicle Review* (September 25, 2009) B7–B9.

Carriel, Mary Turner. *The Life of Jonathan Baldwin Turner.* Urbana: University of Illinois Press, 1961.

Cayton, Andrew R. L., and Gray, Susan E. *The American Midwest: Essays on Regional History.* Midwestern History and Culture. Bloomington: Indiana University Press, 2001.

Chaney, Charles. "Diversity: A Study in Illinois Baptist History to 1907." *Foundations* 7 (1964) 41–54.

Cherry, Conrad. *Hurrying toward Zion: Universities, Divinity Schools, and American Protestantism.* Bloomington: Indiana University Press, 1995.

Collins, Gail. *America's Women: Four Hundred Years of Dolls, Drudges, Helpmates, and Heroines.* New York, NY: HarperCollins, 2003.

Conner, John T., convenor, and Dieter T. Hessel, editor. *The Agricultural Mission of Churches and Land-Grant Universities.* Ames: Iowa State University Press, 1980.

Cope, Alexis. *History of the Ohio State University.* Volume 1, *1870–1910.* Edited by T. C. Mendenhall. Columbus: Ohio State University Press, 1920.

Cremin, Lawrence. *American Education: The Colonial Experience, 1607–1783.* New York: Harper & Row, 1970.

———. *American Education: The National Experience, 1783–1876.* New York: Harper & Row, 1980.

Curti, Merle, and Vernon Carstensen. *The University of Wisconsin: 1848–1925.* Madison: University of Wisconsin Press, 1949.

Danhof, Clarence H. *Changes in Agriculture in the Northern United States, 1820–1870.* Cambridge: Harvard University Press, 1969.

Davis, James Michael. "Frontier and Religious Influences on Higher Education, 1796–1860." PhD diss., Northern Illinois University, 1975.

Dayton, Donald W. *Discovering an Evangelical Heritage*. Peabody, MA: Hendrickson, 1988.

Delumeau, Jean. *History of Paradise: The Garden of Eden in Myth and Tradition*. Translated by Matthew O'Connell. Urbana: University of Illinois Press, 2000.

DeMartini, Joseph R. "Student Protest During Two Periods in the History of the University of Illinois: 1867–1894 and 1929–1942." PhD diss., University of Illinois, 1974.

Dil, Anwar. *Norman Borlaug on World Hunger*. San Diego: Bookservice International, 1997.

Dombrowski, James. *The Early Days of Christian Socialism in America*. New York: Octagon Books, 1966.

Dorrien, Gary J. *Reconstructing the Common Good: Theology and the Social Order*. Maryknoll, NY: Orbis, 1990.

———. *The Making of American Liberal Theology: Imagining Progressive Religion, 1805–1900*. Louisville: Westminster John Knox, 2001.

Eddy, Edward Danforth. *Colleges for Our Land and Time*. New York: Harper & Brothers, 1957.

Edmond, J. B. *The Magnificent Charter*. Hicksville, NY: Exposition, 1978.

Edwards, O. C. "The Preaching of Romanticism in America." *American Transcendental Quarterly* 14 (2000) 297–312.

Epstein, Barbara. "Grassroots Environmental Activism: The Toxics Movement and Directions for Social Change." In *Earth, Air, Fire, Water: Humanistic Studies of the Environment*, edited by Jil Ker Conway, Kenneth Keviston, and Leo Marx. Amherst: University of Massachusetts Press, 1999, 170–83.

Finney, Gail. *The Counterfeit Idyll: The Garden Ideal and Social Reality in Nineteenth-Century Fiction*. Studien zur deutschen Literatur 81. Tübingen: Niemeyer, 1984.

Fitzgerald, Peter H. "Democracy, Utility, and Two Land-Grant Colleges in the Nineteenth Century: The Rhetoric and the Reality of Reform." PhD diss., Stanford University, 1972.

Gaustad, Edwin S. *The Rise of Adventism: Religion and Society in Mid-Nineteenth-Century America*. New York: Harper and Row, 1974.

Geiger, Roger L. *The American College in the Nineteenth Century*. Vanderbilt Issues in Higher Education. Nashville: Vanderbilt University Press, 2000.

Girling, Katherine Peabody. *Selim Hobard Peabody: A Biography*. Urbana: University of Illinois Press, 1923.

Gordon, Lynn D. *Gender and Higher Education in the Progressive Era*. New Haven: Yale University Press, 1990.

Grant, C. David. *God the Center of Value: Value Theory in the Theology of H. Richard Niebuhr*. Fort Worth: Texas Christian University Press, 1984.

Grassley, Charles. "Public Policy and Feeding a Hungry World." Address at the conference of the Cooperative Baptist Fellowship "Celebration of a New Baptist Covenant." Atlanta, GA, January 30–February 1, 2008.

Gray, James. *The University of Minnesota: 1851–1951*. Minneapolis: University of Minnesota Press, 1951.

Green, the Rev. W. T. "The First Seventy-Five Years 1864–1939." Unpublished Booklet of the First Baptist Church of Champaign. Champaign, IL, 1939.

Gregory, Allene. *John Milton Gregory: A Biography*. Chicago, IL: Covici-McGee, 1923.

Guarnari, Carl J. "The Associationists: Forging a Christian Socialism in Antebellum America." *Church History* 52 (1983) 36–49.

Hancock, Judith Ann. "Jonathan Baldwin Turner (1805–1899) A Study of an Educational Reformer." PhD diss., University of Washington, 1971.

Harrison, Paul M. *Authority and Power in the Free Church Tradition: A Social Case Study of the American Baptist Convention*. Princeton: Princeton University Press, 1959.

Harrold, Philip E. *A Place Somewhat Apart: The Private Worlds of a Late Nineteenth-Century Public University*. Princeton Theological Monograph Series 63. Eugene, OR: Pickwick Publications, 2006.

Hart, D. G. "The Troubled Soul of the Academy: American Learning and the Problem of Religious Studies." *Religion and American Culture* 2 (1992) 49–77.

Hatch, Nathan O. *The Democratization of American Christianity*. New Haven: Yale University Press, 1989.

Hatch, Richard A. *An Early View of the Land-Grant Colleges*. Urbana: University of Illinois Press, 1967.

Hauerwas, Stanley, and John H. Westerhoff, editors. *Schooling Christians: "Holy Experiments" in American Education*. Grand Rapids: Eerdmans, 1992.

Hawkins, Hugh, editor. *The Emerging University and Industrial America*. Lexington, MA: Heath, 1970.

Herscher, Uri D. *Jewish Agricultural Utopias in America, 1880–1910*. Detroit: Wayne State University Press, 1981.

Hesser, Leon. *The Man Who Fed the World: Nobel Peace Prize Laureate Norman Borlaug and His Battle to End World Hunger*. Dallas: Durban, 2006.

Hoeveler, J. David. "The University and the Social Gospel: The Intellectual Origins of the 'Wisconsin Idea.'" *Wisconsin Magazine of History* 59 (1976) 282–98.

Hofstadter, Richard, and C. DeWitt Hardy. *The Development and Scope of Higher Education in the United States*. New York: Columbia University Press, 1952.

Hofstadter, Richard, and Walter P. Metzger. *The Development of Academic Freedom in the United States*. New York: Columbia University Press, 1955.

Hollinger, David A. "The 'Secularization' Question and the United States in the Twentieth Century." *Church History* 70 (2001) 132–43.

Horowitz, Helen Lefkowitz. *Campus Life: Undergraduate Cultures from the End of the Eighteenth Century to the Present*. Chicago: University of Chicago Press, 1988.

Howard, Robert P. *Illinois: A History of the Prairie State*. Grand Rapids, Eerdmans, 1972.

Howard, Thomas Albert. *Protestant Theology and the Making of the Modern German University*. Oxford: Oxford University Press, 2006.

Howden, William D. "'The Pulpit Leads the World': Preachers and Preaching in Nineteenth Century America." *American Transcendental Quarterly* 14 (2000) 169–72.

Inman, D. M. "Professor Jonathan Baldwin Turner and the Granville Convention." *Journal of the Illinois State Historical Society* 17 (1924) 144–50.

James, William. *The Varieties of Religious Experience*. New York: The Modern Library, 1929.

Johnson, Allen, and Dumas Malone, editors. *Dictionary of American Biography*. New York: Scribners, 1931.

Johnson, Daniel Thomas. "Puritan Power in Illinois Higher Education Prior to 1870." PhD diss., University of Wisconsin, 1974.

Johnson, Henry C. "'Down from the Mountain': Secularization and the Higher Learning in America." *The Review of Politics* 54 (1992) 551–88.

Johnson, Henry C. and Erwin V. Johanningmeier. *Teachers for the Prairie: The University of Illinois and the Schools, 1868–1945*. Urbana: University of Illinois Press, 1972.

Kaestle, Carl F. "Ideology and American Educational History." *History of Education Quarterly* 22 (1982) 123–37.

Kammen, Carol. *Cornell: Glorious to View*. Ithaca: Cornell University Library, 2003.

Kelsey, David H. *Between Athens and Berlin: The Theological Education Debate*. Grand Rapids: Eerdmans, 1993.

Kersey, Harry A., Jr. "John Milton Gregory as a Midwestern Educator: 1852–1880." PhD diss., University of Illinois, 1965.

———. *John Milton Gregory and the University of Illinois*. Urbana: University of Illinois Press, 1968.

Kiefer, Christie W. *The Mantle of Maturity: A History of Ideas about Character Development*. SUNY Series in Medical Anthropology. Albany: State University of New York Press, 1988.

Kilde, Jeanne Halgren. *When Church Became Theatre: The Transformation of Evangelical Architecture and Worship in Nineteenth Century America*. New York: Oxford University Press, 2002.

Kiler, Charles Albert. *On the Banks of the Boneyard*. Urbana: Illini Union Bookstore, 1942.

Kimmel, Michael. *Manhood in America: A Cultural History*. New York: Free Press, 1996.

Kuykendall, Dean W. "The Land-Grant College: A Study in Transition." PhD diss., Harvard University, 1946.

Ladd, Tony, and James A. Mathisen. *Muscular Christianity: Evangelical Protestants and the Development of American Sport*. Grand Rapids: Baker Books, 1999.

Leavelle, Tracy Neal. "'Bad Things' and 'Good Hearts': Mediation, Meaning, and the Language of Illinois Christianity." *Church History* 76 (2007) 363–94.

Leslie, W. Bruce. *Gentlemen and Scholars: College and Community in the "Age of the University," 1865–1917*. University Park: Pennsylvania State University Press, 1992.

Longfield, Bradley J. "From Evangelicalism to Liberalism: Public Midwestern Universities in Nineteenth-Century America." In *The Secularization of the Academy*, edited by George Marsden and Bradley J. Longfield, 46–73. Religion in America Series. New York: Oxford University Press, 1992.

Madden, Etta M., and Martha L. Finch. *Eating in Eden: Food and American Utopias*. Lincoln: University of Nebraska Press, 2006.

Mandelker, Ira L. *Religion, Society, and Utopia in Nineteenth-Century America*. Amherst: University of Massachusetts Press, 1984.

Mansfield, Harvey C. *Manliness*. New Haven: Yale University Press, 2006.

Marsden, George M. *Fundamentalism and American Culture*. New York: Oxford University Press, 1980.

———. *The Soul of the American University: From Protestant Establishment to Established Nonbelief*. New York: Oxford University Press, 1994.

———. *The Outrageous Idea of Christian Scholarship*. New York: Oxford University Press, 1997.
Marsden, George M., and Bradley J. Longfield. *The Secularization of the Academy*. New York: Oxford University Press, 1992.
Martin, Hugh. *Christian Social Reformers of the Nineteenth Century by James Adderley*. London: Student Christian Movement, 1927.
Marty, Martin E. "The Inner History." *Christian Century* 116/23 (1999) 831.
Marx, Leo. *The Machine in the Garden: Technology and the Pastoral Ideal in America*. Galaxy Book 179. New York: Oxford University Press, 1970.
McCauley, Lena M. "Taft Completes on Alma Mater Group." *Chicago Post*, 6 June 1922.
McClay, Wilfred M. "Thoughts on 'That Embarrassing Dream.'" *Fides et Historia* 39 (2007) 71.
McClendon, James William. *Biography as Theology: How Life Stories Can Remake Today's Theology*. New edition. Philadelphia: Trinity, 1990.
———. *Systematic Theology*. Vol. 3, *Witness*. Nashville: Abingdon, 2000.
McCollum, Dannel. "ETC." *The Champaign-Urbana News Gazette*, 5 May 2000.
Merrill, George D. "Land and Education: The Origin and History of Land-Grants for the Support of Education." PhD diss., University of Southern California, 1964.
Miller, Perry. *The Life of the Mind in America: From the Revolution to the Civil War*. New York: Harper & Row, 1965.
Moores, Richard Gordon. *Fields of Rich Toil: The Development of the University of Illinois College of Agriculture*. Urbana: University of Illinois Press, 1970.
Moore, William D. "Constructions of Religion: Toward an Understanding of Nineteenth Century American Spaces and Places of Devotion." In *Sacred Spaces*, edited by Virginia Chieffo Raguin and Mary Ann Powers, 59–65. Worcester, MA: Trustees of the College of the Holy Cross, 2002.
Moorhead, James H. *World Without End: Mainstream American Protestant Visions of the Last Things, 1880–1925*. Religion in North America 28. Bloomington: Indiana University Press, 1999.
Morgan, William H. *Student Religion during Fifty Years: Programs and Policies of the Intercollegiate Y.M.C.A.* New York: Association Press, 1935.
Nelson, Louis P. "'Building Confessions': Architecture and Meaning in Nineteenth Century Places of Worship." In *Sacred Spaces*, edited by Virginia Chieffo Raguin and Mary Ann Powers, 11–26. Worcester, MA: Trustees of the College of the Holy Cross, 2002.
Nevins, Allan. *Illinois*. New York: Oxford University Press, 1917.
———. *The State Universities and Democracy*. Urbana: University of Illinois Press, 1962.
News Gazette. A Century in Pictures. Champaign: The News Gazette, 2000.
Noll, Mark A. *A History of Christianity in the United States and Canada*. Grand Rapids: Eerdmans, 1991.
———. *America's God: From Jonathan Edwards to Abraham Lincoln*. New York: Oxford University Press, 2002.
Nordhoff, Charles. *The Communistic Societies of the United States [1875]*. New York: Shocken, 1965.
Noyes, John Humphrey. *History of American Socialisms [1870]*. New York: Hillary House, 1961.

Orsi, Robert A. *Between Heaven and Earth: The Religious Worlds People Make and the Scholars Who Study Them.* Princeton: Princeton University Press, 2005.

Patton, Cornelius Howard, and Walter Taylor Field. *Eight O'Clock Chapel: A Study of New England College Life in the Eighties.* New York: Houghton Mifflin, 1927.

Pauli, Kenneth W. "Evidence of Popular Support for the Land Grant College Act of 1862 as Revealed in Selected Speeches in New England, 1850-1860." PhD diss., Stanford University, 1960.

Peterson, Merrill D. *The Jefferson Image in the American Mind.* New York: Oxford University Press, 1960.

———. *Thomas Jefferson and the New Nation: A Biography.* New York: Oxford University Press, 1970.

Peters, Scott J. *The Promise of Association: A History of the Mission and Work of the Y.M.C.A. at the University of Illinois, 1873-1997.* Champaign: University YMCA. 1997.

Phillips, Paul T. *A Kingdom on Earth: Anglo-American Social Christianity, 1880-1940.* University Park: Pennsylvania State University Press, 1996.

Phillips, Sarah T. "Antebellum Agriculture Reform, Republican Ideology, and Sectional Tension." *Agricultural History* 74 (2000) 799-822.

Pitts, Bill. "Personal and the Social Christianity in Rauschenbusch's Thought." *American Baptist Quarterly* 26 (2007) 138-60.

Pitzer, Donald E., editor. *America's Communal Utopias.* Chapel Hill: University of North Carolina Press, 1997.

Potts, David B. "American Colleges in the Nineteenth Century: From Localism to Denominationalism." *History of Education Quarterly* 11 (1971) 363-80.

Powell, Burt E. *Semi-Centennial History of the University of Illinois, Volume I: The Movement for Industrial Education and the Establishment of the University, 1840-1870.* Urbana: University of Illinois, 1918.

Putney, Clifford. *Muscular Christianity: Manhood and Sports in Protestant America, 1880-1920.* Cambridge: Harvard University Press, 2001.

Raven, Charles E. *Christian Socialism, 1848-1854.* London: MacMillan, 1920.

Reuben, Julie A. *The Making of the Modern University: Intellectual Transformation and the Marginalization of Morality.* Chicago: University of Chicago Press, 1996.

Roberts, Jon H. *Darwinism and the Divine in America: Protestant Intellectuals and Organic Evolution, 1859-1900.* History of American Thought and Culture. Madison: University of Wisconsin Press, 1988.

Roberts, Jon H. and James Turner. *The Sacred and the Secular University.* Princeton: Princeton University Press, 2000.

Ross, Earle D. *Democracy's College.* Ames: Iowa State College Press, 1942.

———. *The Land-Grant Idea at Iowa State College; A Centennial Trial Balance, 1858-1958.* Illustration selection and commentary by Dorothy Kehlenbeck. Ames: Iowa State College Press, 1958.

———. "The Manual Labor Experiment in the Land Grant College." *Mississippi Valley Historical Review* 21 (1935) 513-28.

———. "Religious Influences in the Development of State Colleges and Universities." *Indiana Magazine of History* 46 (1950) 343-62.

Rotundo, E. Anthony. *American Manhood: Transformations in Masculinity from the Revolution to the Modern Era.* New York: Basic, 1993.

Rudolph, Frederick. *The American College and University: A History*. New York: Vintage, 1962.
Sayer, Willam. "The Evolution of the Morrill Act of 1862." PhD diss., Boston University, 1948.
Scott, Franklin W. *The Semi-Centennial Alumni Record of the University of Illinois*. Urbana: University of Illinois, 1918.
Scott, Roy V. "Grangerism in Champaign County, Illinois, 1873–1877." *Mid-America: An Historical Review* 43 (1961) 139–63.
———. *The Reluctant Farmer: The Rise of Agricultural Extension Education to 1914*. Urbana: University of Illinois Press, 1970.
Selby, Paul. "The Part of Illinoisans in the National Education Movement, 1851–1862." *Transactions of the Illinois State Historical Society* 9 (1904) 214–29.
Setran, David P. *The College "Y": Student Religion in the Era of Secularization*. New York: Palgrave Macmillan, 2007.
Shannon, Fred A. *The Farmer's Last Frontier: Agriculture, 1860–1897*. New York: Farrar & Rinehart, 1945.
Shepardson, Whitney H. *Agricultural Education in the United States*. New York: MacMillan, 1929.
Shor, Francis Robert. *Utopianism and Radicalism in a Reforming America, 1888–1918*. Contributions in American History 178. Westport, CT: Greenwood, 1997.
Simpson, Thomas W. "Mormons Study 'Abroad': Brigham Young's Romance with American Higher Education, 1867–1877." *Church History* 76 (2007) 778–98.
Smith, Brett Hunn. "Envisioning and Embodying a Public, Protestant Paideia at the University of Illinois, 1867–1880." PhD diss., Northwestern University, 2002.
Smith, Brett H. "'Men,' Not 'Monks': Teaching 'Christian Culture' at the Illinois Industrial University." *Fides et Historia* 38 (2006) 69–86.
———. "Reversing the Curse: Agricultural Millennialism at the Illinois Industrial University." *Church History* 73 (2004) 759–91.
Smith, Henry Nash. *Virgin Land: The American West as Symbol and Myth*. Cambridge: Harvard University Press, 1950.
Smith, Mark M. "The Touch of an Uncommon Man." *The Chronicle Review*, 22 February 2008, B6–B8.
Solberg, Winton U. "The Conflict between Religion and Secularism at the University of Illinois, 1867–1894." *American Quarterly* 18 (1966) 183–99.
———. *The University of Illinois, 1867–1894: An Intellectual and Cultural History*. Urbana: University of Illinois Press, 1968.
Solomon, Barbara Miller. *In the Company of Educated Women*. New Haven: Yale University Press, 1985.
Sommerville, C. John. *The Decline of the Secular University: Why the Academy Needs Religion*. New York: Oxford University Press, 2006.
———. "Secular Society/Religious Population: Our Tacit Rules for Using the Term 'Secularization.'" *Journal for the Scientific Study of Religion* 37 (1998) 249–53.
Steingraber, Sandra. *Living Downstream: A Scientist's Personal Investigation of Cancer and the Environment*. New York: Vintage, 1998.
Stephens, Carl. *Illini Years: A Picture History of the University of Illinois*. Urbana: University of Illinois Press, 1950.
Sutton, Robert P. *Communal Utopias and the American Experience: Religious Communities, 1732–2000*. Westport, CT: Prager, 2003.

Tewksbury, Donald G. *The Founding of American Colleges and Universities before the Civil War, with Particular Reference to the Religious Influences Bearing upon the College Movement.* New York: Teachers College, Columbia University, Contributions to Education 543 (1932).

Thompson, Willard. "The Philosophy and History of the Land Grant Colleges and Universities in the United States." PhD diss., New York University, 1934.

Tilton, Leon Deming, and Thomas Edward O'Donnell. *History of the Growth and Development of the Campus of the University of Illinois.* Urbana: University of Illinois Press, 1930.

Townsend, Kim. *Manhood at Harvard: William James and Others.* New York: Norton, 1996.

True, Alfred C. *A History of Agricultural Education in the United States, 1785–1925.* Washington, DC: Government Printing Office, 1929.

Tyler, Alice Felt. *Freedom's Ferment: Phases of American Social History to 1860.* Minneapolis: University of Minnesota Press, 1944.

Vasquez, Mark G. "'Correctly Forming Public Opinion': Religious Rhetoric, Social Change, and the Myth of Self Culture." *American Transcendental Quarterly* 14 (2000) 173–92.

Vesey, Laurence. *The Emergence of the American University.* Chicago: University of Chicago Press, 1965.

Wells, Ronald. "Donald Yerxa's 'Dream': A Reply." *Fides et Historia* 39 (2007) 67–70.

Welter, Rush. *Popular Education and Democratic Thought in America.* New York: Columbia University Press, 1962.

Widder, Keith R. *Michigan Agricultural College: The Evolution of a Land-Grant Philosophy, 1855–1925.* East Lansing: Michigan State University Press, 2005.

Williams, Raymond. *Culture and Society 1780–1950.* London: Penguin, 1984.

Yerxa, Donald A. "That Embarassing Dream: Big Questions and the Limits of History." *Fides et Historia* 39 (2007) 53–65.

www.ingramcontent.com/pod-product-compliance
Lightning Source LLC
Chambersburg PA
CBHW072219240426
43670CB00038B/2118